Certain Success

By

Norval A. Hawkins

Certain Success
by Norval A. Hawkins

Copyright © 2023

All Rights reserved.

ISBN: 978-93-59956-74-9
Published by

DOUBLE 9 BOOKS

2/13-B, Ansari Road
Daryaganj, New Delhi – 110002
info@double9books.com
www.double9books.com
Tel. 011-40042856

ABOUT THE AUTHOR

Renowned for his prowess as an author and motivational speaker, Norval A. Hawkins has solidified his standing in the realm of private development and achievement techniques. With years of devoted training, he has emerged as a guiding force, guidance people toward realizing their fullest capacity and motivating them to actively pursue their dreams. Hawkins' effect is profound, having stimulated infinite people to capture manipulate of their lives. At the core of his influential frame of labor is "Certain Success," a testomony to Hawkins' unwavering commitment to empowering others. This book serves as a complete guide, reflecting his dedication to helping individuals navigate their particular paths to success. Through a wealth of revel in and insights, Hawkins imparts precious classes, encouraging readers to set ambitious dreams and persevere thru challenges. Beyond the written word, Hawkins extends his motivational have an impact on via dynamic speeches and training periods, creating a long-lasting impact on those in search of personal improvement. His knowledge in success coaching has positioned him as a sought-after parent within the field, making Norval A. Hawkins a beacon of proposal for those desiring to gain positive fulfillment of their lives.

CONTENTS

To Begin With— 7

How to Study Certain Success with The Selling Process 15

CHAPTER I
The Universal Need For Sales Knowledge 18

CHAPTER II
The Man-Stuff You Have For Sale 37

CHAPTER III
Skill In Selling Your Best Self 62

CHAPTER IV
Preparing to Make Your Success Certain 78

CHAPTER V
Your Prospects 89

CHAPTER VI
Gaining Your Chance 102

CHAPTER VII
Knowledge of Other Men 119

CHAPTER VIII
The Knock At The Door Of Opportunity and
The Invitation To Come In 136

CHAPTER IX
Getting Yourself Wanted 154

CHAPTER X
Obstacles In Your Way 170

CHAPTER XI
The Goal of Success 189

CHAPTER XII
The Celebration Stage 208

To Begin With—

Salesmanship Essential to Assure Success

There are particular characteristics one can have, and particular things one can do, that will make *failure* in life *certain*.

Why, then, should not the possession of particular opposite characteristics, and the doing of particular opposite things, result as *certainly* in *success*, which is the antithesis of failure?

That is a logical, common-sense question. The purpose of this book and its companion volume, "The Selling Process," is to answer it convincingly for you.

Success *can* be made certain; not, however, by the mere *possession* of particular characteristics, nor by just *doing* particular things.

Your success in life can be *assured*; but only if you supplement your qualifications and make everything you do most effective *by using continually, whatever your vocation, the art of salesmanship.*

Why Are Some Men Failures Who Deserve to Succeed?

Life can hold nothing but *failure* for the ill-natured, unsociable, disgusting tramp who is known to be ignorant, lazy, shiftless, a spendthrift, a liar, and an all-around crook. Such a worthless man will make a complete failure of life because he is so *dis*-qualified to succeed.

On the other hand certain success ought to be achieved by the good-natured, intelligent, reliable man who continually wins friends; the truthful man who has a fine reputation for thrift, honesty, neatness, and love for his work. He seems entirely worthy of success. Yet for reasons that baffle himself and his friends it sometimes happens that such a man is unsuccessful.

The defeat in life of one who appears so deserving of victory seems to prove that success cannot be *assured* by the development of individual characteristics and by doing specific things. But such a wholly negative conclusion would be wrong. When a worthy man fails, he loses out because he lacks an essential *positive* factor of certain success—the ability to *sell* his capabilities. *By mastering the selling process this failure can turn himself into a success.*

Self-advertised Disqualifications Unrecognized Capabilities

We are sure of the failure of the man who is utterly disqualified to succeed; not because he *has* particular faults, but because they *self-advertise and sell the idea* of his disqualifications for success. His characteristics and actions make on our minds an impression of his general worthlessness. Defects are apt to attract attention, while perfection often passes unnoticed.

Millions of worthy men, otherwise qualified for success, have failed solely because their merits were not appreciated and rewarded as they would have been if recognized. Capabilities, like goods, are *profitless* until they are *sold*. Therefore the man who deserves to win out in life can make his victory *sure* only by learning and practicing with skill the certain success methods of the master salesman.

The Duty to Succeed

Down through all the ages has come the *duty* to succeed. It was enjoined in the Parable of the Talents. No one has the right to do less than his best. Then only can he claim full justification for his existence. The Creator accepts no excuses for failure. Every personal quality, and every opportunity to succeed that a man has, must be used, to entitle him to the rewards of success. He owes not only to himself and to his fellows, but also to God, the obligation of developing his *utmost capability*. If he does not pay dividends on the divine investment in him, his dereliction is justly punished by failure in life. Sometimes he even forfeits the right to live.

Success Cannot be Copied

Many ambitious people, who recognize their duty to succeed but do not know how to go about it, make a common mistake in thinking. They believe the secret of certain success can be learned from *examples*; that success can be *copied*. So men who have succeeded conspicuously are often asked to state and explain their rules, for the benefit of other men who regard them as oracles.

Other Men's Formulas

Doubtless you have read much about Marshall Field, J. Pierpont Morgan, Charles M. Schwab, and similar outstanding business men. You have studied their principles of success. You have tried to practice their methods. But somehow the most careful following of their directions has not made you a multi-millionaire, nor can you see riches as a prospect. Naturally you are both disappointed and puzzled. Perhaps you have tested faithfully for years various formulas of success extracted from the advice of successful men. Yet *you* have failed, or have achieved only partial and unsatisfying success. You have been unable to solve the problem that you once felt so sure could be worked out by the rules you mastered.

Maybe you have become discouraged and have given up, in disgust, your ambition for achievement. Very likely you have said to yourself, "Success is so much a matter of luck and circumstances, there's no way to make sure of it. I've done everything that Marshall Field, J. Pierpont Morgan, and Charles M. Schwab have counseled; but I'm still plugging along on an ordinary salary. Rules for certain success are bunk. Luck has to break right for a man."

The Element of Luck

Unquestionably good luck *has* brought success to some men who would have failed without its aid. It is equally beyond doubt that bad luck has prevented other men from achieving their ambitions. Of course *such* successes and failures do not fall within any rules. They are altogether exceptional, and neither prove nor disprove general principles.

Eliminating the factor of luck, good or bad, the success of any normal, deserving man *can* be made certain *to the extent of his individual capacity.* Some men have different or bigger capacities than others; hence not all successes will be of the same kind, or alike in extent. But any normal, deserving man can assure himself as great a success as he is fitted to achieve. It is necessary, however, that he do more than *develop his utmost capability.* He must learn to employ skillful salesmanship, in order to *market* his "goods of sale," or personal qualifications, *most profitably.*

Sales Skill Necessary

Each of us has to make *his own pattern* of success. "The individual should develop his individuality," instead of attempting to imitate anybody else. It is even more necessary for him to *use* most effectively all the natural powers he builds up.

A man can assure his success only if he learns how to utilize his personal qualifications *so as to create and control his opportunities* to succeed. He should be able to *bring himself to good luck,* and not expect anybody or any event to bring good luck to him.

One cannot make the most effective use of his capabilities, he cannot create and control his chances to succeed, until he develops skill in salesmanship, which is necessary to market his qualifications profitably. He must practice "selling himself" until the habit of using sales skill in everything he does and says becomes second nature to him. Sales skill is the *dynamic* factor of success. It transforms potential powers into actual accomplishments. It enables the qualified man to turn his individual capabilities to best account.

Opportunity A Constant Companion

Sometimes a man says, as an excuse for his failure, "I never had a chance." The truth is that Opportunity is a constant companion to every man. Each of us has *within himself* limitless wealth. All normal people are rich in ability. It is possible for anyone to become more prosperous. *He need only turn his possibilities into realities.* When a man capable of accumulating riches continues poor, he is like the shipwrecked discoverer of a bonanza gold mine on an uncharted island. He cannot exchange his potential wealth for the things he desires; because he is unable to market his raw gold.

Similarly you who have not yet succeeded are *potentially* rich. If you possess the generally recognized fundamentals of success; such as characteristic honesty, intelligence, energy, etc., you are not handicapped for want of a market. Even though you now may seem to lack some of the essential qualifications, you are capable of succeeding. Every necessary characteristic of the successful man is *latent* in your nature and can be brought out by development. You have not yet done your utmost with the best that is in you.

Your Market Not Lacking

First you should resolve to make yourself completely *worthy* to succeed. Meanwhile you should be learning how to sell your "goods." On every hand there are markets in which qualities like yours are being sold successfully by other men. Undoubtedly there will be a purchaser for the best that is in you when you bring it out; provided you present your "goods of sale" in the most skillful way. All about you are highly prosperous people with no more innate merits than you have. Certainly the market for your particular abilities is within reach. Golden opportunities of which you have not taken the fullest advantage surround you and touch your daily activities. If you have not grasped your chance, it was because you did not *know how* to reach out with all your capabilities. In other words, possessing the fundamental qualifications for success, you have stood in the midst of the world's need for such capabilities as yours, *but you have not gone through the selling process.*

You have failed thus far to achieve your ambition, simply because *you have been an unsuccessful salesman of yourself* to the world.

Perhaps you never have thought of yourself as a salesman. You may not have realized the importance *to you* of knowing and practicing the principles of skillful selling. Only one per cent of the people in the United States *call* themselves salesmen or saleswomen. Yet in order to succeed, each of us must sell his or her particular qualifications. Your knowledge and use of the selling process are essential to assure your success in life.

Master Salesmen Made, Not Born

The best commercial executives agree that the most effective selling representative of a house is not the "natural born" salesman, but the salesman who is *made* highly efficient by training. So every big, successful business conducts a course in salesmanship. Thorough tests have proved that particular principles and methods of selling are sure to produce the highest average of orders. Therefore these principles and methods are followed as *standard practice* in the sales department.

That is, in order to *assure* the success of an individual salesman, he is required and aided to develop particular qualifications and to do certain things that master executives have learned will get the orders and hold the trade of buyers. The qualified professional salesman is drilled thoroughly in tested principles and methods of selling. He is trained to use this standard sales knowledge skillfully. As a result he works in the field with complete confidence.

Why should he doubt that he will succeed? He knows his own limitations and capabilities; knows the true worth of his line; knows there is a market in his territory; knows how to sell in the ways that have been proved most effective; and knows that practice of right salesmanship will make him skillful in getting and holding business. Verily such "knowledge is power."

Certain Success With the Selling Process

Your success in selling *yourself* can be made as certain as is a successful career to the first-class professional salesman. This book and its companion volume will explain in detail salesmanship ways to develop your best capabilities most effectively. You will be given the principles and methods employed by the expert salesman in marketing any kind of right goods. You will also be shown how to sell yourself by adapting his practices to your "goods of sale."

When you comprehend, and employ as second nature, the usages of the finest sales art, your success in life, like that of the master professional salesman, will be *certain.*

Ideas of Goods Not the Goods Themselves Are Sold

If you have not *called* yourself a salesman, perhaps you doubt the value to you of skill in selling. All you have to market is the best that is in yourself.

Your ambition may be to succeed as a doctor, or lawyer, or preacher, or clerk, or mechanic, or farmer, or banker. You do not see how salesmanship could assure *your* success, however much it might help some one with commercial ambitions.

If you think it would not be worth while for you to master the selling process, since you do not expect to engage in the *profession* of selling, you misconceive the functions and work of the salesman. You have thought he sells "*goods;*" and that as you do not deal in commodities, you would have no practical use for the selling process he employs to assure his success. But even the shoe salesman, or grocery salesman, or real estate salesman, or insurance salesman does not really sell *goods*. He sells *ideas about* goods. Similarly you sell ideas about yourself in order to succeed.

When the Goods and the Ideas Are Different

A sale is often completed in business without any inspection of the actual "goods" by the purchaser; as when a quantity of standard sheet copper is specified, or when the salesman describes a piece of machinery or shows a picture of it with a catalogue number. The "goods" are to be delivered later. However, the *selling process is finished;* though only the mind's eye of the buyer has seen what he anticipates getting on his order. The salesman has presented nothing except *certain ideas* to the mental vision of the prospect. But these ideas have been sold so realistically to the imagination of the purchaser that he gives his order for what he *expects*.

Suppose the goods delivered later do not correspond with the particular ideas about them that have been sold. For example, the sheet copper furnished is not as specified in the contract, or the machine shipped is not the same as the salesman pictured when he got the order for it. Then there has been *no sale* of the different "goods." The intending purchaser bought *particular ideas*. He will not accept the delivery of *goods unlike the ideas sold* to him.

Know Your Prospect's Idea

Another illustration. A real estate salesman describes a bungalow to a prospect for a home. He shows plans and specifications, with accurate dimensions; there is no misrepresentation of any detail. The salesman especially emphasizes, what is his own belief, that the bungalow would make a "cozy" home. The prospect decides to buy the property. He says, "If it is as you describe it, I'll take that place." *The sale to his mind has been completed.* All that remains is delivery of a bungalow corresponding to the ideas sold. The delighted salesman escorts the buyer to the "cozy home." But the empty rooms do not confirm the idea emphasized to the prospect.

The salesman cannot furnish them convincingly with his imaginative "cozy" word pictures. He has made the mistake of omitting to learn the other man's conception of a cozy home before selling the expectation of coziness. He is shocked when the sale is declared annulled with the prospect's contradiction of his description, "There's nothing cozy about this place." The intending buyer of a home feels there has been a misrepresentation; though the bungalow is exactly like the plans and specifications shown to him. He was sold an idea that "the goods" have not delivered; so he declares the sale off. A sale is a success only when *true ideas* are sold, and afterward are delivered by *the goods*.

Selling Ideas About Yourself

If you "have the goods" and would succeed *certainly* in your chosen vocation, you must *sell* to the world or to individual buyers *true ideas* about your particular qualifications for success—true ideas regarding *your best capabilities* and the *value* of your services. Your "goods of sale" may be your muscular power; your brain energy; your talents, skill, integrity, and knowledge in this capacity or in that. Whatever qualities you possess, it is necessary that some one be sold the idea of their full worth, or you cannot succeed. No matter how valuable your services *might* be, they have only potential worth until another man, or some business, or the world at large *perceives desirable possibilities in you and buys the expectation that you will "deliver the goods."*

Probably you have said to yourself, "If I had the chance, I know I could deliver the goods." We will grant that you are able to make delivery. However, *before you will be given a chance* you must get across to the mind of some prospective buyer of muscular power, or brain energy, or other capabilities such as you could supply, the true idea that *you have* "the goods" he needs and that your qualifications would be a satisfactory purchase *for him*.

In other words, it is necessary that you use *the selling process* effectively, with thorough scientific knowledge and a high degree of art, *in order to make certain of gaining your opportunity* for success. You have no doubt that you can succeed if you get the chance. But you have not realized, perhaps, that *you can make yourself the master of your own destiny by first learning and then practicing until it becomes second nature to you the sure, salesmanship way to gain the opportunities you deserve.* After you *comprehend* the sure process, you can soon develop *skill in actually selling* to other men true ideas of the best that is in you.

The Secret of Certain Success

The secret of *certain success* in life for you, then, *whatever your vocation or ambition*, lies in knowing HOW to sell true ideas of your best capability in the right market or field of service. The chapters of the present book, supplemented by the contents of the companion volume, "The Selling Process," should reveal to you clearly every principal detail of this secret.

No 100% Salesmen

Before you proceed further with the study of successful salesmanship as analyzed in these pages, avoid a possible misconception of masterly selling. Even the most efficient salesman does not get *all* the orders for which he tries. By his knowledge and skill his average of failures is minimized; therefore everybody recognizes him as a great success.

So, however well you comprehend the selling process, and however skillfully you use it in your career, you will not *always* accomplish the particular purpose to which you apply your salesmanship. But you will markedly lessen the number and importance of your failures to do the things you attempt. You will also increase to an extraordinary degree the quantity, quality, and profitable results of your successful efforts. You will make a grand average so high that you will feel you are a real success. Others, too, will so regard you.

The Master Key

Therefore, whatever your life ambition, study the selling process until you understand it thoroughly; then perfect your skill by daily practice in selling your ideas, and ideas about yourself, to other people. When you know HOW to sell true ideas of your best capability in your chosen market or field of service, and have become expert in *applying* what you have learned, you can use salesmanship continually in your everyday work. You should feel *absolute assurance* that with its aid you can open the treasure house of your desires.

This universal master key that fits all locks now between you and success can be made by your own hands and head. You have begun to shape it for your future use.

How to Study Certain Success with The Selling Process

Suggestion To Salesmen

The professional salesman or saleswoman who undertakes the thorough study of both this book and its companion volume, might better read first "The Selling Process," the chapters of which apply especially to his or her vocation.

If you are a "salesman," therefore, begin your study with the introduction to that book. When you have read "The Selling Process" once, start "Certain Success" and master it. Then re-read the other book in the light of the new ideas that will have been shed upon its contents by the present text.

The practical value of "Certain Success" and "The Selling Process" to you as a salesman will be multiplied a hundredfold if both are kept handy for *continual reference*. The marginal index should enable you to find quickly any point regarding which you want to refresh your recollection. This set of books was not written to collect dust on a library shelf. No salesman can get the full worth out of the pages unless he *uses* "Certain Success" and "The Selling Process" *as working tools*.

If Your Vocation Is Not Selling

If you are not engaged in selling as a vocation, and have not realized before that you must be a good salesman or saleswoman in order to achieve your life ambition, commence mastering the secret of certain success with the selling process by reading thoroughly the book now in your hands. This preliminary study will increase your ability to read intelligently the more technical contents of "The Selling Process." Do not skip or slight any portion of either book. You cannot afford to miss a single bit of information regarding the sure way to succeed.

Purpose and Scope of the Two Books

This is the first publication of "Certain Success," but five large editions of "The Selling Process" were required in 1919 and 1920 to supply the demand from all over the world. The two books, each complete in itself, now are issued together under the double title, CERTAIN SUCCESS WITH

THE SELLING PROCESS; though either "Certain Success" or "The Selling Process" may be ordered alone.

My chief purpose in preparing this set has been to stimulate each reader's comprehension of the value of skillful salesmanship *to him*. All of us who are ambitious to make the most of the best that is in us need to be first-class salesmen, whether we market "goods" or our personal capabilities. As has been emphasized repeatedly in this preface, *every one who would succeed in life must know HOW to sell his qualifications to the highest advantage*. Poor salesmanship is responsible for most of the failures of people who really *deserve* to succeed. It is almost surely fatal to ambitious hopes in any trade, profession, or business.

CERTAIN SUCCESS WITH THE SELLING PROCESS covers in outline the whole subject of Salesmanship. But the scope of this set does not afford room to give here a minutely detailed exposition of the special processes of making sales in particular businesses. I have compiled for you, rather, the *general principles* of effective selling that may be *universally applied*. "Certain Success" and "The Selling Process" are handbooks of fundamental ideas which each reader, by his individual thinking, should amplify and fit to his own work or ambition.

Real Study Required

The fine art of successful salesmanship cannot be mastered in a few hours of casual reading. You will not be able, immediately after glancing through these books, to unlock every long-desired golden opportunity with absolute assurance. CERTAIN SUCCESS WITH THE SELLING PROCESS must be *studied out*. You should keep them always at hand like your bank books, and draw on the contents for your salesmanship needs from day to day.

You will get only a smattering of the secret of certain success if you just skim over the chapters, and skip whatever requires you to think hard in order to comprehend it all. But if you dig into the meaning of each sentence for the full idea, you will enrich yourself with constantly increasing power and skill in selling. *So you will surely become a real success.*

Tested Working Tools

The principles and methods of successful salesmanship summarized in these companion books, though they will be new to most readers, are not mere personal theories. They all have been demonstrated and tested in actual practice during my twelve years experience as Commercial and General Sales Manager of the Ford Motor Company. Under my direction in the course of that period Ford sales were multiplied one hundred thirty-two times—from 6,181 to 815,912 cars a year. The fundamental principles and methods that I have tested and proved to be most successful in selling automobiles and good will should work equally well in any profession, or business, or trade; and for any normal, intelligent man or woman who uses them continually.

Dollars and Cents Value

Since the first publication of "The Selling Process" thousands of enthusiastic readers of the book have voluntarily borne witness to its practical, dollars-and-cents value to them in their daily work. Preachers, doctors, lawyers, bank officials, clerks, book-keepers, mechanics, laborers; as well as business executives and sales managers and salesmen—men and women in scores of widely different vocations—unite in testifying to their increased earning power and fuller satisfaction in living and working. They credit these results to their study and continued use of "The Selling Process." The value of that book will be at least doubled by the supplemental reading of "Certain Success." Therefore the two are now published as a set of working tools for any ambitious man or woman who is resolved to *earn* success.

NORVAL A. HAWKINS

Majestic Building,
Detroit, Michigan.

CHAPTER I
The Universal Need For Sales Knowledge

Analysis of Secret of Certain Success

The Secret of Certain Success has four principal elements. It comprises:

(1) Knowing how to sell

(2) The true idea

(3) Of one's best capabilities

(4) In the right market or field of service.

Your success will be in direct proportion to your thorough knowledge and continual use of *all four parts* of the whole secret. No matter how great your effort, an entire lack of one or more of these principal elements of Certain Success will cause partial or utter failure in your life ambition. You will be like a man who tries to open a safe with a four-combination lock, though he knows only two or three of the numbers.

No one, however well fitted for success elsewhere, can succeed in the *wrong field*, or in rendering services for which *he* is not qualified. Nor is complete success attainable by a man unless he develops the *best* that is in him. Even if he brings to the right market his utmost ability, he may fail miserably by making a *false impression* that he is unfitted for the opportunity he wants. Or he may be overlooked because he does not make the *true* impression of his fitness.

Evidently, in order to gain a *chance* to succeed, anyone must first *sell* to the fullest advantage the idea that he is *the* man for the opportunity already waiting or for the new opening he makes for himself. Of course he cannot do this *surely* unless he *knows how*. Therefore sales knowledge is *universally needed* to complement the three other principal elements of the complete secret of certain success.

Reasons for Failures

When we try to explain the failure of any man who seems worthy to have succeeded, we nearly always say, in substance, one of three things about his case:

"He is a square peg in a round hole;" by which we usually mean he is a right man in the wrong place.

Or, "He is capable of filling a better position;" a more polite way of saying that a man has outgrown his present job but has not developed ability to get a bigger one.

Oftenest, probably, we declare, "He isn't appreciated."

Very rarely is a worthy man's failure in life ascribed to the commonest cause—*his personal inefficiency in selling* to the world comprehension of his especial qualifications for success.

What Failures Realize

If a man is a square peg in a round hole, he should realize that his particular qualities must be fitted into the right field for them before he can succeed. A natural "organizer" cannot achieve his ambitions if he works alone at a routine task.

No sensible man would aspire to fill a better position than he holds, unless he had developed a capacity beyond the limitations of his present work. The shipping clerk who craves the higher salary of a correspondent knows he cannot hope for the desired promotion if he has not learned to write good business letters.

However deserving of advancement a man may be, he realizes he has but a slim chance to succeed if his worth is unrecognized. So he wants appreciation from his chief. He knows that unless his worth is perceived and truly valued, some one else, who may be less qualified, is apt to be selected for the "Manager's" job he desires. Such "injustices" have poisoned countless disappointed hopes with bitterest resentment.

The deserving man who fails because he is a misfit in his particular position, the worthy man who is limited to a small career because the work he does lacks scope for the use of all his ability; the third good man who has been kept down for the reason that his chief is blind to his qualifications for promotion—all three of these failures understand pretty clearly the reasons for their non-success.

When Lack of Salesmanship Causes Failure

It is very different in the case of the capable man who fails because he has been *inefficient in selling true impressions* of his qualifications for success. A private secretary, for illustration, might be thoroughly competent for managerial duties; but by his self-effacement in his present job he might make the false impression that he was wanting in executive capacity. He would be given a chance as manager if he were effective in creating a true impression of his administrative ability. Such a capable man, if he has little or no scientific knowledge of the selling *process* is apt also to lack comprehension of the value *to him* of knowing *how to sell ideas*. He does not happen to call himself a salesman. Therefore he has never studied with personal interest the fine art of selling. He does not realize that *ignorance of salesmanship,* and *consequent non-use of the selling process, almost always are responsible for the merely partial success or the downright failure in life of the man who deserves to win, but who loses out.*

Who Is To Blame for Failure

One may feel able to "deliver the goods," were he given the chance. He may know where his best capability is greatly needed and would be highly appreciated if recognized. Yet the door of opportunity may not open to his deserving hand, however hard he tries to win his way in. His failure seems to him altogether unfair, the rankest injustice from Fortune.

If a man knows he is completely fitted to fill a higher position, he feels considerable self-confidence when he first applies for it. But his real ability may not be recognized by his chief. The ambitious man may be denied the coveted chance to take the step upward to the bigger opportunities for which he rightly believes himself qualified. If his deserts and his utmost efforts do not win the promotion he desires, he grows discouraged. He loses the taste of zest for his work. His earlier optimism oozes away. After awhile his ambition slumps. Then he resigns himself sullenly to the conviction that he is a failure *but is not to blame.*

Dynamic Quality Lacking

Leaving out of consideration most exceptional, unpreventable bad luck, the worthy man who fails in life *is* to blame. He is not, as he thinks, a victim of circumstances or ill-fate. His failure is due to his ignorance of the first of the four principal factors of the secret of certain success. *Potentially* qualified to succeed, he does not have the absolutely necessary *dynamic* element. He lacks an essential characteristic of the self-made successful man, a characteristic which any one of intelligence can learn how to develop—*a high degree of capability in gaining his own opportunities to succeed.*

He does not know *how to sell true ideas about himself;* though he may realize the importance of making the best impression possible. So, however, he tries, he cannot get his deserved chances to succeed. He could secure them *easily* if he comprehended the selling process of the master salesman, and used it with skill. This process of masterly selling is the key to certain success for the fully qualified man in any vocation.

Making and Governing One's Own Good Luck

A capable applicant will invariably be given a chance to succeed, if he takes the best that is in him to a man who has need of such services as he could render, and then *sells the true idea of his ability*. He has mastered *all four principal elements of the complete secret of certain success*. Consequently he is able to create and to control his opportunities to succeed. He makes and governs his own good luck.

Everywhere the most desirable positions in the business world are in need of men who can fill them. Only the poorer jobs are crowded. But when Opportunity has to seek the man, the *right* one is often overlooked. The golden chance is gained by another—less qualified and less worthy, perhaps; but *a better salesman of himself*. The fully competent man, however, can *assure* his success by becoming proficient in selling true ideas of his best capability in the right market or field of service. The master salesman of himself makes his own chances to succeed, and therefore runs no risk of being overlooked by Opportunity.

Success Way Is Charted

Master salesmen of ideas about "goods" use *particular selling processes* to get their ideas across *surely* to the minds of prospective buyers. The professional salesman, therefore, has plainly charted the way to certain success in any vocation, for the man who has developed the best that is in him. If you are a candidate for a position, do not let a prospective employer *buy* your services at *his* valuation, for he is certain to under-estimate you. *Sell* him true ideas of your merits. Set a fair price on your *worth*, and *get* across to his mind the true idea that you would be worth that much *to him*. Such skillful salesmanship used by an applicant for a position can be depended on to make the best possible impression of his desirability; just as the practiced art of the professional salesman enables him to present the qualities and values of his goods in the most favorable light. The *masterly selling process* is not very difficult to learn. Proficiency in its use can be gained gradually by any one who practices consciously every day the actual sale of ideas in the artistic way.

Knowledge of Salesmanship Develops Confidence

As was stated in the Introduction to this book, it has been proved conclusively in business that particular principles and methods of selling are certain to produce the highest average of closed orders. In other words, success for the professional salesman is *assured* if he develops certain qualifications, and if he does certain things; all within the capacity of any normal, intelligent man. Scientific sales executives know positively, as the result of comparative tests, that the salesman who develops these personal qualifications, and who does these things, should get his quota of business and hold it. Hence, as has been said, specific training is given in the sales schools of the most successful businesses, along the lines of best selling practice.

Practical Principles

When the individual salesman who has been so trained commences work in his territory, he learns in his experiences with buyers that the principles and methods he has been taught are actually *most effective*. Assuming that he has developed his *best capabilities* pretty fully, and that he has become fairly *skillful* in using what he knows about how to sell his line, he works with continually growing confidence that he will succeed. Why should he doubt his complete selling power? He knows there is a *field for his goods* in this territory. He knows clearly and vividly *what ideas* he wants to get across to the minds of prospective buyers. He knows—most important of all—*just how* to make convincing and attractive impressions of the desirability and true value of what he presents for purchase. He comprehends the *most effective ways* to show prospects both their *need* for his goods and that he has come, with a real purpose of service, to *satisfy* that need.

You, the non-professional salesman of yourself, will sell *your* "goods of sale" with similar complete confidence in your power to gain and to control your opportunities for success—if you, too, use the right selling process.

This set of books explains and demonstrates in detail the principles and methods of *the successful salesman of ideas*. The Introduction and twelve Chapters of the present series apply the selling process especially to *the sale of ideas about one's self*, with particular relation to *self-advancement* in the world. "The Selling Process," companion book to "Certain Success," shows the master *professional* salesman at work, getting orders with *assurance*.

Hard Study Necessary

The fact that you have proceeded thus far in reading "Certain Success" proves you have an earnest purpose to make the most of your present opportunity to learn *how* to succeed with certainty. We will assume that you have developed your individual ability pretty fully, and that you know where there is a field for such services as you are sure you could render if afforded the chance. Surely, then, your ambition in life, whatever it may be, is a sufficient incentive to the most thorough study of the principles and methods of successful salesmanship. Do not merely *read* this set of books. MASTER "Certain Success" and "The Selling Process" to make yourself the master of your own destiny.

Again and again, lest at any time while you study you might fall below 100% in *absolute assurance,* you will read in these chapters the assertion that your success can be made *certain.* This statement is not an exaggeration It is necessary that you accept it literally throughout your reading of this set of books. Do not take it "with a grain of salt." The taste of the declaration that the selling process makes success sure will become familiar after these many repetitions. Realize when you come upon the repeated idea as you proceed with your study that your continued reading should frequently be reenforced by a steadily growing conviction that you *are* mastering the sure way to succeed. You believe in yourself more than you did when you began to read this book. This increasing faith should develop to complete confidence when you have dug *into* the text of both "Certain Success" and "The Selling Process," and have dug *out* every idea in the twenty-four chapters.

Salesmanship Not a Science But an Art

At the outset of your present study comprehend that salesmanship is not a *science.* Rather, it is an *art.* Like every other art, however, it has a *related* science. Selling is a *process. Knowledge about the principles and methods* that make the process most effective is the related *science.* But such knowledge supplies only the best foundation for building success by the *actual practice* of most effective salesmanship. The master salesman practices the scientific principles and methods he has learned until the *skillful use* of his knowledge in every-day selling becomes *second nature* to him. Thus, and thus only, is his *art* perfected.

You will gain *knowledge* from these books about *how* to sell with assurance the true idea of your best capabilities—about *how* to sell any "goods of sale" unfailingly. But you can develop the *skill* necessary to the *actual achievement* of certain success only if you *continually use* what you learn about the selling process. You must perfect your selling *art* by the intelligent employment of every *word* and *tone* and *act* of your life to attract other men to you, and to impress on them convincingly true ideas of your particular ability.

Be a Salesman Every Minute

The master professional salesman is "always on the job" with his three means of self-expression, to get across to prospects true ideas of the desirability and value of his goods. He is a salesman *every minute,* and in *everything* he does or says. You can become as efficient as he, in selling ideas about *your* "goods of sale," if your proficiency becomes as *easy and natural* as his. Such ease is the *sure* result of sufficient right practice.

You have countless opportunities daily to make use of the selling process. In each expression of yourself—in your every word, tone, and act—you convey *some* idea of your particular character and ability. You should *know how* to make *true, attractive* impressions of your *best* self; and how to avoid making *untrue* and *unfavorable* impressions by what you do and say. Then, when you have *learned* the most effective *way* to sell ideas about yourself that you want other people to have, it is necessary that you *use* the selling process consciously all the time until you grow into the habit of using it unconsciously, as your second nature. Once you are accustomed to *acting the salesman continually*, it will be no more difficult for *you* to be "always on the job" selling right ideas of your qualifications for success, than it is for the *professional* user of the selling process to be a salesman "every minute."

Your "Goods of Sale"

As already has been emphasized, "the goods of sale" in your case are your *best* capabilities. You need first of all to *know* your true self, before you can sell true ideas about your qualifications for success. Your *true* self is your *best* self. You are untrue to yourself, you balk your own ambition to succeed, unless you develop to the *utmost of your capacity* your particular salable qualities.

You do not need qualities *you* now wholly lack. You should not attempt to "salt" the gold mine in yourself with the characteristics of *other* men who have succeeded by the development and use of capabilities that were natural to *them*, but that would be unnatural to *you*. It is worse than futile—it is foolish for you to imitate anybody else. Just be *your* best self. Make the most of what *you* have that is salable. You require no more to assure your success.

Selling the Truth About Your Best Self

Every individual has distinct characteristics, and is capable of doing particular things, of which he may be genuinely proud if he fully develops and uses his personal qualifications. *When all the truth about his best possible self is skillfully made known to others*, chances for success are certain to be opened to the ambitious man. If he lacks the salesmanship key, the doors of opportunity may always remain closed, however well he deserves to be welcomed.

You possess "goods of sale" that have real *quality*, that are *durable*, that will render *service* and afford pleasurable satisfaction to others. *Your* goods can be sold as *surely* as quality phonographs, durable automobile tires, serviceable clothes, or pleasing books.

Maybe you can "deliver the goods" with smiles, or hearty tones, or ready acts of kindness. Any one can easily be friendly. But have you developed *all your ability* to smile genuinely? Have you cultivated the hearty tone of real kindness so that now it is *unnatural* for you ever to speak in any other way? Do you perform friendly acts of consideration for others on *every* occasion, as second nature?

If your honest answers to such questions must be negative, you are not a good salesman of your best self all the time.

Your Salable Qualities

Your most salable quality may be dependability, rather than quick thinking. If this is the case, concentrate your salesmanship on making impressions of the true idea of *your reliability*. Your greatest success will be achieved in some field of service where dependableness is a primary essential. You may be *naturally unfitted* to make a star reporter, but *peculiarly qualified* to develop into the cashier of a bank.

Should you happen to be unattractive in features, your job is to transform your homeliness into a *likable* quality—not to try to make yourself appear handsome. If you are wholly inexperienced, that need not be a detriment to your success in the field you want to enter. When you have mastered the selling process, your very greenness can be presented before the mind of a prospective employer as the best of reasons for engaging you. You will be able to make yourself appear desirable because you *are* green in that field, and therefore have no wrong ideas to "unlearn."

Know All of Yourself

You can greatly improve your chances to get the job for which you are best adapted, if you use the reciprocal selling process employed by the professional salesman when he sells his services to a house. He meets the head of the concern as his man-equal, and does not just offer himself "for hire." Such a consciousness of your man-equality when you are face to face with a prospective employer can result only from certain, analytical *knowledge of your best self,* complemented by *knowing how to sell* the true idea of your particular desirability and worth.

Very likely you think you are seriously *handicapped* in many ways. Having made no detailed analysis of yourself from a salesman's view-point, you do not appreciate fully the number and the market value of the *advantages* you might have. Probably some of your best, most salable qualities are latent or but partly developed.

Chart Necessary

List *your* particular "goods of sale." Put down on a chart, not only the qualities you have now, but all the additional ones you feel *capable of developing*. Then you will realize vividly that you possess many abilities, some undeveloped yet, which are always needed in the world. You know that such qualities *should* be readily salable, to the mutual benefit of yourself and of buyers. You are learning the selling process in order to make certain that *you can* sell the best that is in *you*, as other men are selling themselves successfully.

Complete your chart by listing your various *defects*. Then study out ways to use even *your particular faults* differently than you have been handling them; so that they will help you, instead of being hindrances to your success. Think of some people you know, and of how they have turned their physical "liabilities" into "assets" of popularity.

The very first sales knowledge you need is of exactly what *you* have to sell. You cannot see *all* of yourself, your good and bad points—yourself as you *are*, and as you *might be*—unless you make a detailed chart of your "goods of sale." One of the most important immediate effects of such a self-analysis will be increased self-respect. Your handicaps will shrink, and the peculiar advantages you have will grow before your eyes. You should feel new confidence in your own ability.

Man-Equality

With this confidence will come a feeling that you are not the inferior of another man who has achieved a larger measure of success than you have gained. When you start the sale of true ideas of your best self to an employer-buyer of such services as you are capable of rendering, you will have an innate consciousness of your man-equality with him. You should realize that this sale of yourself, like all other true sales, is to be a transaction of reciprocal benefits, and should be conducted on the basis of mutual respect.

It is your right to take pains that the prospective buyer of your services shall sell himself to you as the boss you want to work with. Expect him to sell himself to you as a desirable employer just as thoroughly and satisfyingly as you intend to sell yourself to him as a worthy applicant for an opportunity in his business. When you have definite, sure knowledge of your capability and service value, you certainly should not be willing to take "any old job."

There is no better way to make the impression of *your desirability* as an employee than to demonstrate that you are *choosing* your employment intelligently. In explaining your choice, give specific reasons for your selection of this particular opening. Show that you comprehend *what is to be done.* Give some indication of your ability to do it *efficiently* and *satisfactorily.* Suggest the *worth* of your services when you shall have proved your fitness.

Require Employer to Sell You the Job

The ordinary man who applies for a job in the ordinary way is accepted or turned down wholly at the discretion of the employer. If you use the selling process skillfully, you will suggest that *you* are out of the ordinary class. Of course, you should demonstrate in your salesmanship that you are not over-rating your ability. The other man must be made to feel you have sound reasons for your bearing of equality and self-confidence when you seek to make sure that in his business you will have your best chance to succeed. By showing him that you are taking intelligent precautions against making a mistake in your employment, you indicate conclusively that you are not merely a "floater," but that you have a purpose "to stick and make good."

In the same measure that you require proof of a desirable personality in an employer, you should make sure that the work is exactly what you expect. See that your prospective "new boss" sells you the job at the same time you are selling him your services. If he perceives in you the one man who best fits his needs, he will put forth every effort to buy your services. Every employer will respect the man who states, with salesmanship, a sound reason for selecting and seeking connection with a business house; since such a man gives promise of making the sort of dependable, loyal worker that every business values and appreciates.

Sell to Satisfy Real Needs

The true salesman sells to satisfy *a real need* of the buyer. Therefore, when you have charted your salable qualities, select the field of service in which such capability as you possess is needed. That, you may be sure, is *your* right market—the field where you are *certain* to succeed. Enter it, and no other field. Apply there for a place of opportunity to serve; with the absolute confidence of a good salesman come to satisfy a want, and conscious of his individual fitness "to deliver the goods."

You may not get just what you desire at the first attempt. The best professional salesman often has to make *repeated* efforts to close orders. But in the end, if you "have the goods," that are needed where you bring them, *and you know how to sell true ideas of your best self* (as you *will* know after mastering the selling process) you will be sure of getting sufficient opportunities to succeed. You will be as certain about getting enough chances as the first-class professional salesman is certain of attaining his full quota of business despite some turn-downs. *Success is a matter of making a good batting average.*

Parts of Complete Process

Remember as you read that you are studying *a completed process.* An unfinished sales effort is not *a sale* at all. You will not be a *certainly successful* salesman until you perfect your knowledge and skill in *all the steps* of salesmanship. You can learn only a single part of sales efficiency at a time. The relative significance of each point, its full importance in the entire selling process, will not be comprehended until you have read at least once all there is in this set of books. When you re-study the successive chapters, the details you may at first understand but vaguely in a disconnected way will be clear. You will comprehend them as various elements of salesmanship which must be fitted together to complete the process of selling.

Thus far in the present chapter we have been considering principally the "goods of sale." We have been looking at our subject from the *material* aspect. Now let us turn our attention to the mental view of sales.

Mental Nature of Selling Process

In the effective selling process the skilled salesman is able to be the *controlling* party. *He makes the other man think as he thinks.* As has been stated repeatedly, he sells *ideas*, not goods. So the *real nature* of any sale is mental, not material. You must "deliver the goods" to the *mind* of the man to whom you wish to sell your best capabilities. You should use the same process as the professional salesman, who works to control the *thoughts* of his prospect regarding the line of goods presented. Hence when you plan to make sure of getting a desired position, it is necessary that you know *exactly how* to put true ideas about yourself into the head of the person whom you have chosen as your prospective employer. Further, you need to know *precisely what* psychological effects you can secure with certainty by using skillful salesmanship.

Three Sales Mediums

Ideas of your best capability may be sold through three mediums— advertising, correspondence, and personal selling. Take advantage of all three, wherever and whenever possible, to gain your chance for success. Use these mediums with *real salesmanship.*

Advertising

If you advertise for a position, think out in detail the impression of your true best self that you wish to make on the minds of readers. Put *your personality* into the advertising medium in such carefully selected language as will reach *the needs of particular employers,* and will not appear to be just a broadside of words shot into the air without aim. Indicate clearly that *you* are not seeking "any old job so long as the salary is good." Analyze and know *just what* you suggest about yourself in print. Many a successful business man has sold himself through the door of his initial big opportunity by real salesmanship in his advertisement of his capabilities.

Correspondence

Each letter you write should be regarded as "a sales letter." It makes an impression, true or false, of *you.* Take the greatest pains to have that impression what you want it to be. Never be slovenly or careless in writing to *anyone on any subject.* Put genuine salesmanship into all your letters *consciously;* instead of conveying ideas unwittingly, without realizing what the reader is likely to think of you and the things you write. You can scatter impressions of your best self broadcast over the earth by using your ordinary correspondence as a medium of salesmanship. So you can open both nearby and far distant opportunities for the future; even while you still are training yourself to make the most of these chances you hope to gain.

Good sales letters are so rare that the ability to write them has erroneously been called "a gift." It is not. Any one of educated intelligence can write his ideas; *provided he has clear, definite thought-images in his own mind.* But cloudy thinking reflects only a blur on paper.

Using Sales Letters

A letter that plainly conveys true ideas is a sales letter; for it gets across to the mind of the recipient a clear, definite mental impression of the writer's real personality and thoughts.

In all your correspondence, throughout the period of preparation for your chosen life career, send out true ideas of your best capability. If you do, you doubtless will find the door of your desired opportunity open by the time you are fully prepared to knock. Successful business is always ready in advance to welcome "comers;" whenever and wherever they are sighted. Therefore project your personality far and wide through your letters. Employ the medium of correspondence, with salesmanship knowledge and skill, even when you write the most ordinary messages to your acquaintances or to strangers. That is, *think out certain ways to sell particular ideas about yourself;* then incorporate these bits of salesmanship in your letters.

A young man in his senior year at college selected a large corporation as his prospective employer. He did not know any of the executives of the company, but he worked out a plan to get acquainted through letters. He was especially desirous of entering the field of foreign trade, and had made a fairly comprehensive study of the export business. He wrote to the president of the corporation, gave a brief outline of articles and books he had read; then complimented the great company by declaring that he realized the knowledge he had acquired was theoretical and abstract, and that he wished to gain practical, concrete ideas by studying the methods of the corporation. He enclosed with his letter ten cents in postage stamps, and requested that he be sent any forms, instruction sheets, sales bulletins, etc., the president was willing to let him have for study.

Getting A Future Chance

His letter was referred to the vice-president in charge of sales, who in turn passed it on to a department manager with instructions to supply the matter requested. In the course of a week the college student received a bulky package. Meanwhile a letter had been sent from the department head which stated that the vice-president in charge of sales had referred to him the request for forms, instruction sheets, etc., and that they would be forwarded under separate cover.

The student took advantage of the three opportunities opened to conduct correspondence with the executives of the corporation. He first wrote courteous, carefully worded "thank-you" letters to the president, vice-president, and department head. These were all in his own hand, so that his good penmanship might make an individual impression. After these letters were dispatched the student mastered the material that had been sent to him. Then he wrote three supplemental letters of appreciation, and made concise comments on some of the methods of the corporation, with comparisons from his previous reading of books and articles on foreign trade. He stated that he intended to make further investigation along these particular lines and that if he learned anything he thought might be interesting to the company he would write what he found out. In the course of a month he sent a letter which detailed his investigations. This he addressed to the department head only. But he also penned brief letters to the president and vice-president, in which he informed them that he had written in detail to the department head.

Effect of Follow-up Letters

The correspondence continued throughout the remainder of the student's senior year at college. The letters from the business men soon evidenced more than formal courtesy. They grew personal and indicated real interest. A month before his graduation the student was invited to call at the company's office after Commencement. He went, made an excellent impression in interviews with the vice-president in charge of sales and the department head, and though the ink on his sheepskin was not yet dry, he gained his object. He was engaged by the corporation and began training as a prospective representative of the company in foreign territory.

Thus through the correspondence medium of salesmanship a young man who had no advantage of personal influence or acquaintance secured exactly the chance he wanted. Similar opportunities are open to any one.

Personal Selling

Every moment of your life when you are in the presence of other people, you have chances to sell true ideas about the best that is in you. You will not need to seek such opportunities for personal salesmanship. Chances come to you continually to make good impressions on the minds of the men and women you meet from day to day.

Be a skillful salesman of true ideas about yourself always, even in the most casual relations you have with other people. Sell the best possible impressions of yourself to passers-by on the street, to your fellow riders in cars, to clerks and customers of stores you visit, to your home and business associates. Put selling skill, as second nature, into each word, tone, and action of your social and business life.

Realize that in whatever you do or say, consciously or unconsciously, you *are* selling ideas about your capability or your incapacity. You are making more or less definite impressions—you are affecting your opportunities to succeed, and are forming good or bad habits—all the time. *Control the effects of your words, tones, and acts by saying and doing, consciously and intelligently, only what will aid in selling true ideas of your best capabilities..*

Practical Psychology

Of course you already know that each word and tone and act of your life makes *some* impression on the people who hear or see you. But probably you have not realized fully that *particular ways* of saying and doing things have *distinct and different effects*, each governed by an exact law of psychology. You perhaps do not know now *just what* impression is made by a certain word, or tone, or act. To be a master salesman of yourself you need to study the science of mind sufficiently to acquire *working knowledge* of common mental actions and reactions. Familiarity with at least the general principles of psychology is of the utmost importance in using the selling process effectively.

Do not shy from study of the science of mind because it is an "ology" and therefore may seem hard. *You are a psychologist already.* You know that certain things you do and say make agreeable or unfavorable impressions on other people. In a *general* way you know *why*. It is necessary only that you analyze *specifically* what you realize now rather indefinitely. If you do not care to study a *book* on psychology, just use your own mind as your psychological laboratory for continual self-analysis.

Answer for yourself such questions as, "Exactly what effect will this particular word, or tone, or act have—and just why?" You can work out pretty well the *practical knowledge of psychology* you must have in order to sell ideas about your capabilities most effectively. You simply need to apply *purposeful intelligence* in everything you do and say; instead of making impressions without comprehending that by each word and tone and act of daily living you are influencing, favorably or adversely, your chances to succeed.

Three Factors of Selling Process

Think of yourself as one of the *three factors* of the selling process. The *goods of sale* are your best capabilities, of course. The second factor is the *prospective buyer*, the man who has need of such qualities or services as you could supply. The *agent of sale*, or third factor, is yourself. If you will keep in mind always the conception of yourself as *the uniting link* between your "goods of sale" and the prospective buyer, you can be a salesman of yourself every minute. At any moment except when you are alone you may encounter and influence a possible buyer of your best capabilities. You are continually within sight and hearing of people whose impressions of you might affect your chances to succeed in life. Therefore always be alert to grasp every sales opportunity within your reach.

Twelve Steps

It will be essential, also, that you have knowledge of the successive *steps* of the selling process, as well as knowledge of your goods of sale and knowledge of practical mind science. Otherwise you might omit inadvertently to use some round of the ladder to certain success, and tumble to failure. These steps are so important to understand that the last nine chapters of the companion book are devoted to them exclusively. It will suffice here just to state what they are.

1. Preparation For Selling;
2. Prospecting;
3. The Plan Of Approach;
4. Securing An Audience;
5. Sizing Up The Buyer;
6. Gaining Attention;

7. Awakening Interest;

8. The Creation Of Desire;

9. Handling Objections;

10. The Process Of Decision;

11. Obtaining Signature or Assent;

12. The Get-Away That Leads To Future Orders.

Five Degrees of Effort

Another element of necessary knowledge about the selling process is the classification of sales according to the five degrees of effort required to close them.

1. A sale completed by response to the mere demand of the buyer.

Example—While a street car strike is on you are driving, an automobile down town. A man in a hurry to catch a train stops you and says, "I'll give you two dollars to take me to the station." You transport him in response to his call for your services.

Distinguish Degrees of Effort

2. A sale completed by the buyer's acceptance on presentation only.

Example—A man is walking along a country road in the summer time. He sees a sign in the door-yard of a farmhouse; BERRY PICKERS WANTED. He presents himself as a candidate and the farmer at once engages his services.

3. A sale completed immediately after a desire of the buyer has been created by a definite, intentional effort of the salesman.

Example—A man out of work wants a job that will employ his physical strength. He encounters three men who are struggling to load a very heavy box onto a truck. He takes off his coat and proves his strength by the ease with which the box is lifted when he helps. He inquires which of the three men is the truck boss; and asks for a job. He is hired because he has made the boss want the aid of his strength in handling heavy loads.

4. A sale completed only after persuasion of the buyer.

Example—Assume that the truck boss in the next preceding illustration refuses at first to hire the applicant who has demonstrated his strength. It is necessary then for the man out of a job to talk his prospective boss into the idea that he needs a fourth man in his gang.

5. A sale completed only after a decision by the buyer as to the comparative benefits of purchasing or of not buying.

Example—You and another candidate apply for the same position in an office. You appear to be about equal in capability. The employer "weighs you in the balance" against the other applicant. This is a sale requiring the fifth degree of effort. Manifestly you will need to use a very high quality of skill to get into the mind of the prospective buyer of services the idea that you are likely to be of more value as an employee than your competitor for the place. Then you must skillfully prompt him to accept your application.

Difficult Sales Most Worth Making

When you appreciate exactly how sales differ in the degrees of effort necessary to close them, you will realize the wisdom of preparing to sell your particular qualities and services *with full comprehension of all the difficulties commonly met* by candidates for desirable positions.

Countless men have died failures because they used throughout their lives only the first or second degrees of effort. Consequently all their attempts to get good jobs were futile. The non-success of millions of other worthy men has been due to their use of no more than the third or fourth degrees of selling effort.

Sales of The Fifth Degree of Difficulty

Sales of the fifth degree of difficulty sometimes demand knowledge and skillful use of the entire selling process. *They are the sales most worth making.* The applicant for a new position or for a promotion is *certain to succeed* in his purpose if he knows how to complete a sale of the true idea of his best capabilities. In order to do this he must control the *weighing process* of the buyer; and be skillful in *prompting acceptance* of his "goods of sale."

When you *master* and reduce to *every-day practice* the fundamental principles you can learn from this set of books, you will be assured of making a successful average in handling sales of the fifth degree of effort.

They are sales of the kind the *professional* salesman makes with complete confidence every day. *His* methods, applied to the marketing of *your* goods of sale, will work such wonders for you that you soon should build up self-confidence equal to the matter-of-fact assurance of the master salesman of clothing, insurance, and other *materials* of sale. He *knows* when he begins a season or starts on a trip that he will make a good batting average.

Desired Results In Selling

Comprehend, further, exactly what *results* are desired by the skilled salesman whose work is based on scientific principles.

The *immediate* results desired are:

First, *confidence*;

Second, *acceptance* of the ideas brought by the salesman.

One who is unfamiliar with the scientific principles underlying the skillful practice of the right selling process is unlikely to realize that the *first* sales effort should be concentrated on *winning the prospective buyer's confidence in the salesman and in the goods of sale*. Failures in selling are often due to the fault of the salesman who works primarily for but the *second* of the immediate results to be desired; the acceptance of his proposition — the acceptance of his personal capabilities and services, for instance. He neglects, as a *preliminary* to securing acceptance, to gain the *confidence* of the other man. When you undertake to sell your particular good qualities and your services to a prospective employer, do not make the mistake in salesmanship of omitting the process of first winning his *belief* in you.

Repeat Sales

Besides the two *immediate* results desired by the skillful salesman, there is a *permanent* result to be worked for — an enduring consequence desired from the present gains made. That permanent result wanted is *the opening of other opportunities for future sales*.

Complete success in life is not assured when the *original* sale of one's best capabilities is closed successfully. Gaining the *initial* desired chance does not make it certain that one will succeed in his *entire career*. The first sale is faulty if it does not include a lead to future opportunities "to deliver the goods."

The right selling process is continuous. Where one sale ends, another should be already started. A great many failures of capable men can be ascribed to short-sighted concentration on immediate chances. *One who would make certain of the success of his whole life must ever look ahead to the next possible opportunity for the sale of the true idea of his best capabilities, meanwhile making the most of his present chance.*

Service Purpose In Selling

In order to get the right viewpoint for further study of the selling process, you, *the salesman of yourself,* need to comprehend clearly the fundamental *purpose* of all true salesmanship. *It should be the service of the buyer in satisfying his real needs.*

Few salesmen *know* what sales service *is,* and *how* it should be rendered. Service is the very soul of the certain success selling process. Service must be studied *as a purpose* until the principles underlying the fullest satisfaction of the buyer's real needs are mastered, and all false misconceptions of service are cleared away from the salesman's idea of his obligation to the purchaser of his goods of sale.

Sales Knowledge Universally Needed

This brief summary of the principal essentials of sales knowledge has been outlined in order to impress on you the practically *universal need for a better understanding of the selling process.* Certainly you are convinced now that it will pay *you* to know HOW to sell. Then let us look next at *yourself* in a different light—as a subject of study in sales-*man*-ship.

CHAPTER II
The Man-Stuff You Have For Sale

The Man Sales-Man Ship

Your *knowledge* of sales principles and methods, and your *skill* in selling ideas must be combined with right sales-*manhood* if your *complete* success in sales-man-ship is to be made certain. Particular *man* qualities are necessary to make you a master *salesman* in your chosen field. "A good man obtaineth favor." So we will study now the elements of character required for the most effective sales-*man*-ship, and how to develop them.

We shall not consider "Man" in the abstract, nor exceptional ideals of manhood. Our thought of the sales *man* will be concentrated on qualities *you* have or can develop, that are necessary to make *you* most efficient in selling ideas about *yourself*.

Some radical *changes* in your present character may be required. But you will need principally to *grow* in order to attain the full stature of sales manhood that is necessary to gain complete success. If your manliness is dwarfed now, you cannot succeed largely in selling true ideas of your best and biggest capabilities, until you rid yourself of the character faults that are stunting your growth as a sales *man*.

The Little Man Out-of-Date

Realize at the outset that the time has passed forever when the *little* man, with the narrowly selfish outlook for "Number One," might succeed. The demand of the future will be, however, not so much for BIG men as for big MEN. The world no longer looks up to Kaisers and Czars. Success has ceased to be merely a towering figure. Hereafter the one sure way to succeed will lead through the door of *brotherly understanding of the other fellow,* into the *common heart of mankind.* Only salesmanship can open that door with certainty.

We are entering a new business era, where the old individualistic methods of attaining so-called "success" will be worse than useless. Many of them even now are forbidden by law. All the practices of the "profiteer" and his ilk are discountenanced by far-seeing people. Men of vision perceive that the size of To-morrow's Success will be measured in direct proportion to its quality of *human service*.

"SERVICE" is the motto of the highest salesmanship. Therefore, in shaping your plans to succeed, start with the resolve to make yourself a truly big sales MAN. Do not copy the little, selfish models of Yesterday. Study the signs of the times. To be out-of-date is equivalent to being a failure.

Pint and Bushel Men

You will need to be big in ability, in imagination, in energy, in your ideals—but most of all you must be big in MANHOOD. If you are little and selfish in your life purpose, you cannot be certain of success in selling to a truly BIG man the idea that you are fully qualified for his service. Before making any attempt to sell yourself into a desirable position, take pains to develop as much *man quality* as characterizes your prospective employer. You cannot comprehend him if you fall short of his standard of manhood. To-day the biggest buyers of brains and brawn recognize their obligations of human brotherhood. If you are little and self-centered, how can you reach into the mind and heart and soul of another man who is genuinely BIG? How can you impel him to think as you wish?

The little man even doubts the existence of big manhood. He cannot comprehend such size. A pint measure, however much it is stretched, is utterly unable to contain a bushel. But the larger measure easily holds either a pint or a bushel. Similarly if you are big in *manhood*, you can comprehend alike the little man and the big man. You will be able to deal successfully with both.

The Clothing Of Manhood

It is not sufficient, however, that you grow to the full stature of your biggest man possibilities. It is necessary also that you be *clothed in the characteristics of manhood* in order to be *recognized* as a man. When you were only an infant, you were safety-pinned into a square of cloth once doubled triangularly. You graduated to rompers at a year and a half or two. Then you put on knee-pants, and afterward youth's long trousers. Now you wear the clothes of a full-grown man. You would not think of dressing in knickerbockers, or rompers, or—something younger, to present your qualities and services for sale. Yet your outer garb is much less important to the success of your salesmanship than is your *clothing of manhood*.

What is Your Man Power?

If you hope to assure yourself of man's-size success in life, plan that wherever you are you will make the instant impression that you are "every inch a man," not just an overgrown baby or boy. Follow the example of

Paul, that incomparably great salesman of the new ideas of Christianity. He wrote in his powerful first sales letter to the Corinthian field, "When I became a man, I put away childish things." *Compel respect* by your sound virility. Have a well-founded consciousness that in manhood you are the equal of any other man, and you can make everybody you meet feel you are a man *all through*.

What is your size as a sales *man* now?

Ask yourself this question, and answer it frankly. In order to make sure of selling yourself into the opportunities you want, you must take your own measure and fit your manhood to the selling process you have begun to learn. Beyond a doubt you are now a sales man of *some* size. You are selling your physical or mental powers, your services of this kind or that, with a degree of efficiency directly proportionate to your man-power.

The ¼ m.p. Man

If you are only a ¼ m.p. salesman at present, you lack three-fourths of the man capacity needed to handle with certain success all the opportunities of full-size manhood. You were not limited by Nature to ¼ m.p. size. You were born with *full man capacity*. You are like a gasoline motor developing but a quarter of the power it was designed to produce—not because of any structural fault in the engine, but simply for the reason that it does not function *now* as it was intended to operate, and as it can be made to work *in the future* if it is overhauled and put in perfect condition. The full power capacity originally built *into* the motor needs to be brought *out*. Likewise *your* man-power plant requires to be made as efficient as possible, in order to assure you of full man-capability for achieving success.

Maybe your chief fault is poor fuel, and what you most need is good "gas." You have not been filling up your mind with the right ideas. Or, perhaps, your piston rings leak; and you lack the high compression of determined persistence. Another fault might be in your carburetor—you are not a good "mixer." Or your spark of enthusiasm may be weak. It is possible, too, that your fine points are caked over by the carbon of accumulated bad habits. Maybe you have a cracked cylinder—your health is partly broken down. The fault is in your timer, perhaps. You are not "on the job" when you should be.

Your Manhood Can Be Re-built

No matter what ails your particular engine, *it can be repaired or rebuilt into a full one-manpower motor of efficiency*. If you limp and pound along with but a quarter of your capability, it is your own fault for not overhauling your power plant. Don't continue as a ¼ m.p. man and blame anybody else, or curse your bad luck because you can't make speed and carry the load necessary to succeed. *Stop trying to go on crippled or clogged in manhood.* Run yourself into the repair shop right away and "get fixed."

You can make your manhood over.

There is full-man capability in you. You can get it all out and put it to work for your success.

You have the ability to re-make your *character* entirely, without changing *your individual nature.*

You must accomplish transformation into *your best self* before you can make the most of your opportunities to sell your abilities and services. It will not suffice that you just are *willing,* or *desire,* to become a first-class salesman of your particular "goods of sale." Merely acquiring information or *knowledge* of the selling process is not enough to assure your success in life. Even the most skillful *practice* of all the sales principles and methods you learn will be insufficient to guarantee your success—if you do not develop your full *man capacity* for sales-man-ship.

Essentials of the Master Sales Man

The result of the necessary changes and growth in *your* manhood will be an enlarged conception of *all* men—your greater capacity to understand and to handle *any one else* successfully.

It is entirely possible for you to develop and cultivate every essential quality of the master sales-*man,* and still to be just *yourself.*

Good Appearance

The high grade professional salesman makes the best *appearance* of which he is capable. Surely you can do that, too. You can train yourself to grace and ease in your bearing. However unsatisfactory your features may be, you certainly are capable of looking pleasant, and therefore of being attractive. It is possible for you to have well-kept hands and hair; to wear suitable, clean clothes; to be neat.

Physical Capacity

First-class salesmanship requires, too, a high degree of *physical capacity* for the most effective performance of the selling process. You need health, virility, energy, liveliness, and endurance, in order to sell effectively *the idea that you are physically able* to fill the job you want most. Physical incapacity is a handicap in almost any vocation. It can be remedied. It *must* be remedied as fully as possible in your case. You may not be very robust naturally, *but you can make the most of the constitution you have,* with certain success as the incentive for your fullest possible physical development. Few of us are as well as we *might* be.

Mental Equipment

Whatever your physical shortcomings, there can be no doubt that you are capable of developing all the essential *mental* equipment of the successful salesman. You only need to comprehend a few elemental laws of mind science; and then to *train* yourself to the utmost of your particular ability—in perceptive power, alertness, accuracy, punctuality, memory, imagination, concentration, adaptability to circumstances, stability, self-control, determination, tact, diplomacy, and good judgment.

Does this seem like a long list of difficult accomplishments? Examine the items, and realize how easy it is to develop these mental qualities of masterly sales*man*ship.

Perception is simply looking at things with your mind as well as with your eyes.

Alertness is no more than mental sharp ears.

Accuracy results from taking pains to be right.

Punctuality is a habit of mind that anyone can develop.

Memory is acquired by practice in remembering things.

You use *some* imagination every day—use *all* your imaginative power.

Likewise you occasionally concentrate your thoughts. More exercise in concentration will develop this mental characteristic.

You adapt yourself to circumstances when necessary, or when you choose. You can train yourself so that you will be prepared to meet anything that may happen.

You have a degree of stability of character, otherwise you never would accomplish anything. Increase your steadfastness by sticking to more purposes.

Similarly determination, self-control, tact, diplomacy, and good judgment are merely the natural results of *continual practice* to develop these mental qualities.

Emotional Qualities

The principal *emotional* or *heart* qualities required in masterly selling are ambition, hopefulness, optimism, enthusiasm, cheerfulness, self-confidence, courage, persistence, patience, earnestness, sympathy, frankness, expressiveness, humor, loyalty, and love of others. Think of these one by one, and realize how many of them you already possess to a considerable degree.

You may not be optimistic; perhaps you lack self-confidence, or maybe you are wanting in courage. But with the possible exception of these three "heart" qualities of the master salesman, you are not deficient now in the emotional essentials of successful salesmanship. You need only a *higher degree* of each.

Develop all your capability in the other qualities, and you will find you have become an optimist. Your self-confidence, too, will grow as fast as you increase your ability. When you are full of optimism and self-confidence, you will not find it difficult to create courage within yourself. *Then you will have the complete emotional equipment of a master salesman.* The exact way to develop courage with certainty is explained in the second chapter of "The Selling Process," with especial reference to the professional salesman, who *must* meet his prospects courageously in all circumstances if he would succeed.

Ethical Essentials

Nor is it hard for you to qualify yourself *ethically* for mastery of the selling process. Surely your intentions are right. You mean to be honest and truthful. You can be of good moral character. You expect to be reliable. It should be easy for you to love your chosen work.

Spiritual Capacity

There remains, finally, the essential of *spiritual capacity* for selling. It comprises idealism, vision, faith, desire to serve, ability to understand other men. Perhaps you are deficient in some of these spiritual qualities now. But with idealism all about you in the spirit of the world cannot you, too, lift your eyes to higher purposes than the satisfaction of merely selfish desires? Are you not able to look broadly, instead of narrowly at life? You know you must have faith—that you cannot make sure of success if you doubt. Your mission as a true salesman of yourself should be to serve your prospects by satisfying their real needs for the abilities you have. Love of others results from serving them with what you can supply that they lack.

In no respect, then, from personal good appearance to spiritual capacity, need you be other than *your best possible self* to qualify for certain success with the selling process.

Change and Growth Necessary

Reference has been made repeatedly in these pages to the necessity for *change* and *growth* in your man character before you can become a master salesman of your full capability for success. Of course you cannot change your *nature* into a different *nature*; any more than one form of life can be transformed into an entirely distinct form of life. It is impossible to develop a carrot into a calla, or to make a dog of a pig. But the *elements* of any particular form of life may be altered, most radically.

Develop Use, Activity and Quality Of Elements

So you can develop: (1) the *use*; (2) the *degree of activity*; (3) the *quality*, of any element in your present salesman equipment.

For example, it is generally recognized that suitable clothes help to create a good impression. Therefore you should *use* to the *highest degree of activity* and of *quality* what you know about the effect of dress in helping to create a good impression. But, to particularize, do you (*use* your knowledge) polish your shoes, even if it is no more than flicking off the dust with your handkerchief, every chance (*highest degree of activity*) you get when they need it? And when you polish your shoes in the morning preparatory to starting your day's work, do you just give them "a lick and a promise," or do you "make 'em shine?" (Highest degree of *quality*.)

Animal Training

The "stupid" pig can be taught to do as phenomenal tricks as the "intelligent" dog. It is possible to train a pig so that he will appear to be able to discriminate among colors, to tell time, even to perform simple operations in arithmetic. At the circus or vaudeville we sit in wonder while the "educated" stupid pig, alertly afraid of the trainer's whip, performs stunts of seeming *intelligence*. Under the stimulus of fear he acts like a quick-thinking dog. In truth he *has* been changed by training, from the *pig characteristic* of utter stupidity to the *dog characteristic* of rudimentary intelligence. But in *nature and form* he remains just a pig. If you should see him among other pigs in a pen, you never would mistake the "educated" pig for a fat puppy.

In the trained pig the *use* of his pig mind is developed to an unusual degree of *activity* and of *quality* to save himself from punishment and to gain the tidbits that reward his performance of tricks. The purpose of the trainer is accomplished by changing and developing the *mind functioning* of the pig. No trainer would attempt to change the *nature* of a pig—to develop a pig into an elephant, a different *creature*. Only *characteristics* can be changed or developed.

Plant Development

Luther Burbank has accomplished with plants even more extraordinary changes and developments in characteristics than have been achieved by the most expert trainers of animals. He could not make a carrot into a calla; but he did take the dwarf natural calla plant and develop it into a splendid lily that bears flowers measuring a foot across the petal. He also multiplied the characteristic colors of the natural calla and has evolved great blossoms of a score of shades, from pure white to jet black.

The noted plant wizard developed, too, the naturally small, hard, dry, sour prune and transformed it into a juicy, sweet fruit that is bigger and more delicious than our common plum.

He also succeeded in altering radically an element of the natural walnut, which had a characteristic covering skin of bitter tannin over the meat inside the nut shell. For countless centuries walnut trees had been in the habit of covering the meat of their nuts with this tannin skin. Luther Burbank trained selected walnut trees to give up this fixed bad habit, and to produce nuts the meats of which were not enveloped in bitter coverings.

Man Making

Since expert trainers have been able to accomplish such marvelous changes and developments in the characteristics of lower animals and plants—not changes in the form of life, but alterations so nearly miraculous that they seem almost to be changes in nature—is there the least doubt that you, a *man*, excelling every other animal, and every plant in consciousness and intelligence, are capable of the most radical, elemental changes in your present self?

Cannot *you*, then, certainly develop and *use* to a much higher degree of *activity* and *quality* the MAN characteristics you now possess? Of course you can! You need but to learn the *science of yourself*—to get full knowledge of what you are and of what you might be—by studying the *big, best qualities in you*. After that you will need *to make the most* of what you learn about your true self. Intensive self-study will reveal to you all the possibilities of your enlarged and bettered personality. When you know you have developed your biggest, best manhood, you certainly will feel increased power to sell your "goods."

Of all living creatures, Man is the most adaptable, is capable of the greatest development, and responsive in the highest degree to desires from within and to influences from outside himself. Only a stupidly ignorant man would hold to the belief that the elements of his character cannot be radically changed and developed. At present you may be handicapped with what you have considered "natural disqualifications" for success. Then *study* yourself thoroughly, *one detail at a time*. Follow this self-analysis by intelligent practice in the active use of your best qualities, and determine to *change* your "disqualifications" into *salable characteristics* that will help you to succeed.

No Normal Man Lacks Qualifications For Success

Certainly a slouch can straighten up, wash his dirty hands and face, dress neatly, and suggest proper regard for his appearance. The physical weakling is able to build considerable strength into himself. Dullards, unless their brains are stunted, may develop surprising intellectual keenness. Careless men can train themselves to painstaking accuracy. Individuals who are habitually late may become models of punctuality. The man of flighty thoughts can concentrate. It is possible to control a quick, bad temper. Tact, diplomacy, and good judgment can be learned and used efficiently by the countless thousands of people who now are tactless, undiplomatic, and characterized by poor judgment.

So it is with the principal emotional, ethical, and spiritual qualities of the master salesman. *You* have them *all*, elementally. *Certainly you can develop any selected element to higher activity and use it* to help you sell true ideas of your best capabilities.

Maybe you have fought long and vainly for self-confidence, for courage, for will power. Perhaps you have realized for years that you are slow in perception, and have struggled to make yourself take mental snap-shots of details and conditions. You have wished and willed and worked to be agreeable and courteous; yet perhaps you lose friends by your characteristic disagreeableness and lack of courtesy. If, in spite of all you so far have done to improve yourself, you have been unable to get rid of your faults and defects, you are apt to question the statement that you *certainly can* develop such qualities as you most desire.

Decision Will Power Hard Work Insufficient

No doubt you have *decided*, probably you have *willed*, very likely you have made a *persistent struggle* to change your characteristics. You honestly have tried hard to grow, and to increase your man capacity. Consequently your failure may have left you rather hopeless about ever succeeding as you once expected to succeed. Perhaps you have given up your case as "too tough a job." We will assume that you are not so young as you wish you were, and that you have committed to memory the fatalistic, hoary lie, "You can't teach an old dog new tricks." But recall the fixed habit of bitterness the walnut had for centuries, the color and size of the natural calla, the sour taste of the little wild prune, which the plant wizard changed most radically without using any "wizardry" at all. He just *applied scientific knowledge* in his training of walnut trees and callas and prunes and other forms of vegetable life. Have you tried his method of development? Do you know exactly what he did?

If Luther Burbank had merely *desired* and *willed* that the walnut should give up its old bad habit, he never could have accomplished the job of development. He might have *insisted persistently* for a life-time that the little, sour, dry prune should become more luscious and larger than the plum; but it would have remained the same in size and other characteristics as it always had been, despite his continued determination. Desire, will, and persistence were but preliminary steps toward the complete accomplishment of his purpose with the prune.

Luther Burbank's Method

Burbank worked out in his mind and by actual experiments *distinctive methods* of development—*development and changes along particular, definite lines*. He selected for the prune he *wanted to produce,* (an imagined, ideal prune) certain desirable qualities of the plum—the best plum characteristics. He studied *what produced these particular qualities in plums*. Then with his exact, scientific knowledge of the *similarity in nature* of the plum and the prune, and his equally definite knowledge of the *differences in their characteristics*, supplemented by his knowledge of *exactly what produced* the difference in the two fruits, he started his experiments with natural prune trees.

He led specimens through a pre-determined scientific process of training. He succeeded in getting his experimental prune trees to develop discriminatively, almost as if they had the power of choice, *particular plum qualities in preference to others*. But the result was not a transformation of the prune trees into plum trees. The fruit of the tree he evolved was just a *perfected* prune. He simply developed *all the capability* the prune had originally to be *like* a plum in deliciousness.

Natural Growth Without Struggle

Note just here one very important feature of the Burbank method of plant development and change. It did not involve any *struggle* or *hard work* on the part of his trees. He merely provided *natural*, but scientifically *selected* conditions and food; knowing that his prunes then would grow naturally in the particular ways he wanted them to develop, and in no other ways at variance with his plan.

Perhaps the primary fault in your ineffective effort to develop yourself into the man you want to be, is that it has been a *struggle*. *Natural* growth always is *easy*. Growth involves a struggle only when one or more of the *means* of natural growth are lacking. Luther Burbank wished his prune trees to develop certain selected qualities of the plum. Therefore he provided his wild prunes with the same means he had used effectively *with plums* to increase *their* lusciousness. He knew these means should have a *similar* effect on *prunes*. When he had provided the natural means of discriminative development, he left the rest to the *natural growth* of his prune trees. They began to develop the selected plum qualities *easily*, and generation after generation became more and more like plums.

Two Bases Of Growth Mind and Body

Now let us consider briefly: first, the *bases* of natural, easy growth of selected man qualities; second, the *processes* that take place in the development of desired man qualities, some of which may not have seemed to exist previous to the evolutionary training; third, the training *methods* that should be employed to make these processes most effective and to produce the particular results wanted and no others.

There are *two bases of development in every one*—the inner and the outer man. The *real himself* is the inner man, which psychologists call the "Ego." But there is something else in the make-up of every man, his *body*. Each of us recognizes his body—not as *himself*, not as his ego—but as *belonging to* the real, or inner himself. A man thinks and says, "*my* body" just as he considers and refers to anything else that is his.

The discrimination between the two parts of "*You*" must be understood at the very start of your self-development. All your plans for the growth of the characteristics you need to assure your success should be based on comprehension of your *duality*. The two "You's" in yourself not only are distinctly *different*, but they are also very intimately *related* in all their functions. Neither your "ego" nor your body is independent of the other part of your duality. So, of course, both must co-operate fully in every *process* of your self-development; and your *training methods* should be planned for the bettered growth of your inner and outer man *as a team*.

Team-work Processes

You understand now that your growth should be on a dual basis; that you have two different men to develop, not just one; and that they must be handled *discriminatively*, but *together*.

Next it is necessary that you know in *exactly what ways* the activities of the mind man, or ego, are related to the activities of his body, or the physical man. Otherwise you cannot comprehend the team-work processes by which any desired qualities of manhood can be developed from their rudiments. Perhaps the reason you have not yet succeeded fully is that you have been a "one-horse" man and have not trained your dual self to be an effective *mind-and-body* team pulling together. It takes both mind and body to bring to market successfully all the "best capability" of a man.

Training Methods

Evidently, as a pre-requisite to self-development, one should have knowledge of the particular processes that result *surely* in natural, easy, rapid growth. Otherwise he would be more than likely to employ a wrong or only partly right *method of training*. So as a student of yourself you need to start with comprehension of your two *bases* of development, mind and body. It is necessary next that you acquire scientific knowledge of the distinct but related *processes* of developing your two selves severally to work together as a team. Then you must learn the particular *methods* of coöperative mental and physical training that are most effective in accomplishing the man growth you desire.

Neither Mind Nor Body A Unit

Not only have you two selves, but neither "You" is a *single unit*. Your mind, as well as your body, is made up of distinctly different but very intimately related and associated *parts*. Your "mind" cannot be developed as a *whole*. Its parts must be severally bettered and strengthened in coordination, just as the physical man is developed by training his various muscles.

You know you have *distinct sets of muscles* which all together make up your *composite body*. Perhaps, however, you have not realized before that your *mind* is not a *unit*, but is made up of innumerable distinct "mind centers," each of which functions as independently of the others as your set of eye muscles operates independently of the set of muscles governing the movements of one of your fingers. And possibly you do not know that each *mind* center has a distinct *brain* center, which functions for that *particular part alone* of your whole mind. *Each associated mind-and-brain center* also has direct, distinct nerve connections *with only one set of muscles*.

In fact, you are "a many-minded, many-bodied" man—a collection of mental and physical *parts*, a composite man rather than a man unit. These several parts are in large measure practically *independent* of one another.

One set of body parts "belongs to" only its particular associated set of mind parts, or mind center.

Independent Mind and Body Centers

If you were constituted otherwise, your life would be very precarious; for the injury or destruction of even a minor part of your body would be fatal to the whole unit. As it is, you can lose a finger without affecting your eye-sight in the least. So you might suffer a localized brain injury that would completely paralyze a finger, without impairing your sight at all. Either the mind center that governs a finger, or the set of muscles in that finger can be affected without necessarily reacting upon any *other* mind center or any *other* set of muscles.

Interrelation Of the Ego And Physical Man

But if the mind center that governs a certain set of muscles is affected, that set of muscles also is directly affected and at once. Likewise if anything happens to a particular set of muscles, the reaction is instantly transmitted to its associated mind center through the "direct wire" nerves and brain center which particularly serve that part of the mind.

Great scientists have studied mental and physical phenomena in inter-relation and have learned certain facts. For example, it is known that "the mind" not only affects the general functions of "the body," but also the rate of bodily activity and the chemistry of body tissues. Long-continued hard thinking actually does "wear a man out." It consumes blood and brain tissue. It "slows him up." It may impair his digestion and appetite. We all know these things, but the scientists know just *why* we feel *physically* tired after using only our *minds*.

They have learned also that every activity of the *mind* has a direct effect on the *brain substance*. That is, each mind operation *through* the brain *changes* its physical structure in some degree. Mental effort or relaxation increases or decreases the amount of blood in the brain. When you have been using your mind very hard, your head "feels heavy," and it *is* unusually heavy then on account of the extra amount of blood weight. Even the temperature of the brain, particularly of that portion of the brain which is especially functioning at a given moment, is changed with every mental effort.

Slow Muscles Slow Mind

There is abundant scientific proof that the quality and quantity of muscle, brain, and nerve (*physical*) activity in a particular individual are accompanied by corresponding qualities and quantities of *mental* activity. That is, when a person's muscle action, nerve response, and brain action are sluggish, his *mind* also develops a characteristic of slow action. And vice versa.

We say of a certain acquaintance that he has an alert mind. But his "ego," or mental self, could not act quickly and alertly if his *brain*, the physical instrument of his *mind*, did not receive and transmit impressions swiftly to his mentality. The *brain* does not *think*. It is as purely physical as any other part of the body. It just *handles*, or transmits in and out, to and from the *mind*, the various impressions sent *in* by different sense muscles, and the mental reflexes or impulses sent *out* by the innumerable mind centers. Your mind works *through* your brain. Of course, therefore, the quality and quantity of mental work *you* are capable of doing are limited by the degree of handling-or-transmitting *efficiency* characteristic of *your* particular brain structure.

Value of Practical Psychology

Any interference with the *brain* quality or quantity of an individual naturally interferes with his normal *mental* functioning. If a particular part of a man's brain is injured, the associated mind center is harmed likewise and his mental *quality* is affected in proportion. Should a certain portion of his brain be cut out, the total *quantity* of his mental powers would be correspondingly reduced. We all know these things about the brain and the mind. But only a few scientists are familiar with many *details* of the *inter-relation of mind and brain and muscles*, which should be known to all people who want to make the most of themselves. The salesman of himself needs to understand his "goods" thoroughly; so as we study the selling process that completes the secret of certain success, we dig into *practical psychology* a little way now in order to stimulate in you a desire for further exploration of that gold mine of opportunities.

Physical Manifestations of Ideas

The mind depends on the brain, in coordination with the nerves and muscles, to *express* thoughts. That is how your *inner* or "ego" sales-man gets his ideas *out* of your physical salesman, and *shows them* to the minds of prospective buyers. You can make another person conscious of your thoughts only by some *perceptible physical manifestation* of the idea you wish to convey to him. Evidently, then, in order to succeed in developing your big sales manhood and in making effective impressions of it on others, you must learn both *how to think the ideas of big manhood into your own mind* most effectively and how to *show them outwardly* with masterly skill. The first process is man development; the second is sales-*man*-ship, or *manhood self-expression for the purpose of controlling the ideas of other men.*

Selling A Thought

There is but one way to indicate or express what is going on in your mind. Your thoughts can be physically shown only by *muscular action* of some kind. Brain and nerve action are hidden, but muscle action can be perceived. If your *muscular action* expresses exactly the *idea* you desire and will and use it to manifest, your mind is able to get its *thought* across to another mind—*to sell* the idea.

Conversely, if your muscle action—your outer, perceptible self—expresses something *different* from your thought intention, your mind has failed to make the true impression of your idea. It may be that an impression directly contradictory to your thought has been made by your muscles working at cross purposes. So the truth in your mind won't get across to the other man's mind—not because your *idea* was untrue, but because it has not been *physically interpreted* by your muscles as you *intended*. For example, you might stand so much in awe of a man you greatly admire that you would avoid speaking to him, and in consequence would appear to him indifferent or cold. Your physical appearance would belie your intentions.

Perhaps, if you have failed in life or have only partially succeeded, despite the qualifications you possess for complete success, your *muscles* may be principally to blame. The parts of your idea-selling equipment that *can be perceived in action* probably have not "delivered the goods" of sale correctly.

How Knowledge is Accumulated

Not only is your mind absolutely dependent on the muscular system of your body for any true *expression* of the real *you* inside; it likewise must depend on the activity of your various sets of muscles to get all the *incoming* sense impressions that make up whatever *knowledge* you have.

Have you realized how your present fund of information was accumulated? Everything you know came into your conscious mind originally through impressions first made on your various "sense" muscles, and then transmitted by nerve telegraph to directly connected brain centers, which in turn passed on to their associated mind centers these original impressions of new ideas. Many repetitions of similar sense impressions were needed to register permanently in your mind your first conceptions of different colors, scents, etc. Thus you learned to think. The process was *started*—not by your *mind*—but by your various "sense" muscles. These received from your environment impressions of heat, cold, softness, hardness, etc., and passed them in to associated brain-mind centers, which thus commenced to collect knowledge about the world which you entered with a mind *absolutely empty of* ideas.

If a child might be born with a good brain, but with his general muscular system completely paralyzed, *he could learn nothing at all* regarding the world. He would have no conscious mind. No sense impression of smell, light, taste, sound, or feeling could be received by the brain of such a child; for no original perceptions of any kind could be taken in. He would be like a complete telegraph system with every branch office closed. No intelligence would be transmitted; since no message could be even filed for sending. Because of the paralysis of the sensory muscles, the child's conscious mind would remain blank.

Each Mind-Center Must Be Developed Specifically

Recall now that you have a *multiplex,* not a single brain. That is, your so-called "brain" is made up of innumerable, distinct "brain centers" which function quite independently of one another. No particular unit requires help from any of the others in order to do its especial work with full efficiency. *Each center attends only to its specific business in your life.* It rests, or relaxes from activity, when it has nothing to do; or when the particular muscles it governs are not in use. And, of course, when a certain *brain* center rests or is inactive, its associated *mind* center also rests or is inactive.

As already has been stated, the mind of a man is built up, *through* the brain instrument, by the *sense impressions* transmitted to his consciousness. In other words, *all he knows with his mind first came into his mental capacity from outside impressions of things and ideas.* The fewer the impressions that come into the mind through the brain, the less does a man know. And only the impressions that come into a *particular* mind center develop *that* center. (For example, the development of keenest eyesight by many *optical* impressions would not affect at all a man's ability to discriminate among the tones of music, would not give him "a good *ear*.")

Weak or Undeveloped Centers

It is evident, therefore, that if a *particular brain center* temporarily or permanently is deprived of right and sufficient exercise in transmitting sense impressions, *its coordinated mind center* will be stunted in its growth or starved for lack of mental food. This is why a man is awkward in using his native tongue when he returns to the country of his birth after a long residence among people of a different nation where that language was not spoken. But a little exercise of his brain in transmitting again the sound of his native tongue will quickly stimulate his mind with the renewed supply of this particular mental food to which it formerly was accustomed. In a few weeks he will use the old language naturally; whereas another man, who never had spoken it, would require years to build up such full knowledge from a start of complete ignorance of the language.

Evidently, too, a *weak*, undeveloped brain center would be incapable of receiving *strong* mental impulses from its coordinated mind center, and of transmitting them in full strength to the particular muscles governed by that mind center. This is why, if a man's *brain center* of courage is undeveloped, even the most courageous *thoughts* will not make his body *act* bravely. His legs may run away against his will to fight. The physical instrument of his mind (his brain), and also certain associated sets of muscles, must be sufficiently exercised in the *action* of courage to build up within him the *physical structure* of fearlessness that will be instantly responsive to a *mental attitude* of bravery.

Right Exercise for Development

If for any reason the brain instrument is weak or undeveloped, it can handle only weakly either in-coming messages to the ego from the senses, or out-going impulses from the mind to the muscles. So, because of this undeveloped brain instrument, the full capability of neither the inner nor the outer man can be built up and put to use. Obviously, therefore, if one is ambitious to succeed, he needs to know and to practice the *coordinated mind-brain-muscle exercises* that will increase the quantity and better the quality of his man capacity. Since he is a "many-minded, many-bodied" man, *general* physical and mental exercise will not develop the *particular* qualities required to assure his success. Each and every mind-brain-muscle set must be built up individually by *specific* exercises which strengthen *that particular unit* of the multiplex man. Then, of course, all his units should be taught to work *together* to make his success certain with his all-around capability fully developed and coordinated.

The Discriminative-Restrictive Method

Luther Burbank worked out "discriminative-restrictive" methods of growth that may be applied as successfully to men as to plants. He could not have built up the ability of a prune tree to produce *delicious* fruit if he had not fed into the tree structure, or instrument of production, a sufficient quantity and high quality of the *particular plant foods of deliciousness*. He restricted his experimental prune trees to the development of specific delicious qualities, by giving them no food except that *discriminatively* selected for his purpose. That is, he made them develop in one way and in one way only, when he was making a particular test.

Similarly, as has been stated before, you can develop the specific *man* qualities you need to succeed. You must *feed* to a particular mind center, through the related brain center, *selected sense impressions*. These can come only from the coordinated set of *muscles* governed by that mind-brain center. Then you should *exercise* the specific brain center and set of muscles in the production of mental reflexes, or the mind fruit. Acts of courage, for example, are the fruit of brave thoughts.

Brain Development

A particular brain center, of course, will be strengthened both by the *food* of sense impressions it is given, and by the *exercise* of handling messages to and from the mind. The brain, or physical instrument of the mind, is like an intermediary or go-between of the ego and the body. It is of the utmost importance that it should do its work efficiently. Otherwise the full capability of neither the outer nor the inner man can be utilized.

If Brown passes something to Jones, who passes it along to Smith; then Smith passes it back to Jones to be re-passed to Brown—Jones, the middle agent of transmission or handling instrument, whom we are comparing to the brain, might be so awkward, slow, and inefficient as a go-between that the possible ability of Brown and Smith in passing would be nullified or greatly hampered. But if the inefficiency of Jones is blamable to his inexperience, it evidently can be changed to efficiency by *sufficient right exercise* in passing. The more of that sort of work he does, in either direction, the better passer will Jones become.

His exercise, however, must be *in passing* things, if *passing* capability is to be developed. He would not become a better and quicker *passer* by any amount of exercise in taking things apart, or in inspecting things—wholly dissimilar functions.

Training in Passing

Moreover, Jones would not become an expert passer of *glassware* as a result of practice in passing *bricks*, for the two kinds of things are not handled alike. Indeed, the man accustomed to passing bricks might be more likely to break glassware than another man who previously had no particular skill in passing anything. The expert brick-passer would be apt to forget sometimes that he was passing glass. His muscles might treat the fragile ware with the rough habit acquired in passing bricks.

Plainly, discriminative-restrictive methods of training are required to perfect capability in any *particular* kind of physical passing; however much skill in *general* passing may have been developed. If Jones should become expert in passing pails of liquid, he would nevertheless need to train himself anew in order to pass frozen liquid efficiently in the form of cakes of ice. And, to particularize still more, it would be necessary for him to learn how to pass different liquids. Water and thick molasses in pails should not be handled alike.

Similarly the various brain centers, as passers of different sense impressions and mental reflexes in and out, require, each of them—like Jones—the *specific* exercises that will develop *their several particular* abilities. The *individual brain unit* (as of courage, memory, judgment, etc.) is strengthened only by handling the in and out business of *its* coordinated muscles and mind center. Also, while a particular set of muscles and coordinate mind center are strengthening their brain center by the exercise they give *it*, they are both being developed by the same exercise of passing along sense impressions and thoughts to each other through the brain—like Smith and Brown.

The Process Of Growth

Returning to the comparison of Burbank's methods with man development, we perceive again how the principle of discriminative-selective training is applied to accomplish the growth of certain characteristics needed to assure a man's success. The plant wizard in his initial tests gave to his undeveloped prune trees particular food and conditions and treatment selected for the purpose of imparting specific qualities of deliciousness. A prune *somewhat improved* in deliciousness was the first result. Then from the product of that *improved* prune he started *another* cycle of development. He fed the selected food of deliciousness to the improved prune tree, and a fruit *more* delicious resulted. His work was simply plant breeding by the discriminative-restrictive method. Brain breeding is a similar process of *particularized, cumulative* development.

Begin With Specific Training of The Outer Man

All the foregoing rather complicated explanation of "psychological processes" has seemed necessary to make a clear impression of the *right training methods* for building within you any quality you need to assure your success. You must begin by training your *outer* man.

You can develop a particular mind-brain center (such as the center of courage) only by the discriminative-restrictive training of those portions of your *body* which are directly related in activity and responsiveness to that mind-brain unit of the multiplex YOU. Training of *any other* set of muscles will not develop the particular mind-brain center you want to build up, and would be a wrong procedure.

You should *begin* with specific training of particular sets of *sensory muscles* because, as we have seen, that is the *natural* order of the process of growth. It is how you began to learn everything you know. You can increase and improve your present limited, conscious knowledge most effectively by taking into your mind from your *trained* particular senses *more and better* impressions than you ever have taken in before.

Developing Persistence

Suppose your success has been hindered by your lack of persistence. You need to develop *that quality* in particular. Let us see how the discriminative-restrictive principle should be applied specifically to assure you of building *persistence* within yourself.

First it is necessary that you discriminate between *this one* quality and *all others*; especially between it and the quality of *determination*. Very *different* training methods are required to develop persistence and determination respectively. When you are just "determined" to do a thing, your jaw muscles, your arm and back muscles, perhaps all your commonly known muscles, will be hardened *as long as you remain determined, but no longer.* They will relax when the occasion for determination has passed. The habit of instantly tensing your muscles temporarily whenever you need to be determined will very greatly strengthen and improve the efficiency of your brain-mind center of *determination*. But that *temporary* hardening of your muscles will only slightly affect the development in you of *characteristic persistence*.

Developing Determination

Hence the training of your muscles for building the habit of determination within you should be concentrated on exercise in *changing swiftly* from comparative laxity to *muscular tension*. That is, in order to accustom your *mind* to hardening with *determined thoughts* whenever determination is needed, you should train your *muscles* to harden *in coordination*, and thus to support your mental determination by the complementary *physical suggestion* of the same quality.

You do not need to use determination *all the time*; so it will be sufficient if your muscles are taught to be *quickly responsive* to determination of mind on any occasion. (You know it helps you to carry out a resolution if you stiffen your body at the moment you make up your mind to do a thing, but *continued* stiffness of the body in determination would be a strain likely to weaken your power of action unless backed by a tremendous, stored-up reserve strength of muscles.) Begin your practice for the development of determination, then, by training your muscles to tauten the instant you think determinedly. Your brain-mind center of determination will also be strengthened by the exercise that builds up the supporting habit of muscle action in coordination. Millions of men have failed in life because their determined thoughts were not reenforced by stiffened backbones.

Discrimination Between Determination and Persistence

Now let us discriminate between muscle training to develop the characteristic of *persistence* and the training already described for the building of determination. In order to strengthen your persistence, you must transmit through the distinct brain center of persistence to the corresponding mind center, the impression of muscles *permanently developed in firmness*, not just capable of temporary hardening on occasion.

The *characteristically persistent* man has gradually developed his lax-muscled, sagging, baby chin into a jaw that is habitually firm, whether or not he happens to be determined to do anything at a given moment. His muscles do not sag utterly, even when he is asleep. He probably wakes up in the morning with his teeth clenched. So, whenever his coordinated brain-mind center perceives that the quality of persistence is required, and starts to apply it, the *mental impulse* to persist is backed by a *permanent firm muscle structure* that can stand up as long as the mind needs the physical support.

A Slump in Determination

In contrast, the man who is only characteristically *determined*, but who lacks *persistence* in his determination, has developed just the habit of hardening his muscles *for the time* he is determined on doing a particular thing. That does not exercise his muscles sufficiently to make them firm *all* the time, whether under tension or not. Consequently his determination is likely to slump if his resolution is subjected to a long strain. He does not possess muscular structure sufficiently strong to support persistence in his determination.

Habitual lack of firmness in the jaw muscles, as you know, results in a sagging chin; which detrimentally affects the brain-mind center of persistence. A man whose jaw habitually hangs loose may be capable of great *determination* for a while, but he is not *persistent in character*. He might clench his teeth, stiffen his body, and plunge into the surf to rescue a drowning person; but his first resolution to effect the rescue would be weakened by the cold water and by fear. He lacks the quality of the bulldog that will die rather than loose its teeth from another dog's throat.

Muscles Express and Impress Ideas

The coordinated muscles *express* the mental attitude, as we have perceived; and equally they *impress* the mind with *their* attitude. If you have a sagging chin, you are incapable of the mental bulldog grip of persistence. So *tighten up your jaw muscles, and never let them hang utterly loose,* if you are resolved to develop the characteristic of "stick-to-it-iveness." *Begin* with *muscle* training, for your muscles must be utilized to start the process of building up your brain-mind center of persistence.

Developing Perception

When you train the particular sense muscles that transmit external *impressions* to a particular brain-mind unit (the same muscles that reflexively *express* the ideas of that one part of your multiplex ego) you may be absolutely *sure* of developing a particular related characteristic. For example, if you want to sharpen your *perceptive* faculties so that you will see with the *eyes of your mind* much more than the *ordinary* man perceives, exercise your *physical* eyes in taking snap-shots that you can see clearly in detail *with your imagination* when you look away from an object after a glance at it. Try glancing at the furnishings of your room, then shut your eyes and construct a mental picture. When this is definitely clear to you, open your eyes. The reality will be very different from your imagined picture. But *sharpen your perceptive faculties,* develop a "camera eye;" then the reality will be exactly impressed on your mind. Witnesses in court often contradict one another, in all honesty, simply because their ability to perceive actualities is not highly developed. In consequence, they get false mental impressions of happenings or things they severally have seen.

Three Processes Of Mental Development

There are but three *processes* of mental development:

The first process comprises *getting information* from a *sense* to its associated *brain center,* which then makes the *mind* center conscious that particular information has been transmitted to it.

The second process is *organizing* the information in the mind center, with relation to *other* information *previously* brought to the mind.

In the third process the mind center directs its co-related brain center to send out certain *impulses of action* to the corresponding muscular structure.

Let us analyze an illustration of these three processes of mental development. Suppose first you *hear* something that concerns a particular prospect for your "goods of sale." Second, you comprehend the *significance* to you of what you have heard. Third, your mind directs your muscles to make a particular *use* of what you have comprehended. The original mental impression has been *fully developed* because you employed all three processes. If you had not completed the cycle of development, you would have given your mind only partial exercise with what you heard.

In order to become a master salesman, you must *take in* many impressions, perceive their *significance to you* and how you can make use of them, then *act* on your comprehension of what you have learned. There are countless failures in the world who might have been successes if they had not stopped their possible mental development at the first or second stages.

A man might know an encyclopedia of facts, but be a failure.

He might comprehend how to use his knowledge, and still be a failure.

Success comes only to the man who acts most effectively on what he knows.

Right Practice Of the Three Processes

In order to secure quick and effective results, the *practice* of the three necessary processes of development should be:

First, *definitely conscious*. You need to *know just what* quality you want to develop in yourself.

Second, *discriminative*. You must learn the *differences* between what you *want*, and what you *don't want* to develop in particular.

Third, *restrictive*. It is necessary that in your training to develop a certain quality, you *concentrate* your practice on the respects in which this particular quality differs from other qualities.

Most of us are pretty *definitely conscious* of what we want. We know just the qualities we would like to have. But very few people employ most effectively the *discriminative-restrictive methods of training* in their processes of development.

Importance of Differentiation

It is impossible to develop a particular quality fully if you only recognize its *likenesses* to other qualities. *Real mental development is accomplished only as a result of the recognition of differences*. After studying twins for a year, you still might be unable to tell them apart if you were impressed solely with their remarkable similarity to each other. Another man, with a mind discriminatively and restrictively trained to recognize differences, would learn in five minutes to distinguish the individualities of the twins.

Almost phenomenal development can be attained by use of the discriminative-restrictive training method. The minutest distinctions can be perceived if one concentrates his practice for mental growth on the recognition of *differences only*. Individuals who have lost one or more senses become extraordinarily adept in detecting contrasts with their other senses. A normal man, possessed of all his senses, is capable of even greater development of his powers of differentiation.

You know how remarkably a blind man learns to "see" with his fingers and ears. But need you lose the sense of sight before you can comprehend the lesson of his example to you? You realize that you appear to lack many essential qualities of success. Know now that these are all merely *dormant* in you. They can be awakened and developed to an extraordinary degree if you train yourself consciously in the discriminative-restrictive use of all your sense tools. You would do it if you were blind. It certainly should be much easier to accomplish the desired transformation with your eyes open to aid your other senses.

Whatever You Lack Now You Can Develop

The significance of all this is that you need not be permanently handicapped in your sales-*man*-ship by any present lack of particular qualifications for success. *It makes no difference what you happen to be short of now.* By properly coordinating your brain-mind-muscle sets or centers, and by using all three in the processes of your development, *you can make yourself over almost miraculously.* Will power, courage, exact and wise judgment, persistence, patience, rapid thinking, constructive imagination— *any and all qualities you want* CAN be developed in you, even though they now seem not to exist.

Your development is limited only by the practically limitless number of unawakened cells in your brain. Most of your potential mind centers are asleep yet. *You can wake up the slumberers with your various sense muscles, and vigorously exercise them into activity for your success.* You have been handicapped because you have been carrying so many "dead-heads" that ought to be working or paying their way.

Remember that growth of any brain-mind center can be begun and continued only by the exercise of the coordinated set of sense muscles in transmitting impressions from outside yourself and in expressing your thoughts.

Your Limitless Brain Capacity

The number of cells in the human brain has been estimated at from six hundred millions to two billions. The greatest genius who ever lived doubtless had scores of millions of brain cells that remained more or less idle, if not sound asleep, all his life. Nature has furnished you with a plentiful surplus of grey matter in your head. Do not be afraid that you will exhaust or tire out your brains by your self-development. *Put into your work all the brains you can waken with your various senses. And keep the alarm clocks wound up.*

William James, the great psychologist, wrote, "Compared with what we ought to be, we are only half awake. Our fires are damped; our drafts are checked. We are making use of only a small part of our physical and mental resources. There are in every one potential forms of activity that actually are shunted from use. Part of the imperfect vitality under which we labor can thus be easily explained. One part of our mind dams up—even damns up—the other part."

Growth Can Be Assured And Success Made Certain

Can you become a big sales MAN? Of course! You have all the necessary tools to make yourself over in any way you will—your muscles, nerves, brain, and mind. Use them cooperatively, as they were meant to be used, *in their respective sets*—not as if you were a mental-physical unit. *To develop your sales manhood you need only to apply real thinking in the processes of your daily life.* Study out the reasons and effects of all your acts and expressions. Your experimental psychological laboratory should be yourself, undergoing at your hands the transformation from what you are to what it is possible for you to become. Begin making your man-stuff over. Each successive step will be easier to take. *Your growth, when you employ the right processes and methods, is certain.* Therefore your success in making yourself a big sales man can be *assured.*

CHAPTER III
Skill In Selling Your Best Self

Practice Of the Art

If you have developed real capability and first-class manhood, you have "the goods" that are always salable. But you realize now that the mere *possession* of these basic qualifications for success will not insure you against failure in life. You cannot be *certain* of succeeding unless you *know how to sell* true ideas of your best self in the right market or field of service, and until you develop *sales skill* by continual correct practice.

We will assume that you have had little or no selling experience. You are conscious that you entirely lack sales art. Therefore, though in other ways you feel qualified to succeed in life, you may be dubious about your future. Perhaps you realize that *skill in selling* true ideas of your best capabilities is all you need to make your success certain. But you question, "Can I be *sure* of becoming a skillful salesman of myself?" You have no doubt of your ability to *learn* the selling process, but very likely you do not believe you ever could *practice* it with the art of a master salesman. Consequently you are not yet convinced of the certainty of your success.

Success Proportionate To Sales Skill

Of course success cannot be absolutely assured in advance unless *every element* of the secret we have analyzed can be mastered. Hence it is necessary that you now be shown *certain ways* to sell ideas—ways that *cannot fail*, that are adaptable to the sale of *any* right "goods," and that *you* surely can master. You need to feel absolutely confident that *if you follow specific principles and use particular methods, you can impress on any other man true ideas of your best capabilities*. When you become skillful in making good impressions, you certainly will be able to sell yourself into such chances to succeed as fit your individual qualifications.

Your success with the best that is in you can be made directly proportionate to your skill as a salesman of "your goods." Mastery of the art of selling will enable you to cut down to the minimum the possibilities of failure in whatever you undertake. Remember that *success does not demand perfection*.

There never was a 100% salesman. To be a success, you need only *make a good batting average in your opportunities* to sell. It is not necessary to hit 1000 to be a champion batsman in the game of life. Ty Cobb led his league a dozen years with an average under .400.

Technique And Tools

The *foundation* of sales art is *knowledge of selling technique*. So the first step in the process of developing your skill as a salesman of yourself is the study of the *right tools* for making impressions of "true ideas of your best capabilities." You must know, also, the scientific rules that govern the *most effective use* of these right tools. Technique, however, is only the *basic element* of salesmanship. On the foundation of your sales *knowledge* it is necessary to build sales *skill* that will completely cover up your technique. Your perfected sales art should seem, and really be *second nature* to you.

Your salesmanship probably will be crude until you overcome the awkwardness of handling unfamiliar tools, or familiar tools in ways that are new to you. But "practice makes perfect." The use of the right technique in selling true ideas about your best self will soon become natural.

Making Success Easy

The *skillful* sale of ideas is accomplished *without waste of time or energy in the selling process*. The unskillful, would-be salesman not only fritters away his own time and effort, he also wastes the patience and power of the man to whom he wants to sell his "goods." The sales artist, however, gets his ideas into the mind of a prospect *quickly*, with the least possible *wear and tear* on either party to the sale. No one appreciates a fine salesman so thoroughly as the best buyer. Skill in selling true ideas about your particular qualifications will not only *assure* your success, but will make it *easy* for you to succeed.

Docking Your Sales-man-ship

The skillful salesman is the captain of his own sales-man-ship. But in order to make certain of landing his cargo of right impressions he takes aboard the pilot Science to begin with, and then concentrates on four factors of the art of selling ideas:

First, *discovering and traversing* the best channel into the prospect's mind;

Second, *locating the particular point of interest* upon which the salesman's cargo can be most effectively unloaded;

Third, *maneuvering alongside* this center of the buyer's interest;

Fourth, *securely tying to* the interest pier so that the shipload of ideas may be fully discharged.

The primary aim of the skillful salesman *when making port* is to get safely to the right landing place as soon as possible and with the least danger of failure in his *ultimate purpose* of completing the sale. At this initial stage of the selling process, however, he concentrates his thoughts on the *skillful docking* of his sales-man-ship. The *nature of the cargo* a sailor ship captain brings to port has little or nothing to do with the art of reaching and tying up to the pier. Similarly, whatever his "goods of sale," the skillful *salesman* uses the same principles and methods to dock his salesman-shipload of ideas most effectively in the harbor of the prospect's mind. So the *art* you are studying is *standardized*. When you master it, you can apply it successfully to the sale of your best self or any other "goods of sale."

Reasoning And Argument Are Wrong

Before considering the methods of selling that are most effective, it will be well to get rid of a mistaken idea that is all too common. A great many people regard reasoning power, or the force of pure logic, as an important selling tool. There are so-called salesmen who attempt to "argue" prospects into buying. Unthinking sales executives sometimes instruct their representatives to employ certain "selling arguments." But the methods and language of the debater have no place in the repertory of a *truly artistic* salesman or sales manager.

One debater never *convinces* the other. At best he only can *defeat* his antagonist. In a skillfully finished sale, however, there should be neither victor nor vanquished. The selling process is not a battle of minds. There is no room in it for any spirit of antagonism on the part of the salesman. So in your self-training to sell true ideas of your best capabilities, do not emphasize especially the value of logic and reasoning. If you use them at all in selling yourself, disguise their character most skillfully. *Never suggest that you are debating or arguing your qualifications* with prospective buyers of your mental or physical capacity for service. You cannot browbeat your way into opportunities to succeed.

Most employers buy the expected services of men and women in order to satisfy their own *desires* for particular capabilities. Few will buy against their wishes. In order to sell your qualifications with certain success, you first must make the other man genuinely *want* what you offer. Almost always *mind vision* and *heart hunger* must be stimulated to produce desire. Therefore the most skillful salesman of himself does not use the words, tones, and actions of argument. In preference to cold reason and logic he employs the arts of *mental suggestion* and *emotional persuasion*.

The Force of Suggestion

Suggestion is especially effective in producing desire; because an idea that is merely *suggested,* and not stated, is unlikely to provoke antagonism or resistance. A suggestion is given ready access to the mind of the other man. Usually it gets in without his realizing that a *strange* thought has entered his head from outside. When he becomes conscious of the presence in his mind of an idea that has been only *suggested* to him, he is apt to treat it *as one of his own family of ideas* and not as an intruder. Naturally he is little inclined to oppose a desire that he thinks is *prompted by his own thoughts.* However, he would be disposed to resist the same wish if he realized it had been *injected* into his consciousness.

All of us know the great force of suggestion; but there are very few people who so use words, tones, and movements as to make the *most* of their power of *suggesting* ideas in preference to *stating* them. Probably no tool of salesmanship will be of more help in *assuring* your success than fully developed ability in suggestion, which is the skillful process of getting your ideas into the minds of others *unawares.*

Words Are Doubted

The *words* we use are intended to convey pretty definite meanings to listeners. If we are entirely honest in our words, we expect whatever we say to be taken at its face value as the truth. Yet each of us knows that his own mind seldom accepts without question the statements of other men, however well informed and honest they are reputed to be. You and I mentally reserve the right to believe or to doubt the written or spoken *words* of someone else; because they always enter our minds *consciously.* We know that the words we hear or read come from *outside ourselves.*

The skillful salesman proceeds on the assumption that his words will be stopped at the door of the prospect's mind and examined with more or less suspicion of their sincerity and truth. Therefore the selling artist employs words principally for one purpose—to communicate to the other man information about such *facts* as cannot be introduced to his consciousness otherwise. Some facts can be told only in words. But a master of the selling process uses as few words as possible to convey his meaning. He depends on his *suggestive tones* more than on what he says. He reenforces his speech with accompanying *movements* and muscular *expressions*, to get into the mind of the other man by *suggestive action* the true *ideas behind the words* used.

Similarly when you bring your full capability to the market of your choice, you should not rely upon a mere *declaration* of your qualifications; and upon *word* proof, written or spoken, that you are *the* man for the job. Your words are unlikely to be taken at their face value. Any claims you have a right to make will be discounted heavily if you *say* very much about your own ability. You run the risk of being judged a braggart and egotist when you *talk* up your good points; though you may be telling no more than the plain truth.

Tones and Acts Are Believed

However, if your *tones* of sincerity and self-confidence denote really big manhood; and if your every *act and expression* indicate to a prospective employer that you are entirely capable of filling the job for which you apply, he probably will consider himself very shrewd in sizing you up. Really *you* have suggested to him every idea he has about you, but he will think *he* has *found* in you the very qualifications he desires in an employee. You can do more to sell yourself by the way you walk into a man's office than you could accomplish by bringing him the finest letters of introduction or by "giving him the smoothest line of talk about yourself." He is able to read the principal characteristics of the real You in your poise and movements and in the manner of your speech. *He will believe absolutely any characteristic he himself finds in you. What* you say to him may have little real influence on his judgment of you. But be sure that he will note *how* you speak; and will make up his mind about you from your tones and actions, rather than from your words. He will think the ideas you suggest to him are *his own original discoveries.*

Suggestion By Tones And Acts

Evidently, before you attempt to achieve success, it is very important that you study the *art of suggestion* by tones and actions. When you know the principles, you should practice this art until you make yourself a master of skillful suggestion.

You need to know precisely the *effects* of tone *variations*, the exact *significance* of the *various* tones you can use. It is necessary also for you to comprehend not only that "Every little movement has a meaning all its own," but *just what that meaning is.* When you are equipped with thorough knowledge of *how* to suggest particular ideas through tones and motions, you should practice using the principles and methods of suggestive expression you have learned, until it becomes second nature *always to speak and act with selling art.* Then you will be a skillful salesman, sure of your power to sell true ideas of your best capability wherever you are.

Your success will have been made certain through your sales *art* built on the foundation of your sales *knowledge* by your fully developed sales *manhood*.

Discriminative Selective Method

Your increased selling *skill* will result *naturally,* just as we have seen that you will *grow* naturally in sales *manhood,* if you employ the discriminative-selective method when training your human nature in the art of suggesting your best self. You need first to recognize the exact *differences* of significance among the various tones and movements at your command. Then your self-training in suggestive expression should be concentrated on the *particular ways* of speaking and acting that will best demonstrate your qualifications for success. Of course it is equally important to *eliminate all tones and movements that might suggest unfavorable ideas* about you. To make sure of your success, be certain that everything you do and say tells "the truth, the whole truth, and nothing but the truth" about your capabilities. It is necessary to make sure no word, tone, or movement carries the least suggestion that might possibly leave a false impression of the real You.

Let us make a brief analysis now of words, tones, and acts—*the three means of suggestive expression which are the natural equipment of every man for conveying his ideas to the minds of others.* You cannot employ the discriminative-restrictive method to develop your selling skill unless you know very definitely just *what* your different tools of expression are, and the almost infinite variety of *uses* to which they can be put.

Four Rules About Words

For the reasons already explained, words are of much less value than tones and movements in suggesting ideas the other man will admit to his mind unawares. But the sales efficiency of words can be very much increased if they are chosen with intelligent *discrimination,* and if the choice is *restricted* to words that have four qualifications.

First, they should be *common* words.

Second, *short* words are more forceful than long words.

Third, words of *definite meanings* are preferable to mere generalizations.

Fourth, words that make *vivid* impressions are most effective in suggesting ideas.

Common Words

When you employ words to sell true ideas of your best capability, choose words that everybody understands. Do not "air your knowledge" in uncommon language. Unless you are seeking a position as a philologist in a college, restrict yourself to every-day common speech when selling your personal qualifications. An important element in the skillful sale of ideas is making them as *easy* as possible for the other man to comprehend. If you use unfamiliar words, it sometimes will be hard for him to understand what you mean. *The truly artistic salesman avoids introducing any unnecessary element of difficulty into the selling process.* So you should discriminate against all unusual expressions and restrict yourself to the *common* words that are easy for any man to comprehend.

Short Words

A long word or phrase may convey your idea clearly, but *force* is lost in the drawn-out process. Remember that your *words* will meet the intuitive resistance of the other man's mind before they are admitted to his full belief. You cannot afford to sacrifice the driving-in power of the *short* word. Therefore, when your opinion is asked, it will be better salesmanship to say, "I think" so and so than "It is my impression—"

Definite Words

The *definite* word conveys a *particular meaning* to the mind of the other man, not merely a vague or general idea. Never say, when you apply for a position, "I can do anything." That tells the prospective employer simply *nothing* about your ability. Particularize.

Vivid Words

It is of the utmost importance to make *vivid impressions* with your speech. You should employ words skillfully to produce in the mind of the other man *distinct and lifelike* mental images. He may not credit the words themselves, taken literally and alone. But he will believe in *the pictures the words paint in his mind*; because he will think he himself is the mental artist. He will not be suspicious of his own work. If you apply for a situation in a bank, and the cashier seeks to learn whether or not you are safely conservative in your views, you can suggest in vivid words that you have the qualification he requires. You will make the desired impression if you say to him, "I always carry an umbrella when it looks like rain."

Tone Meanings

Our analysis of the three means of self-expression turns now to *tones*. Rightly selected words are tremendously augmented in selling power when they are *rightly spoken*. Most men employ but a small part of their complete tonal equipment, and are ignorant of the *full sales value* of the portion they use. The master salesman, however, practices the gamut of his natural tones, and utilizes each to produce particular effects. Thus he supplements his mere statements with *suggestive shades of meaning*. The *way* he says a thing has more effect than the words themselves.

Conversely tone *faults* may have a disastrous effect on one's chances to succeed. For illustration, ideas of mind, of feeling, and of power can be correctly expressed by the discriminative use of particular *pitches* of tone. But a wrong pitch, though the words employed might be identical, would convey a directly opposite and false impression.

Mental Pitch

Suppose you are appealing only to the *mind* of your prospective employer—as when you quote figures to him—you should restrict your tone temporarily to the mental pitch. You are just conveying facts now. Therefore the "matter-of-fact" tone best suits the ideas expressed. Since it fits what you are saying, the way you speak impresses the other man with the suggestion that *your tone and words are consistent*. Therefore his mind has no inclination to resist the mental pitch on this occasion. He admits your figures to his conscious belief more readily than he would credit them if spoken in an emotive or power tone. Such tone pitches would strike him as out of place in a mere statement of fact.

Tone Faults

If your prospective employer asks how old you are, and how many years of experience you have had, and you reply in a tone vibrant with emotion or in a deep tone of sternness, the wrong pitch certainly will make a bad impression on him. By employing an inconsistent pitch when stating facts, you might "queer" your chances for the position you most desire. The tone fault in your salesmanship would lie about your real character. The man addressed would think you were foolish to use such a pitch in merely imparting a bit of *information* to his mind. He would expect you to employ for *that* purpose simply a *head* tone, not a chest tone nor an abdominal tone. The head tone, when used to convey matters of *fact*, aids in convincing the *mind* of the other man because *it is the pitch that fits bare facts*—the tone of pure mentality.

When Mental Tone Should Be Used

This mental, or head tone, is most effective in gaining *attention*, in conveying *information*, in arousing the *perceptive faculties* of another mind. *Restrict its use to these purposes only.* The mental tone is not pleasing to the ear. It is pitched high. It suggests arguments and disputes. It is the provocative tone of quarrels. So it should be employed most carefully, with every precaution against giving offense by its *insistence*.

Avoid its use for long at a time. Its very monotony is apt to irritate. The high pitch suggests a mental challenge to the mind of the other man, and hence arouses his mental tendency to opposition. The unskillful *over-use* of head tones may ruin a salesman's best opportunity to gain a coveted object.

There are times, however, when it is necessary that you should insist— briefly. If you do so *artistically*, and do not persist in the high, mental, rasping tone; but change to the lower, emotive, chest tone very soon after your insistence on the other man's attention, you will not hurt your chances. It is the *continued* use of the head tone that is to be avoided.

Emotive Pitch

The *emotive* (chest or heart) pitch dissipates opposition as naturally as the mind tone provokes a quarrel. Even a hot argument can be ended without any lasting ill-feeling if the disputants conclude with hearty expressions of good will for one another. The same words spoken in head tones would increase the antagonism by suggesting sarcasm or insincerity. The resonant chest tone suggests that it comes from the speaker's heart. The *hearer's* heart makes *his* mind believe the heart message conveyed by the emotional pitch of the other man's voice.

Therefore if you want your ideas to penetrate a man's *heart*, don't aim your tone *high* at his head. *Lower* it to the pitch of true friendliness, of comradeship, of human brotherhood. Aim at *his* breast with *your* breast tone. Do not fawn or plead, however, when selling ideas of yourself. You can persuade best by suggesting that you have brought all your manhood to render the other man a real service. This suggestion will induce a feeling of *respect* for you, which will certainly be followed by willingness of the prospect to let you show him you are able "to deliver the goods."

Danger of Over-using Head Tone

Some people suggest by the over-use of head tones that they depend altogether on what they *know* to achieve success. They make the impression that they expect their high degree of *mentality* to open chances for them to succeed. "They know they know" their business; so when they secure opportunities to demonstrate their capabilities, they emphasize too much what they *know*. They are apt to use the mental tone continually. Perhaps the prospective employer needs a man of exactly such knowledge as is possessed by the candidate he is interviewing. But if when presenting his qualifications the applicant rasps the ears of his hearer for a long time with high-pitched head tones, the listener intuitively becomes prejudiced. He is impressed with the suggestion that the speaker is a "know-it-all" fellow.

The employer is likely to turn down his application because of the unskilled tone pitch in which it is made.

Sing-Song Parrot Talk

When a man has talked glibly and fast about superior qualifications he knows he possesses, it dazes him if his exceptional capabilities fail to win him the job for which he is particularly fitted. He cannot comprehend why another applicant who plainly is not so well qualified should be chosen. But his voice has suggested to the employer that everything he said was just "parrot talk." Thousands of bright "parrots" remain failures all their lives for no other reason than their utter inability to get inside the *hearts* of other men. The ordinary canvasser who trudges from house to house with his "sing-song" patter has grown into the bad habit of using head tones almost exclusively. As a natural reflex of the unpleasant impression he makes with his voice, it is a common experience to have a door slammed in his face.

Getting Around Mental Barrier

The master salesman comprehends that the *mentality* of a prospect is a barrier to his *emotional* expression. That is, the mind is an alert sentinel on guard to protect the *heart* from its own impulses to unthinking action. So the skillful salesman when making his "approach" *goes around* the mind side of the prospect to the emotional side, where there is no hostile guard. He knows that "the hearts of all men are akin," and that "the hardest heart has soft spots." He realizes it is bad salesmanship to challenge the sentinel mind of the prospect in a mental tone. So the salesman artist makes *his* tone resonant with chest vibrations that stimulate the direct response of the *other* man's heart. *He works at first to draw out fellow feeling, not to drive his ideas into the head of the prospect.*

Talking Like a Brother

The mere presentation of *thoughts*, or *mental pictures* of goods, is not enough to induce a prospect to buy. The master salesman comprehends that he has to deal with the *dual personality* of the individual he plans to sell. Therefore from the very beginning of his interview he works to open the mind of the other man by first establishing a unity of human feeling between his own heart and the heart of his prospect. He uses the *emotive* tone. He "talks like a brother." Of course he is careful not to exaggerate this show of fellow feeling. He uses a "hearty" tone without appearing in the least degree hypocritical. When their *hearts* are in accord, the other man is prepared to agree *mentally* with the salesman.

Power Pitch

The third pitch of your voice as a salesman is the *power* tone. It can be used skillfully to suggest that you have the force required to succeed. It is the pitch that comes from deep down and that calls into play the powerful abdominal muscles. It is not necessarily a loud tone, however. Often it is low, with a suggestion of immense reserve strength behind it. With the power pitch you can *command* in a simple request which, spoken in a higher tone, might be refused because it would lack the suggestion of force. In order to succeed, you sometimes must employ power. When a situation requires a demonstration of your strong personality, augment the force of your words and acts by using the tone pitch that suggests the power of the big muscles of your waist.

When to Use Power Tone

Employ the emotive tone to convey ideas of your truthfulness and honor. Show your courtesy and kindness with the heart pitch; use it to manifest your real desire to be of service to your prospect. But suggest your solidity and capacity for good judgment by employing the pitch of power. With its aid you can convince your prospect of the enduring quality of your best characteristics; you can deny disparagement or doubt of your ability; you will be able to brush aside unfounded objections; you can compel respect.

Tone Units

The discriminative use of various *units* of tone is as helpful in making suggestive impressions as is the employment of character pitches. The one-tone voice does not augment the force of words. "Yes" said with but one tonal unit is not nearly so powerful as "Y-es" in two tones, the second pitched low. A two-tone "Y-es" with the second unit high-pitched suggests the very opposite of plain "Yes." It implies "No," or a question instead of an affirmation. Sometimes it is advisable to suggest "No" when the word itself if spoken bluntly would give offense. You can convey the idea of skepticism or denial by using two tone units skillfully pitched in saying "Y-es."

While you ordinarily can double the effectiveness of your tone by using two units, and you may treble the effect if you employ three (as in the exclamation A-ha-a!), if you attempted to use more than three units of tone in any ordinary circumstances you would be likely to appear odd or fantastic, if not foolish. So be careful not to over-do the employment of multiple tone units to stress your meaning.

Placing Tones

There is selling value, too, in the *placing* of tones in your mouth. A tone placed far forward indicates lack of thought and instability. It is the tone we associate with "lip judgments." On the contrary, hidden thoughts, unwillingness to tell all you know, are suggested by tones placed far back in your mouth. The middle-of-the-mouth tone makes the impression that the voice is properly balanced, and suggests the associated idea of mind balance. Avoid the extremes in placing your tones, if you would make certain of the most effective use of your voice in selling ideas. Convince and persuade by employing the secure, trustworthy tone of the "happy medium."

Bad Habits

Undoubtedly you have little bad habits that tell lies about you—habits in the use of words, habits of tone, and especially habits of action. When you fully understand the significance of *what* you say, and of *how* you say it, and of the things you *do*—the effects produced on other men—you will *start changing your bad characteristics into good factors* that will certainly help you to succeed. So study yourself most carefully, in order to learn what your habits are, and their meanings.

Significance Of Movements

Ordinarily a man is conscious of his words and tones, but he often *does* things unconsciously. Probably you realize only vaguely or not at all just what your various *actions* suggest to people who observe you. Therefore it is of the greatest importance that you study the significance of *discriminated movements, gestures, and facial expressions* as aids or hindrances to the making of true impressions of your best capabilities. You should *restrict yourself to acts that make the best impressions.*

Movements, and their results, may be analyzed under three heads: *Poise, Pose*, and *Action*.

Poise

It is a phenomenon of psychology that the balancing of the body suggests mental balance. Conversely, if the body is out of balance, there is the suggestion that the mind is no better poised. That is, if a man cannot keep his balance physically, we have an intuition that he is mentally off his equilibrium. Correct poise of course involves correct body support, and suggests a rightly supported mind. *Hence you can make the impression, merely by the way you stand and walk, that you are a person of well-poised judgment.* You may hurt your chances very much if it seems necessary for you to prop your body with your legs. The man who stands with his feet wide apart is out of balance, and is easily tipped over. The impression made by the incorrect poise is that such a man must be unable to stand by himself like normal men. The law of the association of ideas then immediately suggests that his thoughts are similarly unable to stand unless propped.

Incorrect poise of the body has another bad effect in the sale of ideas. It makes the impression of *abnormality*. Being unusual, it distracts attention from the salesman and his capabilities, and turns it to his lack of balance. You realize that in order to sell your ideas effectively you need the *concentrated attention* of your prospect. It will help you to succeed in life if you perfect yourself in the skillful poising of your body and its members so that you will be able to appear perfectly balanced in any normal position.

If you teeter from side to side, or rock back and forth on your heels when you are talking to a man whom you want to impress with your stability of character, you will undermine everything you *say* by what you *do*. Of course you should not stand stiffly. Your leg posts are designed to serve as a flexible pedestal for your body. Your ability to shift your weight from one foot to the other easily without losing your balance suggests associated capability of your mind to keep your judgment in balance. If you have a correctly poised mind, it *can* balance your body.

Pose

The *poses* of your body, too, are suggestive of ideas about your mental make-up. The quiet pose aids in making impressions of the qualities of solidity of purpose, of calmness, of confidence, etc. The active pose is suggestive of enthusiasm, force, hustling, and the like. Your pose should be suited to the vocation you have chosen. In a bank, for instance, the quiet pose of assured efficiency perfectly suits the atmosphere of safety and security. In a factory, on the other hand, you are likely to make a better impression with a much more active pose that matches the energy and speed of manufacturing operations.

You should not, however, take any pose as a *pretense*. Whatever poses you employ to augment the things you say should be used as *means for the better communication of truth, not to falsify* in any degree. And you will need to be extremely careful lest you over-do a particular pose and suggest affectation. Doubtless you have characteristic poses. Analyze yourself. *Determine what your habits of pose mean to other people*. Then make such changes in your characteristic poses as will signify only the best traits you have.

Action

Next we will make a brief study of *actions* from four viewpoints.

First, the *lines* of action;

Second, the *directions* of action;

Third, the *planes* of action;

Fourth, the *tension* or the *laxity* of action.

Lines of Action

All movements are in straight, single curved, or multiple curved *lines of action*. Each of these classes of movements creates a *particular impression* when it is perceived—an impression very different from that produced by movements of either of the other classes. It will help you greatly in your ambition to succeed if you understand the *exact significance* of your every action along the various lines, and if you employ intelligently the right movements to suggest the particular ideas you wish to convey.

The straight gesture always indicates an appeal to mentality. Use it to aim ideas at the other man's *mind*.

The single curve, or wave movement, invariably denotes feeling. Employ it to reach into the breast of the other man and influence his *heart*.

The gesture of double curves signifies power. It should be employed to *dominate* both the mind and actions of the prospect—to *make* him *think* and *do* the things you will.

Directions Of Actions

The different *directions* of actions also suggest various ideas. Your selling purpose is to get ideas over from your mind to the mind of the other man. It is especially important that the direction of your gestures should conform to your sales intention. Every movement you make to aid your purpose should suggest your mental action *toward* the prospect, or *away from* yourself. It should signify that you are taking something out of your mind and offering it to his. Of course you don't *break into* his head with your idea and force him to receive it. You just bring it to the front porch of his mind. Then, if you have been skillful in your salesmanship, *he* will open the door of interest after *you* ring the bell of attention, and will permit your idea to enter his thoughts. But he is unlikely to admit it unless by some indication *from* you *to* him he knows what is expected of him.

If you gesture toward yourself when expressing your thoughts, you do not suggest to the other man that he take in your ideas. Instead you concentrate his attention on your selfishness and your individual opinion. The characteristic gestures of the typical old peddler are displeasing because they are made in the wrong *direction*. He holds his arms close to his body and gesticulates toward himself. He makes the impression that he does not have your interest at heart in the least, but only his own.

Affirmation And Denial

An up-and-down movement suggests something standing. It has the associated significance of vitality or life. Conversely, a side-to-side gesture suggests similarity to things lying down, lack of vitality, or the death of ideas. By holding yourself erect you make a very different impression of your energy than would be made were you to lean to one side. You can affirm a statement by an up-and-down movement of your hand or by a nod of your head. You deny suggestively with a horizontal gesture or by shaking your head from side to side.

Levels of Action

The significance of action on different *planes* or *levels* is seldom appreciated. The level of eye action is of especial importance in suggesting particular ideas.

When you look another person in the eye, you convey to him the idea of direct mental energy. You suggest the straight action of your mind in team-work with his. Your eye action on the same level indicates to him that you are thinking on the *practical* plane.

Lifting Prospect's Thoughts

But if your eyes repeatedly focus above the level of the other man's eyes, you make the impression that you are an *idealist* rather than a practical person. What you say will not seem to him to apply directly to his case. He will not feel the personal, or man-to-man contact of your thoughts. Sometimes, however, it is important to lift your eyes when talking to a prospect, in order to suggest that he lift his thoughts from the level of mere selfishness. By your suggestive eye action on the upper plane you may stimulate in him a higher vision of possibilities or an insight into the future, if he seems inclined to take a strictly practical view of his present needs only.

When you look below the eye level of the other man, you indicate (1) modesty, if the movement is directly down; (2) shame, if the movement is a little to one side and downward; (3) disgust, if your eyes look far down and far to the side.

Tensity and Laxness

The *tensity* or *laxness* of your muscles when you are in the presence of a prospect will suggest to him very diverse ideas. Both tensity and laxity of muscles can be used to good effect in selling. Your muscles should appear somewhat tense when you are *presenting* ideas, in order to make the impression that your mind is fully active. Conversely, by normal relaxation of your muscles when you are *listening*, you suggest the receptivity of your mind and your entire readiness to take in ideas from outside. When you show your muscles are relaxed, you also indicate that you are perfectly at ease and unafraid of objections or criticism. If you were to sit tense under criticism, you would suggest that you felt the necessity of fighting back. But you disarm disparagement of your capabilities when you appear entirely at ease while you listen.

Introduction To Study of Sales Art

The brief outline in this chapter of fundamental principles of selling *skill*, and of the methods by which ideas may be conveyed through artistic suggestion, is just an introduction to your study and comprehension of the successive steps of salesmanship practice which are to be analyzed in the remaining chapters of this book. The limitations of our present space have made it impossible to do more than summarize here the chief factors of art in selling ideas. You will need to master the remainder of the book in order to amplify and to apply most effectively in practice the general principles and methods that have been outlined.

Surely you now are convinced that skill in selling is not a vague mystery, not a natural gift, not something impossible for *you* to attain. Every element of sales art can be analyzed in detail. You are learning *exactly how* to sell the true ideas of your best capability. Practice of what you learn will perfect your salesmanship.

Success Certain

There is absolutely no doubt that you can master the right principles and methods. By continual practice you surely can become skillful in their daily use. When you make yourself adept in the art, you *certainly* will be able to sell your particular qualifications successfully.

CHAPTER IV
Preparing to Make Your Success Certain

Be Ready When Your Chance Comes

Thousands of men have failed in life because they were not ready when their best chances for success came. Some of these golden opportunities slipped away unrecognized. Others, though perceived, could not be grasped. The men to whom they were presented had not prepared to hold and use such chances whenever they might arrive.

If you would make your success a certainty, you must get all ready for it in advance. Then you will not be taken unawares when you find your big chance. If you are thoroughly prepared, you will sight it quickly, realize its full value, and seize it with complete confidence in your ability to make the most of it.

Before you seek it, be sure of your entire readiness for the opportunity you especially want. You can much better afford to wait a little while for *certain* success than to rush, unready, into the field of your choice, risking the likelihood of failure that could be guarded against by intelligent preparation to succeed.

Do Not Start Unprepared

A young man was offered a position of fine opportunity with a great banking house. His ambition was to build his career in that particular organization. But when the duties of the proffered situation were explained to him, he declined to undertake them at once; though he risked the chance that he might not get another such opportunity for employment by the financial institution of his choice.

"I am sorry," he said to the cashier, "but I do not know enough about accounting to fill that job now. It will take six months of hard work evenings to train myself to fit your needs. Please give me other employment in the bank meanwhile, so I'll be able to study the job at close range while getting ready for it."

This was excellent salesmanship. The candidate suggested in his words, tones, and actions that he recognized a real opportunity, that he comprehended all it involved, that he was willing to prepare himself adequately, and that he felt certain of his ability to fill the place after completing the necessary preparation.

The bank, however, was in immediate need of his services in the position offered to him. So the cashier, who had been very well impressed by the young man's attitude, told him to take the place, and offered to supply him with an accountant aide for six months.

Keeping the Opportunity Open

"I would rather not," the applicant persisted in declining. "I mean to keep on climbing toward the top in this bank, once I get started; and I don't want to begin as a cripple. I couldn't give thorough satisfaction now, even with an assistant on the accounting. It is not good business for me to start by making a poor impression. I'd prefer that you do not think of me as a man for whom excuses need to be made. I wish to commence my work in that job, when I am ready, with your complete confidence that I can handle it—not as a weak sister." He smiled winningly.

The failure of so skillful a salesman of ideas was simply *impossible*. There is no getting away from such a high quality of salesmanship. The cashier bought the present and prospective services of the young man who had demonstrated *at the outset* his comprehension of the *first importance of preparation*. The opportunity was kept open six months for the applicant in training, while he fitted himself for his future job. This successful salesman of true ideas of his best capabilities is now a vice-president of the great financial institution.

"But," you say, "suppose the cashier had been unable to wait, would not the young man's over-emphasis of his attitude on preparation have *prevented* him from succeeding in his ambition?"

No! A single turn-down cannot cause the failure of a successful salesman. If that cashier had not appreciated the worth of the candidate, an officer of some other bank certainly would have had a clearer vision of his value. The applicant might have been balked temporarily in his ambition. The best salesman occasionally has to try and try again. But a successful career for that young man was assured in advance. From the very start he was "certain to get there."

On the other hand, if he had risked making a disappointing impression in his new job, he might have taken the first step toward failure. Suppose he had begun the work for which he was unprepared, and then had made serious mistakes due to his unfitness. His record would have been blemished.

His ability might have been questioned. He prevented such possibilities by *making sure his preparation was adequate* before he accepted his big chance.

Preparation Should Be Two-fold

Your preparation for certain success must be two-fold. You need to prepare yourself in ability first *to perceive;* then *to appreciate the full value* of what you see. Golden opportunities are all about you. If you do not recognize them, or if you perceive but slight value in the signs of rich chances to succeed, you will fail because of your unreadiness.

Many a farmer in Oklahoma cursed his "bad luck" after he sold a farm on which a gusher was later discovered. But the oil had been there all the time. The "luckless" farmer simply did not *perceive* the indications of wealth under his plodding feet; or, if he saw signs of oil, he did not realize that they *denoted* the possibility of millions.

Developing Perception

Perception can be broadened almost immeasurably. The physical eye, if normal and thoroughly trained, is fitted to be "all seeing." *So can your mind be made capable of widest vision over all the fields of possible opportunity.* Some are within your present mental view, others you can see only after going farther or climbing higher in knowledge. The biggest possibilities of success cannot be comprehended in their entirety by narrowed mental sight.

The first essential of preparation to succeed is that you *open your eyes fully, and look all around you* for the opportunities within range of your vision. There are so many *close at hand* that your search would better begin right where you are. Even if eventually you seek far for the best chance to succeed, do so with thorough knowledge of what is near by. Before you leave your present environment, have an intelligent conviction that you are capable of a bigger or different success than is to be found within your immediate reach.

Also see and comprehend the especial *difficulties* you will find close at hand. It does not always pay to remain in "the old home town." Often a young man needs to go to a community of strangers to gain appreciation of his ability. It is likely to be hard for him to win success among people who knew him as a boy and who still regard him as immature. He may find it much easier to succeed in a neighboring town.

It is possible to make the greatest success turn aside from beaten paths, leave the accustomed haunts of the successful, and go to a place where no such success ever before has been established. The Mayo brothers compelled their success as world renowned surgeons to come to them at the little city of Rochester, Minnesota. Elbert Hubbard brought fame to East Aurora, New York, by founding there his school of philosophy and the Roycrofters.

Over-specialized Preparation

Almost as common as the mistake of first looking far afield for success opportunities, is the error of *over-particularizing* one's original preparation. If you think now that you want to be a lawyer, you should prepare yourself especially by studying law, of course. But you should not exclude preparation for other vocations. Judge Gary was thoroughly prepared for legal practice. Doubtless when he began his studies of law he expected to continue in his chosen profession. But he did not neglect to prepare himself in general business capability. So when his biggest chance came, he was ready to step out of his law practice and into a manufacturing industry. There he fitted himself for the position of chief executive in the immense United States Steel Corporation.

The ability of a *master* salesman is not limited to getting orders for just one line of goods, or to selling only to certain buyers. He has *all-around* sales knowledge and skill. Though he naturally sells to better advantage in some fields than in others, he can attain a high degree of efficiency in selling anything meritorious, because of his *broad and diversified preparation*.

Varied and Adaptable Preparation

Your preparation for all the possibilities of success you may be able to reach hereafter should be similarly *varied* and *adaptable*; though you will be wise to specialize, in addition, by making more detailed preparation for the vocation of your choice. At twenty the average man cannot *know* for what he is best fitted. He may not be sure even at thirty. The start toward eventual success has often been delayed until middle life. To cite my own case, I prepared myself especially for the career of a certified public accountant, but found my greatest success in the profession of selling. I was able to grasp my biggest opportunity in the sales field because, though I had been devoting my time and energies chiefly to accountancy, I had studied and practiced salesmanship for years in order to market my own services most effectively.

While preparing yourself for success, keep your mental eyes wide open. Perceive any and all chances about you, however much you specialize in your preparation for a selected career.

Preparation In Salesmanship

Comprehend that preparation in *salesmanship* is necessary, whatever vocation you choose. Mastery of the selling process is absolutely essential if you would assure your success in *any* field of ambition. Not only must you *perceive* opportunities to succeed, but you also must know how to *sell yourself into the chances* you see. No matter how much particularized knowledge you may acquire in preparation for a selected career, your success will not be *assured* until you are able to sell your capabilities to the best advantage. You can neither perceive all your possible selling opportunities, nor make the most of them when seen, unless you learn the selling process and develop skill in the actual sale of the best that is in you.

Broad, varied knowledge is required as the foundation for certain success. It cannot be built on a narrow or limited base. Evidently, however, exactly the same amount of knowledge possessed by two men would not make them equally successful. As already has been emphasized, success is not assured by the mere possession of knowledge, *but by the effective ways in which elements of knowledge are fitted to opportunities.*

Abstract And Applied Knowledge

Your abstract knowledge may be valueless. In order to succeed certainly *you must connect the things you have learned with particular people in particular fields of activity.* When you have developed the power of relating your individual ability to every imaginable *use,* your mental eyes will be opened to many opportunities for success that you otherwise might never perceive. Such an association of *what you know and can do* with the various ways your capabilities might be utilized will tremendously augment your self-confidence. When you realize in how many ways it is possible to use your especial talents, you will not be likely to doubt your own *worth.* You will offer your qualifications for sale with complete faith in their value to prospective buyers.

Insurance Against Undervaluation

Thorough preparation in *comprehension of values* is the salesman's best protection against a personal inclination, or an outside temptation, to cut prices. If your preparation for your chosen career has been limited to *gaining knowledge,* and you have not studied its true *worth* to every imaginable prospective buyer, you will be apt often to offer your services for far less than their full value. Conversely sometimes you will be likely to think your services are worth more than they really are. You may fail to close sales because your price is too high. A pre-requisite of good salesmanship is the *right* price. *If your preparation for selling your services has been thorough, you will realize the exact worth of your knowledge and skill.* You will neither suggest inferior value by quoting a cut price on your capabilities, nor demand so much as to indicate the characteristics of displeasing egotism or greed. *If you know what you are truly worth, you will make the right price on your real value.* Then your self-confidence in your worth will lend you power to convince the other man that your services would be a good "buy" for him.

Seeing Into Opportunities

If you can imagine *all the various uses to which your ability might be put,* you will appreciate the full value of every opportunity you perceive. Not only will you see the chances for success that are all about you, but you will *see into* them. When your mind *catches sight* of success chances, they will look *familiar* to you because of their similarity to opportunities you *previously had thought about* and connected with your own qualifications. If you are prepared to perceive and to appreciate fully each indication of a success opportunity that comes within the range of your mental vision, you will promptly begin working a chance "for all it is worth," as if it were a newly discovered gold mine.

Service Purpose In Preparation

Possibly what you have read has unduly impressed you with the idea that the salesman's motive in his preparation is selfish. So perhaps it is well to pause here for the reminder that your primary salesmanship purpose should be true *service.* You are preparing yourself thoroughly in knowledge of your full sales value, *as a measure of success insurance and self-protection.* It is not true sales service to give a buyer value greatly in excess of the price quoted. It is right for you to make sure in advance about your full worth. However, the obligation to render service is the principal element of right salesmanship, and should come before the objective of a good price. *Prepare then primarily to serve your prospect.* Demonstrate your true service purpose, and he will give secondary consideration to the cost of engaging your qualifications for his business.

Pleasing Character

You can serve best if you *please* in rendering service. Therefore prepare your *self,* your *knowledge,* and all your *methods* so that from the moment you make your first impression on a prospective employer, you will please him. Do not prepare for the interview with the purpose of pleasing yourself. What *you* like may be distasteful to the man you want to impress.

Since you cannot tell in advance when or where you may encounter a prospective buyer of your services, you will not be safeguarding every possible chance to succeed unless you wear your "company manners" all the time. You always should dress carefully, act with painstaking courtesy, and conduct yourself as if you might meet a rich relation at any moment. You certainly can expect more wealth from "making yourself solid" with Opportunity than you ever are likely to be willed by a millionaire uncle. It will pay you much better to please Opportunity in general than to ingratiate yourself with any person in particular.

Please Everybody Everywhere Always

"Company manners" that are just "put on" temporarily may be left off on the very occasion when you would want to appear at your best if you only knew that "The Golden Chance" was to be met. Therefore prepare to be *characteristically* pleasing to *everybody, everywhere, and all the time.* Then, no matter where or when or in what guise you come upon Opportunity, you will be sure to please with your *genuineness.*

Innumerable great successes have begun with the making of a pleasing impression on some one whose presence and notice were unknown. You realize that your success is practically impossible if you displease. Preparation to please is of first importance in getting ready to succeed. Your success in the field of your especial ambition will be assured if you win your first chance there by making an *initial* pleasing impression and then *keep right on pleasing.*

Cultivate grace in your movements—for grace is pleasing to everyone. Carry your body naturally, especially your head; with such a bearing that total strangers will feel pleasure when they look at you. *Be a person who pleases at sight.* It is not difficult. No matter what sort of face you have, if it expresses habitually your pleasure in living, it will look pleasant. A look of pleasure is pleasing to others. You like to see some one else enjoying himself thoroughly. Everybody feels the same way. Our own faces brighten when we come upon radiant happiness anywhere.

Details That Please

Please others with your smile. It should not be just an affected smirk, but a smile of *genuine friendliness for all the world.* Please by wearing inconspicuous clothes that are faultless in taste, fit, and cleanliness; and of a quality suited to your vocation. Show also that you take good care of what you wear, for that makes a pleasing impression. *You can please in your dress without arraying yourself in expensive clothes.* Indeed, an over-dressed man is more displeasing to Opportunity than is one poorly dressed. There can be no excuse for foppishness, but a shabby neat appearance may be due to a good reason. Please with the suggestion in your manner that you are getting along well. Do not pretend false prosperity, of course; but *indicate that you feel successful.* Any one finds it unpleasant to be in the company of a failure. *If you would succeed hereafter, avoid making the impression that you have not already succeeded.* "Success breeds success."

Courtesy And Politeness

Be courteous invariably. Learn and observe the rules of politeness. Please by acting the gentleman always. Practice courtesy and politeness in your own home to perfect yourself in these pleasing characteristics. Then you will show them everywhere. Remember that the rest of the world is made up of "somebody else's folks." Courtesy and politeness are not natural attributes. In order to make yourself a master salesman you need to *develop* them to an unusually high degree. You may *intend* to be courteous and polite always, but only the development of the *fixed habit* will fully support your intention.

You cannot be polite, however courteous you mean to be, unless you take pains to prepare yourself with knowledge of the usages of polite people. In order to be polite, it is necessary that you do not only the courteous thing, but the *correct thing.* Your courtesy might displease if it were unsuited to the circumstances. It would not be polite, for example, to invite an orthodox Jew to dinner and then to serve him with a pork tenderloin. Your intention to be a courteous host would not lessen your offense against good manners. Your guest would be incensed by your impoliteness, not pleased by your courteous intention.

Virility Pleases

No quality you have is more generally pleasing than virility—*your man stuff.* Therefore on all occasions show yourself "every inch a man." Moreover, act like a *he*-man. Never appear "sissyfied" in even the slightest degree. Swing your legs from the hips when you walk; don't mince along. The stride of a he-man is strong and free. If yours lacks the qualities of virility, change your habit of walking.

When you make gestures, move your whole arm. A wrist movement suggests effeminacy. It is important, too, that you *train your voice to ring with manliness.* Even a squeaky, weak tone can be made to suggest man stuff if the words are spoken crisply, and the sentences are cleanly cut. Do things with the *ease* that indicates a man's strength, not with evident effort. Perhaps you have not realized that by cultivating grace in your movements you can make impressions of your man power. *Grace means the least possible expenditure of energy in efficient action.* A man can accomplish things with ease and grace that a child or a woman would make hard work of and do awkwardly.

Pleasing Tones

A pleasing tone helps to assure one's success. You may think your voice is a heavy handicap. Perhaps it is high pitched and squeaky; or, on the other hand, a "growly" bass suggestive of ill-nature. Again it may be faltering or hoarse. Such faults are not serious to a master salesman. *If your vocal equipment is physically normal, your voice can be made pleasing.* In order to make your tones agreeable, learn to vibrate them naturally through your *nose.* A mouth tone is displeasing. The so-called "nasal twang" that sounds so unpleasant is a mouth tone *prevented* from free vibration through the nose. Humming, as you know, both *indicates* pleasure and is a pleasant *sound.* It is produced with the mouth closed, by a vibration of the bone structure of the face and of the nasal cavities. Certainly, even if you have a disagreeable voice, you can make your tones *hum,* and thereby render them more pleasing. Adenoids that could be removed—even failure to keep the nose clean—may prevent a man from succeeding. *Whatever hinders the free vibration of tones makes displeasing impressions of the speaker.* When a man has a bad cold in his head that blocks the nasal passages, his voice rasps the ears of a hearer.

Avoid Giving Displeasure

Not only please by *doing* things that give *pleasure;* also *avoid* doing *displeasing* things. For example, when you say or suggest anything to another person you want to influence, remember to be a *salesman* of your ideas. Do not make the impression that you are *teaching.* No adult human being really enjoys being *taught.* Any grown person likes to be treated as an equal, and to have new thoughts conveyed to him without that suggestion of superior intelligence which is characteristic of many teachers when dealing with pupils. Perhaps you have heard Burton Holmes lecture. His enunciation is a delight in its perfection, but he talks "according to the dictionary" so naturally that his correctness does not sound a bit affected.

You feel at home with him. His diction is attractive to you. Another speaker practicing the same exactness of pronunciation, but less artistic in selling his ideas with words, might displease you by his scholarly accents.

Tact

Sometimes it is tactful to speak incorrectly, as a courtesy to the other man. If in the course of your interview with a prospective employer he should mispronounce a word, you would be undiplomatic to emphasize the correct pronunciation in speaking that word yourself. It is not dishonest, but truly polite to reply "My ad'dress is"—instead of pronouncing the word correctly. Do not suggest by over-emphasis of right speech that you wish to pose as one who is *conscious* of his superiority, however well you may realize that you are on a higher plane of intellectuality. We all like a genuinely great man who does not hold himself aloof.

Prepare For All Kinds Of Men

Prepare to meet not only strong men, but weak men; cautious men; very proud men; greedy men. Be ready for reckless men, humble men, men who live to serve others. Be aware in advance of the differences in their *buying motives*. They will not all have the same reasons for giving or for refusing you a chance. *Hence be prepared to adapt your salesmanship to the characteristics of the various kinds of men you are likely to meet.* Though you never should pander to an unworthy motive, study different types of character and *learn how to fit your ability to the peculiar or distinctive traits of possible buyers* of such services as you have for sale. Perhaps an easy-going employer will appreciate your "pep" as much as would a hustler, but he won't like it if you seem to prod *him* with your energy. On the other hand, the employer who is a hustler himself might be keenly pleased should you keep him on the jump to stay even with you.

Success Insurance

Be thorough in *preparing* to sell your capabilities; so that your success may be *insured*. You ride on a first-class railroad with confidence, feeling that every precaution for your safety has been taken. You are at ease when you begin your trip; for you know that track, train, and men in charge all are dependable. Because of the complete readiness of the railroad for your journey, you count on arriving safely at your destination. You have no fears that you may be wrecked en route.

Similarly you should make the most thorough preparation before starting out as a salesman of the best that is in you. You have to grade your own roadbed, and must yourself lay the rails over which your ideas in trains of thought will be carried to the minds of other men. You are fireman, engineer, brakeman, and conductor of this Twentieth Century Limited. *Your destiny as a salesman of yourself is in the hands of no one else.* Before you travel any farther, take all practicable measures to assure your safe arrival, without delay, at the station of Success.

Start Confidently

When you are thoroughly prepared to sell true ideas of your best capabilities, you should start with confidence that you will reach the end of the line safely and on time. Don't attempt to "get there" before making adequate preparation for success. Remember that a railroad does not commence operating through trains until the track is finished.

If you are prepared now for the actual start in salesmanship—if you are packed up and ready to leave for your field of opportunity—ALL ABOARD!

CHAPTER V
Your Prospects

Meaning of "Prospects"

If you were to be asked, "What are your prospects for success?" you probably would answer by stating the things you *expect* or *hope may happen.* We commonly say that a certain man isn't rich, but he has "prospects;" because he has a wealthy aunt who is very fond of him, or he is employed by a business that is growing fast, or he owns property which seems sure to increase in value, or some other good fortune is likely to befall him. The literal meaning of "prospect" is "looking forward." So most of us have come to think of our prospects as just possible occurrences in the future, to the happening of which we may look ahead with considerable hopefulness.

"Prospects," in salesmanship has a very different meaning. The master salesman does not regard himself as merely a "prospect*ee*," but as a prospec*tor*. He thinks of "prospecting" as the gold miner uses the word to describe his activities when he searches for valuable mineral deposits. "Prospects" do not just "happen" in the selling process of achieving success. They do not result from circumstances merely, but *must be accumulated by the activity of the salesman.*

Making Good Luck

"Your Prospects," as the subject of this chapter, does not mean your fondest *hopes*, or confident *expectations*. We are studying the *ways to assure* your success. If your prospects depended on mere happenings, they would be highly uncertain; because what you hope and expect may occur, may never take place in fact. The master salesman does not depend on such prospects. *He makes his own luck* to a very large extent by skillful prospecting; as the trained prospector for gold tremendously increases his chances of discovering a rich lode by thoroughly and intelligently investigating a mining region. We are to consider now the prospects you are capable of *controlling*, the opportunities you can bring within reach by your own exploration of possible fields of success.

We will study *particular things you can do, and exactly how to do them,* to increase the number and quality of your chances to succeed. A trained prospector for gold has more chances to strike it rich than a greenhorn because he knows the indications of valuable minerals, and is skilled in the use of that knowledge. So your opportunities for success will certainly be increased if you know how to search for, to discern, and to make the right use of your prospects.

Prospecting Not Gambling

Do not think, because we have compared prospecting in mining and in selling, that the success of the salesman prospector, *your* success, must be largely a "gamble" anyway, as is the case with the explorer for gold. However experienced and skillful in prospecting the miner may be, he is very uncertain of discovering a bonanza. He cannot be absolutely sure there *is* gold in the region he explores, in paying quantities and practicable for mining. Though he has every reason to feel confident of the richness of a particular field, he may nevertheless be so unfortunate as not to discover the gold lode or profitable placer deposit. He is helpless to control the *existence* of the indications of success. They are predetermined by nature. By no effort of his own is he able to increase or decrease the fixed quantity and quality of the golden chances about him. He can only increase his *likelihood of discovering* gold. Even the most intelligent, skillful prospecting will not make a miner's success certain.

You, the salesman prospector for opportunities to succeed, are not so limited. There are particular things you can do, and particular ways of doing them, that will *assure your finding chances* to make sales of the best that is in you. If you learn the scientific principles of prospecting for opportunities, if you make yourself highly skillful in looking for and digging into the success chances that surround you always, there will be nothing uncertain about your prospects to succeed. You will know *surely* that you *have* prospects, just *what* and *where* they are, and their *full worth* to you.

Of course, prospecting is only *part* of the selling process; so your knowledge and skill as a prospector will not suffice to guarantee your *complete* success. However, at this preliminary stage you can be certain that your search for rich chances to succeed will not be a barren quest.

The present chapter will help you to make sure of gaining for yourself such opportunities as lead to complete success in the field of your choice. We will observe and understand how the skillful salesman prospects for the purpose of increasing his sales efficiency. We will study the principles and methods of prospecting he uses successfully; for his practices, applied to your job of selling yourself, will certainly improve your chances to succeed.

We will see also how your very best prospects can be *created* by masterly salesmanship.

Hard Work Necessary

At the outset comprehend that no other step in the selling process involves so much *hard work* as you will need to do in order to find all your possible chances of success and to make the most of them. It is necessary that you look *intelligently,* most *earnestly,* and *constantly.* You must expect to spend a great deal of time and energy in your quest for prospects. So it is essential to your success as a prospector that the investigation of your field of opportunity be carefully *planned* in order to make the most effective use of the time you spend prospecting. It is vitally important, too, that you develop sufficient physical stamina to do a tremendous amount of hard work. The gold miner has little chance to discover the bonanza he seeks if he searches only a few days or weeks, or if he lacks the strength and endurance required for making a thorough exploration of the mineral region. Similarly it may take a master salesman months of unremitting toil to prospect a sale that he then is able to close in an hour or two.

The Food of Salesmanship

Prospecting supplies the food of salesmanship. The salesman thrives if his prospecting is sufficient and good. He grows thin and weak to the point of failure if it is bad, or inadequate in quantity. Every salesman should realize that prospecting furnishes the nourishment for salesmanship, but some so-called salesmen do practically nothing to ensure themselves an abundant food supply. They merely absorb the tips that come their way. Like sponges they sop up the limited quantity of selling chances they happen to get. That is not the way to feed one's ambition with opportunities.

Comprehend that you must *seek actively* for your best prospects. You should not stop searching until you find what you are looking for. Myriads of men have failed because they did not make *an earnest, hard effort to discover chances* to succeed, or because they *did not persist in the exploration* of their fields of opportunity. You know that other men no more capable than you are succeeding all about you. Certainly, then, *your* chance *exists.* Seek it in your own thoughts and in the circumstances of your every-day living. Put a great deal of time and toil into your search. You cannot afford to loaf on this preliminary job.

Prospect Continually Act Quickly

Every moment you are awake should be used in prospecting; unless it is required for some other part of the process of assuring your success. There is no keener pleasure than the eager, continual search of a miner for gold and of a master salesman for possible big buyers. It is necessary that you feel their thrilling zest for discovery; that you develop their unflagging energy; that you be fired by their ardor for the quest. In order to be a highly successful prospector you will need especially a quality they have in common—"pep."

How eagerly the miner prospector drinks in every bit of news he hears about a new strike! How alertly the master salesman listens to casual gossip that holds a clue which may lead to a sale! But the miner and the salesman prospectors would not benefit in any degree by what they learn through their perception of prospects if they did not then *act* intelligently upon the clues secured. Not only should you keep your eyes and ears open for indications of opportunities to succeed, but you should be ready in advance *to take instant advantage* of any you may discover. What a fool a miner would be if, after finding rich prospects of gold, he were to lose his chance to someone else because he did not know how to file a mining claim! Could there be a greater failure in salesmanship than learning about a big contract to be let, and being unprepared to bid on it? Before doing any *outside* prospecting, be sure you know what you have in *you*. Make certain of your ability to take full advantage of your chances to succeed when you come upon them.

Little Doors To Big Success

Prospects that seem at first glance to be hardly worth following may lead to other prospects. Merely because your ambitions are *big*, do not neglect a chance to make a *little* success. Investigate completely every minor prospect you find. Until you look into it thoroughly, you cannot be sure of all that a clue holds. The indication of an opportunity that seems of slight importance may possibly lead straight to the bonanza lode.

An elevator boy in an office building made up his mind to rise permanently in the world; to get out of the vocation in which he was just going up and down all the time without arriving anywhere in particular. He prospected the tenants of the building, learned all he could about them, and determined who were the biggest men. He studied the directory, asked questions, and finally selected the one big business man to whom he was resolved to sell his capabilities.

Persistent Effort After Prospecting

This man was known to be unapproachable. So, instead of attempting to interview him, the elevator boy prospected to discover his characteristics. He found out exactly what qualities were most likely to please his intended employer. Then he cultivated the tone, manner, and habits of action that he felt certain would impress the difficult prospect most favorably. It took the resolute elevator boy nearly a year of continual, skillful work to make the big business man notice him and distinguish him from the other elevator boys. Six months more were required to develop the big man's attention into thorough interest. But at the end of a year and a half of faithful prospecting, the ambitious youth gained his selected, self-created opportunity to succeed. There was no stopping him after he got his start. In less than a decade he had sold his qualifications so successfully to a group of powerful financiers that he, too, had become a multi-millionaire.

This illustration of persistent effort to gain a desired chance should help to keep you from becoming discouraged about your prospects for success. Bear in mind the old, familiar motto, "If at first you don't succeed, try, try again." Stick to your prospecting when you know you are on the right lead. It has been estimated that the busy bee inserts its proboscis into flowers 3,600,000 times to obtain a single pound of honey. But the bee is the only insect, remember, that *lives on honey.*

No Poor Territory For Success

The poor salesman is apt to complain that his territory is poor. *The good salesman makes any territory good.* So in prospecting your field of immediate opportunities, make the best, not the worst, of your present circumstances. The star base-ball player does not refuse to play on the small-town team because it isn't good enough for him. The great Ty Cobb first made them "sit up and take notice" in a bush league. Undoubtedly he felt then that he was fit for better company, but he put in his best licks and played big-city ball on the small-town team. That was excellent prospecting for the chance he wanted with the best clubs. From the very beginning of his career, Ty Cobb has used masterly salesmanship to get across to the world true ideas of his best capabilities in his chosen field.

To-day there is no poor territory for success. Telegraph and telephone and wireless methods of communication, electric light and power, railroads and inter-urban car service, farm tractors, passenger automobiles, motor trucks, and the airplane have so revolutionized the inter-relations of men that all the former great distances of different locations and view-points have been shortened almost to nothingness. The whole world lives now in a single community of interest. The great war has taught us that each individual is close to everyone else. In your prospecting for success you are not limited by any narrow boundary of opportunities. Wherever you are, newspapers and magazines bring to your door chances for big success. If you search for prospects in everything you read you should be able to reach out all over the earth with your capability. An ambitious man I never had heard of before wrote to me at one time from South Africa to secure a selected territory for the sale of automobiles in a western city of the United

States. From a distance of nearly half the circumference of the earth he got his chance to succeed.

The Fields of Opportunity Are Broad

A clerk in a Los Angeles real estate office received a letter from an acquaintance in Chicago who had spent his summer vacation in Michigan. The Chicago man wrote that the farmers of the Traverse Bay region were made rich by a bumper crop of potatoes just harvested. The Californian saw a chance for success in this bit of information. He worked out his idea and talked it over with his employers. He sold them on it. They sent him East loaded with facts about "the glorious West" and brim-full of Los Angeles peptimism. Aided by cold weather in Michigan that winter, the western real estate man eventually sold California irrigated ranches to a score of Michigan farmers who suddenly had made sufficient money to retire from potato raising, and who were old enough to be strongly attracted by the idea of owning and cultivating land in a more genial climate. Thus a sentence in a letter led straight to the success of the clerk who perceived his prospects and knew how to make the most of them.

Know Local Conditions

While distances have been bridged by modern swift means of communication and transportation, every locality has opportunities for success that are peculiar to it alone. Conversely every locality is handicapped in certain ways. Therefore in your prospecting for success *study the conditions in your especial field*. As a salesman of yourself, you should know your "territory," its advantages and disadvantages in particular respects. Men are doing business in your town. There is no better way to gain a prospect to succeed with a house in your home community than to demonstrate to the head of the concern that you comprehend just what he is "up against" on the one hand, and on the other what "edge" he has on businesses in the same line located elsewhere. You could make no worse mistake, you could injure your own prospects no more, than by showing ignorance of local conditions, or inappreciation of the circumstances in which your prospect's business is being conducted.

Turn to Account What You Learn

Not only should you know as many facts as possible regarding opportunities in your chosen field; it is even more important that, by the use of your *imagination* you relate these facts to *practical ways of turning them to account* for your benefit. In order to derive the maximum of benefit from your prospecting, you must make the *best use* of every item of knowledge you gain. Sometimes the mere *possession* of particular knowledge will increase your chances to succeed. But almost invariably you can multiply the value of what you learn if you *prospect in your own mind for ideas* about putting the facts to the most profitable use.

Do not forget that the primary object of true salesmanship is service to the other fellow. Therefore *prospect your own thoughts with the purpose of making what you know especially valuable to some one else,* your intended employer for instance. In every step of the selling process you should think first of how you can serve your prospect with something that he lacks and needs.

Prospect Needs

Surprisingly few young men who go into business prospect their fields of opportunity to learn what is most wanted there. The great majority take up special professions or enter selected industries just because *they* wish to do chosen things. The master salesman, however, *adapts himself to the circumstances and requirements of his customers,* even at the sacrifice of his personal inclinations. He could not succeed if he sold only what he wanted to sell, or if he confined his salesmanship efforts to a limited number of buyers because he liked them and disliked others. In order to assure your success, *you must learn to like to do what is most needed to be done, and learn to like to serve whoever lacks what you can supply.* Therefore prospect your fields of opportunity to learn what capabilities are principally needed. If you would make your success as easy as possible, look about you first to determine the demand for such services as you are able to render.

Sometimes Go The Round-About Way

Perhaps your prospecting will indicate that it is advisable for you to go a round-about way to your goal of ambition; because the direct route is beset with great difficulties. A young doctor wished to specialize in bacteriology. He realized that it would take the savings of a great many years of general medical practice to equip a complete laboratory of his own. Accordingly he discontinued the practice of his profession; though he went on with his studies. He engaged in business for five years. Thus in a comparatively short time he earned the money he needed to enable him to devote the rest of his life to bacteriological research.

Racial Characteristics

Different territories or fields of opportunity have *various characters,* like different people. It is important to study especially the racial types you are likely to encounter. Many a man has attained success by accumulating discriminative knowledge regarding the national peculiarities of the Latin peoples, Slavs, Teutons, Anglo-Saxons, Magyars, etc.

The Italian has strong likes and dislikes in colors and patterns of goods. To be a good salesman in dealing with him, you should know his preferences and prejudices. If you learn what colors and patterns are most favored in the "Little Italy" of your city, you may be able to employ this bit of knowledge to help you very much in influencing your fellow-residents of Italian descent.

You are aware of the effect produced on the majority of Irishmen by the color green. But take care to learn whether the Irishmen whose political help you would like to win are from the South or the North of the Emerald Isle. They may be Orangemen, and you might "queer" your prospects by going among them wearing a green necktie.

Learn your facts with discrimination; then use them restrictively in the circumstances where they will be most effective in promoting your success.

Temporary Conditions

Prospect to learn not only permanent conditions in your field of opportunity, but also any *temporary* conditions that might affect your chances to succeed. Mental and emotional "waves" sweep over the country and over local communities at times. Billy Sunday's revivals in various great cities brought success opportunities to particular businesses, but had injurious effects on others. You should take such factors into account when studying your prospects.

The manufacturers of that successful innovation, the "Service Flag," took advantage of the sudden demand for such an emblem. When war came, they saw into the future and perceived a new lack. But the need for Service Flags was temporary. Before the war ended they were displayed everywhere. To-day none are seen.

Now there has come into existence The American Legion, which seems certain to be a great political and social power in the United States for generations, as was the G.A.R. after the civil war. Any man who hopes for political success in the course of the next thirty or forty years must prospect the thoughts and feelings of the veterans of 1917-18.

Analyze Individuals

You will have *specific* as well as general prospects. Hence it is essential that you supplement your study of conditions with the *analysis of individuals*. Study men with the greatest care, especially the one man or group of men upon whom you want to impress ideas of your capabilities. Learn all you can regarding the personal characteristics of the individual to whom you hope to sell your services or "goods." Your knowledge of his traits and peculiarities, your familiarity with his life purposes and hobbies, may assure you a chance to succeed with him that otherwise you could not get. A friend of mine is the president of a big ice company, but he is not so much interested in cooling people's food as in warming their hearts with his genuine brotherhood for all men. There isn't much prospect for anybody to sell him "a cold business proposition," even though he is a dealer in ice.

Hobbies

Do not, however, make a "hobby of hobbies." Only the *big* hobbies of your man are worth especial study. Never harp on any of his little idiosyncracies. He may be sensitive about being eccentric. It is bad salesmanship to *pretend* an interest in another person's whims. You cannot use his hobbies to help your prospects *unless you share his feelings* to a considerable degree. My friend who believes and practices the doctrine that all men are brothers would be sure to detect quickly a false humanitarian bent on a selfish purpose to exploit his hobby.

As already has been emphasized, the object of the good salesman when prospecting is to discover the lacks of men who might benefit from the things he has to sell. If you are looking for your prospects with that *service* purpose, you have taken a long preparatory step in the process of selling your qualifications. Find the employer who *needs* your best ability, and your success will be assured the moment you get into his mind the true idea that you are the man he has been looking for.

Prospect Lacks

Undoubtedly you know men to whom success has come because they made other men realize they fitted into particular needs. A young acquaintance of mine foresaw that a manufacturer would want an assistant within a year or two; though the executive himself was unaware that he was developing such a need. My acquaintance got a minor job under him in order to make a good impression in advance. Long before the head of the business realized that he was breaking in a confidential assistant, the young man had qualified for the position he had perceived in prospect.

Your chosen employer may not know of the lack that you have prospected in his business. He may not have the least idea that he wants you. Prospecting his needs is part of *your* job as a salesman of yourself.

An expert accountant sold himself into a fine position as the auditor of a great corporation by anticipating that the Company would need to have its system of book-keeping revolutionized in order to prepare for the Federal income tax. He prospected what was coming to that business; then sold the president comprehension that he lacked an expert accountant he was going to need badly before long.

One of my own experiences as an accountant illustrates the value of specific prospecting. When I was studying accountancy, I bought every authoritative publication on the subject. For one set of forty books I had to send to London. Each volume related to the peculiar accounts, terms, etc. of one business. There was a book on brewery accounting, another on commission house accounting, and so on through the list of forty businesses. To each volume I afterward owed at least one client. For instance, I got a commission to make a cost survey for a tobacco company, largely because I was able to convince the president that I knew a good deal about the tobacco business. I talked intelligently to him regarding the processes of his industry.

Reasons Behind Habits

When you prospect an individual's personal qualities, traits, or hobbies, do not stop after learning the facts. Study out the *reasons behind* habits and opinions. It may help you only a little to know that your intended employer is a Republican or a Democrat; that he is conservative or radical in his social opinions. But your chances of success in dealing with him will be greatly increased if you know exactly *why* he belongs to one or the other political party, and the *reason* he is a "stand-patter" or a "progressive." Use knowledge of why's and wherefore's with the skill of a salesman bent on securing an order from a prospective buyer. But be sure you get the *fundamental facts*, for often "appearances are deceiving."

Your Personal Responsibility

When you look for prospects in your selected field of service-opportunities recognize your *personal responsibility* for the successful development of the chances you find. Before you begin prospecting, realize that *what you make of your opportunities is solely up to you.* Assume all the responsibility for your own success; then you will have no excuse to blame any one else if you fail. Should things not go as you wish, say "It's my own fault," and feel that way. *The true salesman never apologizes to himself.* So if you have not found your prospects, or if you have not made the best use of the chances you have discovered, kick at the man who is responsible. Don't get sore on the world at large.

Follow-ups

Perhaps what has been said thus far has over-emphasized the process of prospecting for the *first* chance to succeed. Maybe it suggests to you that if one can get an opening, the hardest part of the effort to assure success will have been accomplished. But a successful career in salesmanship is not built on single orders closed. The master salesman keeps on selling the same buyer and develops him into a steady customer. He continues all the while to prospect the needs of that buyer, just as thoroughly as if he were planning his first approach.

Your initial success should be completed by after-service. In order to continue progressing toward your goal, you must "deliver the goods" right along. You cannot keep your success growing unless you prospect unremittingly for more and better opportunities to render service. Give satisfaction in larger amount and improved quality from month to month, and year after year. If you would continue to succeed, look ahead always for more prospects and *seek in each of them new chances to broaden your usefulness.*

The Art of Prospecting

If you prospect *skillfully* (with art), your chances to find what you seek will be remarkably increased. So look for your prospects *cheerily.* Be *frank* and *expressive* in your quest. Show your *sympathetic* side, and thus appeal to the *kinder* tendencies of other people. The best way to avoid the world's coldness is by *warming* everybody you meet with your own cordiality. Be *courteous.* Especially cultivate the art of talking *with* people instead of *at* them. Use *tact* and *judgment* in dealing with your prospects.

Thousands of men are shut away from the open minds and hearts of others by doors of concealment and reserve. You need to open such doors. You can do it only by frankness on your own part, which will induce people to feel like telling you their secrets. Frank expression of your opinion, provided it has a sound foundation, will often draw out the hidden opinions of others and reveal to you prospects that you might never discover unaided. Do not, however, be dogmatic or arbitrary in saying what you think. Speak your beliefs casually. Then you will not discourage those honest differences of opinion that enlighten one's own ideas.

Rid your face of sharpness if you would be a good prospector for your best chances to succeed. Avoid "the cutting edge" in your voice and manner when you make inquiries about opportunities you seek. You are likely to be most effective in prospecting if you *cultivate an easy attitude of friendliness.* The master salesman does not set his jaw when prospecting. He uses curved, instead of straight line gestures to supplement his words. He suggests a "ball-bearing" disposition, not "corners."

Sympathetic Attitude

Be a good mixer when looking for your prospects. Learn the art of *companionship.* The first essential is fellow feeling. Therefore do not go about with a chip on your shoulder, but with your face a-smile and your palms open to offer and to receive hand-clasps. Sympathize with the ambitions of other men, with their hopes and dreams. Remember that each part of every work of man, however substantial and enduring it now may be, was once no more than a figment of the imagination of some one's mind. So do not be altogether "practical" when prospecting. It is a mistake to neglect to prospect visions.

Have a Leader

When the master salesman prospects, he uses very effectively a "leader" idea. You know how aggressive stores advertise leaders that draw trade in other things. Your prospecting of your various capabilities should enable you to decide which of your qualifications will make the most effective leader in the case of a certain employer. Do not expect him to perceive *all* your merits immediately. Concentrate his attention and interest on *one or two elements* of your fitness to fill his especial needs. Prospect to make sure which of your possible leaders would be most likely to influence him in your favor. Then *use these selected elements of your character very prominently* to open the door of your initial chance. Countless successes have been founded on well chosen leaders.

A little bake shop in Chicago competes successfully to-day with a great chain-store company that has an immense establishment directly across the street. The shop sells as its leaders home-made English tarts that no chain-store could supply. These draw buyers for groceries and other goods the chain-store sells much cheaper, but which the purchasers of tarts order with their pastry rather than cross the street and divide their marketing.

Summary

Now let us summarize "Your Prospects." They are not far away nor far ahead in time. They are in your own hands right now. You *cannot fail* in life if you recognize and use most effectively all the opportunities available to you at present. You suffer from no lack of chances to succeed. You only need to open your physical eyes and the eyes of your mind to *see* fine prospects every day. Then if you *imaginatively relate your abilities to what you perceive, and plan how you can fit yourself into a chosen place of real service,* you will have begun the selling process successfully. At the outset of your career it is possible for you to reduce difficult obstacles to temporary set-backs that you can get around or overcome.

Success A Matter Of Fractions

There is only a narrow margin of difference between success and failure. *Success is a matter of fractions and decimals, not of big units.* A few thousand American soldiers and marines turned the tide of German victory at Chateau Thierry. "It is the last straw that breaks the camel's back."

If you *begin* the selling process by the finest prospecting, and *keep on* with equal effectiveness throughout all the following steps of salesmanship, you will gain so many more chances than you otherwise could get that *your success in the end will be assured.* The master salesman works with *certainty* that he will secure his quota of orders. He knows in advance that he will succeed; *because he knows sure ways to sell.*

Good prospecting is just a natural process, intelligently comprehended. It is neither mysterious nor hard. It is one of the preliminary, understandable ways to make success not only *sure,* but *easy* to attain.

CHAPTER VI
Gaining Your Chance

Getting Inside The Door

We will assume that you have qualified yourself to succeed; that you have developed your best capabilities in knowledge, in manhood, and in sales skill; that you have completed the general preparation necessary to assure your success in marketing your particular qualifications; and that you also have learned how to find and to make the most of your prospects. After these preliminaries you are ready to take the next step in the selling process, and to begin putting your capabilities, and what you have learned from preparation and prospecting, to *specific use in actual selling*.

In order to succeed, you must not only be *qualified* for some *particular* service work, but you also need *chances to demonstrate* your capabilities and preparedness for effective service. If you stand all your life in complete readiness for success but outside the door of opportunity, you will be a failure despite your exceptional qualifications and preparations for handling chances to succeed. *It is necessary that you get inside the door.* We will study now the *sure* ways and means of entrance.

The Salesman's Advantage Over the Buyer

One great advantage the skillful salesman has over even the best buyer is that he can *plan* completely *what* he will do and *how* he will do it to accomplish his selling purpose. The prospect is unable to anticipate who will call upon him next; so it is impossible for him to avoid being taken *unawares* by each salesman. He can make only general and hasty preparations at the moment to deal with the particular individual who comes intent on securing his order.

The good salesman, however, works out in advance the most effective ways and means to present his proposition. Each move in the process of selling his ideas to a prospect is carefully studied and practiced beforehand. The effects of different words and tones and acts are exactly weighed. When the thoroughly prepared salesman calls on a possible buyer, he has in mind a flexible program of procedure with which he is perfectly familiar and which he can adapt skillfully to various conditions that his imagination has enabled him to anticipate. Hence the master salesman usually is able to *control the situation*, no matter how shrewd the prospect may be; because the salesman's chance to plan assures him a great advantage over the unprepared or incompletely prepared other party to the sale.

Dominate The Interview with Confidence

If you would likewise "dominate" the man to whom you want to sell your capabilities, prepare "plans of approach" to his interest before calling on him; in order to make sure of presenting your qualifications most strongly. He can oppose your salesmanship with but comparatively weak resistance; because *he has had no such opportunity as you to get all ready for this interview*. The skillful salesman is confident that he can control the selling process he begins. When you seek a selected chance for the success you desire, you should feel similar assurance of ability to sell your services. You will possess this feeling if you prepare your "plan of approach" as the master salesman gets ready for his interview with a prospective buyer.

The Two Entrances

You have to make two distinct "entrances" in order to gain your desired chance to succeed. You need to get *yourself* into the *presence* of the employer you have selected. Then it is essential that you get the *true idea* of your capabilities and preparedness into his *mind*. Your "approach" to his attention and interest, therefore, involves a *double* process. It is important that you plan intelligently the most skillful ways and means of making the *two* entrances; through the *physical* and the *mental* closed doors that now shut you out from the opportunities you have prospected and desire to gain.

No master salesman would call on an important prospect before planning in his own mind how to take the successive steps of the interview expected. Nor would a master salesman neglect to think out in advance several specific methods of getting past any physical barriers he might encounter between the outer door of the general office and the inner sanctum of the man he must meet face to face in order to close a sale.

Ordinary Way Of Getting Job

But when the *unskilled* salesman of his own capabilities seeks a situation, he usually neglects to make careful, detailed plans to reach his prospect in the most effective way. He does not prepare to create the particular impressions that would be most apt to assure him the attention and interest of the employer upon whom he calls. Nearly always when a man out of a job answers an advertisement or follows up a clue to a possible opening for his services, he thinks the most important thing is to "get there first." The only advantage he hopes to gain over other applicants is a position at the head of the line.

Have you ever stopped to analyze the mental attitude of an employer toward the half dozen, dozen, or score of men who answer his advertisement for the services of one man? He thinks, "Here are a lot of fellows out of jobs. Probably most of them are no good, or they wouldn't be out of jobs. They are competing for this place. Each sees there are plenty of others who will be glad to have it. Therefore it is likely that I can get a man without paying him much to start with, and he probably won't be very independent for a while after I hire him. I'll take my pick of the lot, and keep the names and addresses of two or three others in case he doesn't make good."

Shearing The Sheep

Then the employer calls in the applicants as if they were so many sheep to be sheared by sharp cross-examination. Practically every candidate enters the private office with a considerable degree of sheepishness in his feelings, whether he tries to appear at ease or not. The employer first eyes him in keen appraisal. He then proceeds briskly to clip off facts about him. The man sitting behind the desk absolutely dominates the situation. He finishes his questioning, and disposes of the applicant as he pleases.

What chance to gain the desired opportunity for service does each candidate have in such an uncontrolled process of getting a job? He has one-sixth, or one-twelfth, or one-twentieth of a chance for success; according to whether there are six or a dozen or a score of applicants. Also, practically without exception, men who come seeking a position and find that it has been filled make no further efforts to secure the opportunity for which they have applied; though the successful candidate may not make good and the position may soon be vacant again. Your own experience and observation have made familiar to you this common way of looking for jobs. You know that in such cases the employer has all the advantage. Certainly the applicants who try to gain a chance to work by this method use no *salesmanship* at all.

The Salesman's Method

How would a "salesman" candidate for such a situation proceed? First, he would avoid the mistake of presenting himself as *merely one of a crowd* of competing applicants. He would *make his particular personality stand out*. Before calling, he would do some prospecting to discover just what capabilities were needed to fill the position advertised. Then he would plan different ways of tackling the prospective employer. When all ready, but not before, he would go to the address.

If he should find a crowd there, he would not merge with it. He would avoid stating his business immediately in the outer office, rather than identify himself with the other candidates waiting. He would have a plan to get an interview later, after the dispersal of the crowd. If he should be told then that the position had been filled, he would go right ahead with his selling program regardless of the rebuff. He would proceed to sell the boss the idea that *he* was an especially well fitted man for the job. He would assume that no one else could give such satisfaction.

Nevertheless the employer might feel that he had no place open for the latest candidate. In this event the applicant would demonstrate with salesmanship that he was the sort of person it is worth while for any business man to keep track of. Such a real "salesman" of his own capabilities, if put off for the time being, would be reasonably sure to get his desired chance the next time that employer might require such services as he could supply.

A Salesman Cost Clerk

A young acquaintance of mine wanted to secure a chance in the office of a prominent manufacturing corporation, under a certain executive whom he regarded as the most capable business man in the city. The company had advertised for a minor clerk in the cost department, which was managed by the particular executive. My acquaintance called, and found seven other applicants waiting in the general office. He did not join them, but sent in his card to the busy head of the cost department with the penciled request, "May I see you for twenty seconds in order to make a personal inquiry?" He was promptly admitted to the private office, and then stated his purpose in calling. He was careful to be extremely brief.

"My name is James A. Ward. I believe, Mr. Blank, I am the man you want for the clerkship in your cost section. In order to save your time, may I have permission to make some inquiries of the chief clerk in that department, to learn just what qualifications are required and what the work is? Then when you talk with me, it will be unnecessary for you to explain details."

Securing A Stand-in

Taken unawares, the executive was not prepared to refuse the courteous request. Moreover, he was impressed with the distinctive attitude of the young man. He instructed that the candidate be taken to the cost department. There my acquaintance made an excellent impression on the cost accountant and several clerks. Thus in advance of any other applicant he secured a "stand-in" with a number of persons who might influence the judgment of their chief in selecting a new man. When he had learned the nature of the work to be done, Ward did not make the mistake of thrusting himself again into the sanctum. Instead, he wrote a note to the executive on whom he had called first.

"Dear Mr. Blank:

> I know now exactly what the job in the cost department is, and that I can fill it. But I should like to think over the best ways to give you complete satisfaction, before talking with you about it. Please telephone to me at Main 4683 when it will be convenient for you to see me.
>
> Respectfuly,
> James A. Ward."

The young man sent his note into the private office and left at once. There now were nine applicants on the anxious seat in the reception room. Ward did not wish to be asked to wait his turn. He felt sure the executive would inquire of the costs manager about him, and he got away from the office quickly so that there would be an opportunity for his chosen prospective employer to receive the full effect of the good impression made in the cost department.

Giving Opportunity A Chance to Catch Up

My acquaintance was not at all worried lest some other candidate be chosen in his absence. The measures of salesmanship he had taken made it practically certain that the executive would not employ any one else before talking to him. Ward went to his room and waited for the telephone call he was sure would come. While he sat expecting it, he used the time to think out the best ways to approach the big man with whom he wanted to work.

The salesman candidate was summoned in about an hour. None of the applicants ahead of him had come prepared with any definite plans. Therefore my acquaintance, who knew in advance just what the conditions were and who had decided exactly how he would present his particular capabilities, found it easy to secure the chance he desired. He is earning a salary of four thousand dollars a year now, and is on his way up to a five-or-six-figure job. He will get there, "as sure as shooting." A salesman like that cannot be kept down.

Turning Failure Into Success

I asked Ward one day what he would have done if the telephone call he expected had not come. He replied that he would have gone to see the executive next morning anyhow, and that he had planned carefully how he would approach him.

"I'd have sent in a note that I was ready to report some ideas I had worked out regarding his cost-keeping as a result of the thinking I had done since learning his system. He wouldn't have refused to see me, even if he had hired some one else meanwhile. Then I'd have told him the very things that got me the job. They would have assured me a chance in his office, whether he had a place for me right then or not," Ward asserted positively. "If that plan of mine hadn't succeeded," he amended, "I'd have known he wasn't the kind of man I wanted to work for, after all. But it turned out exactly as I knew it would," my friend ended with a grin.

Can you imagine a man of such sales ability failing to get a chance almost anywhere? Yet Ward did only what any one, with a little forethought, might have done in the circumstances. Analyze the selling process he used, and you will perceive that there was nothing marvelous about it—it was all perfectly natural. Is there any good reason why *you* cannot employ similar methods to gain the chance you want?

Service Purpose is Essence of Salesmanship

Let us dig into what Ward did, and find the "essence" of his salesmanship in the ways and means he employed to assure his two "entrances," to the presence and into the mind of the executive. *He was successful principally because he made the impression that he had come with a purpose of rendering real service to the other man.* His plan of approach assured him the opportunity he wanted because it was designed to serve the head of the department in his need for particular capabilities. *Very rarely will any one refuse a needed service.* So, coming with a purpose of service, Ward made certain in advance that he would be welcomed to his opportunity. The essence of a successful plan of approach to the mind of any prospect is *a carefully thought-out idea of how to supply him with exactly what he lacks.*

Just as the service purpose well planned is the key to the door of a man's *mind*; so is it the "Open Sesame" to his *presence*. Plan how to bring to the attention of a prospect your real service motive in coming to him, and how at the same time you can indicate to him your capabilities; then you will be as sure as was my ingenious acquaintance that no office door will long remain closed to you. *You only need to use the processes of the master salesman to gain any chance you want.* You will succeed almost always in your immediate object; and if you are unsuccessful in your first or second sales attempt you will be absolutely certain to get some other good opportunity very soon.

Make a "Vacancy" For Yourself

It is not necessary to wait until the employer for whom you have chosen to work advertises a job. You should plan ways and means of gaining an entrance into his business organization, regardless of any "vacancy" he may have in mind. Plan exactly how you can serve him. Prospect for a need that he may not realize himself. Afterward work out a particular method of showing him clearly *what he lacks*, and that *you are the man* to fill the vacancy you yourself have discovered and revealed to him.

An elderly man who was down on his luck and who, on account of his grey hair, had been unable to get various kinds of work he had sought, devised a novel plan of approach that gained him a coveted chance in a big department store. He came to the main office and reached the sales manager without difficulty by appearing to be just a customer of the store. Then he whisked from under his coat a pasteboard sign on which he had printed, PORTER WANTED—TO KEEP SIDEWALK CLEAN.

"I'm after that job, sir," he explained his presence.

The sales manager waved the old man away.

"You're in the wrong place," he said curtly. "Employment office is on the top floor."

"I made the sign myself," the applicant declared, standing his ground. "The employment manager—you—no one in this store has realized, I think, how filthy your sidewalk is. If you will come down with me and look at it, I'm sure you will want to have it cleaned and will instruct that I be given the chance. It is hurting your sales, as it is now. Kept clean, as I would keep it, it would be a fine advertisement of the store's policies, and would help sales."

The old man's plan of entrance gained him his initial opportunity. He swept the sidewalk only two weeks. Then the sales manager made a place for him behind a counter, where he is serving customers with satisfaction to-day.

Distinguishing Characteristic Of Masterly Salesmanship

You will recall that in a previous chapter the *ability to discriminate* was stated as the *distinguishing characteristic* of masterly salesmanship. The ability to perceive differences, and skill in emphasizing them, will *assure* success in selling either ideas or goods.

The discriminative-restrictive study of anything is certain to give one a much clearer and more definite understanding of it than could be secured by a study of its likeness to something else. If, when describing two people, you *compare* their points of *resemblance*, you do not paint a clear picture of either. But if you *restrict* your comments to the *differences* in their features, you will portray a pretty definite mental image of each.

"Different" Ways Win

You have been given several examples of ways and means to gain an entrance into the presence and into the mind of an employer. You will note that each applicant *restricted* his plans of approach to methods that were entirely *different* from those ordinarily used in getting a job. The purpose of the salesman in every case was to bring out the difference between him and competing candidates for the situation. The selling processes described were successful because *discriminative-restrictive principles of skill were employed to bring to the attention and interest of the prospect the service capabilities of the one applicant, in distinction from all others.*

When you plan to gain the chance you most want, you can assure yourself of success if you will work out in your own mind how to do *something effective that is different* from the methods commonly used in attempts to gain opportunities, and that will impress your *real service purpose* in applying for your chance.

First think out clearly *what the other man needs.* Distinguish exactly in your thoughts between what is *lacking* in his organization, and what he *already has.* Then when planning to gain an entrance to the presence and the mind of your prospect, restrict your thoughts to ways and means of indicating and suggesting that *you know precisely what service is wanted.* Prepare to show him that you don't have merely a vague, indefinite idea of a job *like* other jobs. Plan to indicate that you are not just about the *same* as ordinary men who apply for positions. Be ready to make the first impression that you are *a particular man with individual ideas and distinctive capability.* If you can prove that, you will be certain to gain your chance through good salesmanship of the true idea of your qualifications.

Plan Approach To Fit the Particular Man

When planning his approach, the master salesman combines his earlier work of preparation and his prospecting. He re-organizes in his mind all the information he previously has gained for his own benefit. Now he reviews his knowledge *from the standpoint of the prospect.* He plans to use what he has learned in the ways that seem to him most likely to fit the mentality, impulses, feelings, conditions, and real needs of the man he wants to influence to accept his proposition.

Having thus planned to *fit his knowledge to an individual prospect,* the skillful salesman arranges constructively in his own mind *particular, definite points of contact* with the mind of this one other man. He plans restrictively. That is, he works out only the approach ideas that are likely to fit the characteristics of the certain man on whom he intends to call. He also discards ways and means that are not *especially adapted* to this prospect.

Different Effects on Different People

Of course the master salesman purposes to make the best possible impression always; but he recognizes that words, tones, and actions which would create a favorable impression on one prospect might make an opposite impression on another. For instance, a jolly manner and expression help in gaining an entrance to the friendly consideration of a good-natured man, but would be likely to affect a cynical dyspeptic disagreeably.

The intelligence and skill used by the master professional salesman of goods in planning ways and means to gain his sales chances, can be used in the same way just as effectively by *you* when planning *your* approach to the presence and mind of any one related to your opportunities for success. Before you apply for the job you want, or before you present your qualifications for promotion or an increased salary, *make in advance a discriminative selection of ideas that will be likely to prove most effective in accomplishing your purpose* with your employer prospect. Then, when you interview him, *restrict* your presentation of your case to these discriminatively selected strong points of your particular capability.

Contrast Selfish and Service Purposes

You should suggest contrasts between yourself and ordinary job seekers or employees. When you present your qualifications for a promotion or for a raise, you will be *sure* of succeeding if you are able to get across to your employer's mind the true idea that your services in the future may be *different and deserving of more reward* than the services for which you have previously been paid.

When an employee asks for more money because other men are being paid higher wages in the same office, or because he has prospects of better pay elsewhere, or even because of increased costs of living, he makes an *unfavorable* impression on the man from whom he requests a raise. His purpose in presenting his claims is evidently selfish. He appears to be looking out only for Number One, and the employer naturally looks out for *his* Number One when responding. By using methods that suggest a wholly selfish purpose, the applicant decreases his chances of gaining what he desires. Yet most employees ask for raises in just this way.

The Quid Pro Quo

Contrast the impression made when an employee approaches the boss with a carefully planned demonstration of his *capability for increased service*, as the basis of a proposal that he be promoted or given a higher salary. He comes into "the old man's" office with an attitude that produces a *favorable* impression. When he explains exactly what he is doing, or can do if permitted, that is deserving of more reward than he has been receiving, he presents the idea of a "quid pro quo" to his "prospect," just as the salesman of goods presents the idea of *value* in fair exchange for *price*.

If the service now being rendered by the employee, or the new service he wishes permission to render, is really worth more money to the employer, the applicant for a raise is practically certain to get it, provided he has chosen a fair boss. And, of course, a good salesman of himself does not go to work in the first place until he has prospected the squareness and fair-mindedness of the employer.

The Saleswoman Secretary

A young woman was employed in a secretarial capacity shortly before the world war began. In the course of the next two years her salary was voluntarily doubled by her employer. But her necessary expenses increased in proportion; so she was able to save no more money (in purchasing power) than it would have been possible for her to put in the bank if there had been no increase either in her earnings or in the cost of living. That is, if the war had not happened, and she had continued at work for two years without any raise at all, she would have been practically as well off at the end of that time as she actually found herself with her doubled pay.

As the months of her employment passed, she had made herself progressively much more valuable to her employer. She was rendering him now a very large amount of high-grade service. But in effect she was being paid no more money than when she was engaged. The young woman knew her employer intended to be fair with her. Undoubtedly he felt he had treated her well by voluntarily doubling her salary in two years. If she had gone to him and had asked for more pay in the manner of the ordinary applicant for a raise; if she had stated her request without skillfully showing the difference between actual conditions and his misconception of the facts; she likely would have made an unfavorable impression. But she was a good saleswoman of her ideas. She made a discriminative-restrictive plan of approach to gain her object, and used first-class selling skill to get into her employer's mind a true conception of her worth to him.

Opening the Boss's Eyes

She compiled from her budget the exact amount of increased living costs. The comparative figures of two years showed that her necessary expenses were approximately double what they had been before the war. Then she used the percentage ratio to demonstrate in neat typewriting that approximately all of her salary increases had gone to some one else, and had not remained in her hands. On another sheet she typed a summary of the most important business responsibilities she carried for her employer at present, but which she had not been qualified nor trusted to bear when she was first engaged. The secretary brought the two exhibits to the desk of the business man, laid them before him with brief explanations of what they represented, and concluded with a simple personal statement which she worded most carefully.

The Approach That Commands Respect

"Mr. Blank, I know you mean to be perfectly square with me. So I want you to realize what has been the actual purchasing power of the salary I have received, and what I have done with it. This percentage slip shows that my additional pay was all used for additional expenses. I have been unable to increase my savings. I really have been paid only for the same kind of services I was able to render when you employed me. Now I know how to do all these additional things." She pointed to the list typed on the second sheet of paper. "In effect, I haven't been paid anything for them, you see. I am sure you have not appreciated the difference between the increased service I have rendered, and the buying power of the raises you have meant to give me but which have all gone to some one else. Please study these lists. I believe you will feel that I am earning a larger salary and really am worth more to you than two years ago."

Her "different" approach gained the secretary not only an immediate increase of fifty per cent in her salary; but five hundred dollars back pay that her fair-minded employer was convinced she should have received.

Such an approach commands the respect of the prospect. It is the approach of an equal, not of an inferior. *So greatly does it reduce the chances of failure that the salesman is practically certain to succeed in his purpose.*

Initiative Is Yours

Recognize that the *initiative* in gaining your chance should be in your own hands. Do not wait for any opportunity to come to you. "Go to it." Go prepared to control the situation you have planned to create, but be ready also to meet *unexpected possibilities*. The object of the master salesman in his preparation is not only to make the selling process *easy*, but also to meet any *difficulties* he can foresee that may arise to block him. He is ready to take full advantage of favorable conditions he has planned to meet, and is equally ready for turn-downs. If you use the discriminative-restrictive method to gain admission to the presence and into the mind of your prospect, it is altogether unlikely that you will be denied the chance you seek. Nevertheless *go loaded for refusals*. Be ready with the quick come-back to every turn-down you can imagine.

A clerk in a real estate office wanted an opportunity to prove that he was capable of selling. Times were very hard, and the firm had flatly announced that it would not promote anybody or grant any raises. But this clerk, who had made up his mind to secure a salesman's job, carefully prepared a plan of approach before he went to the president's office. His ostensible purpose was to get a raise; so he had worked out an ingenious reply to every objection he could imagine his employer might make to paying him more money. But he really wanted a different job, not just a larger salary.

Come-backs To Turn Downs

He tackled the "old man" at a selected time when he knew the president would not be busy. One after another, in quick succession, he came back at every reason given for turning him down on his application for additional pay. Finally the cornered employer stated frankly that the clerk was entitled to a raise, but as frankly said it could not be granted because of general business conditions. The applicant, having gained his immediate object by proving his worth, then switched to the second part of his plan of approach.

"I didn't expect more money for my clerical work, but haven't I proved to you by the way I handle turn-downs that I possess the qualifications of a salesman? It would be just as hard for a prospect to say 'No' to me as it has been for you. I don't want a raise. I want a chance at selling real estate. Give me a drawing account equal to my present salary, and I'll earn it in commissions. I'm going to make it hard for anybody to get away from me after I tackle him to buy a lot or a house."

Of course the clerk got his chance.

Touch Tender Spots

Another important detail of good salesmanship in planning to approach opportunities to succeed, is *touching the tender spots of the subordinates* in the office of the big man you want to reach. Also plan to touch tender spots in *him*. You can do it with a courteous bow, or with the tone of respect. Employ the *personal appeal*—that is, make *contact* between *your personality* and the personality of the *other party* you desire to influence. There is no better way than by manifesting your *real friendliness*. One who comes as a friend is able to feel and to appear *at ease*. The bearing of perfect ease makes the excellent impression of *true equality in manhood,* and helps very greatly in gaining for one a chance to succeed.

Strength and Resourcefulness

Sometimes self-respect will require you to use very forceful methods to secure the opportunity you desire. A snippy clerk may refuse you admittance to the private office. The big man himself may send out word that he will not receive you, or perhaps he will attempt to dismiss you brusquely after you are granted an audience. So be prepared to manifest your *strength,* as well as your *resourcefulness,* should such *force* of personality be needed in any imaginable situation. If you have planned exactly how you will show your strength, you will make the impression when you manifest it actually that you are strong in fact, and not just a bluffer. Often you can prove your strength by looking another person fearlessly in the eye.

Four Essentials of Good Approach

It is evident from what has already been outlined that to make a successful approach one needs particular qualifications. There are four essentials: First, *mental alertness in perceiving;* Second, *good memory for retaining the impressions received;* Third, *constructive imagination* in planning the approach; Fourth, *friendly courage* in securing an audience and in making the actual approach to the mind of the other man.

All your senses must be *wide awake* if you are to *perceive every point of difference* that can be used effectively to sell your particular ideas in contrast with ordinary ideas.

It is necessary not only that you *see* distinctions clearly, but that you be able to *remember them instantly,* when you need to use them in selling your ideas.

You cannot make any certainly successful plan to deal with a future possible chance unless you *cultivate your power of imagination by working out in advance every conceivable situation that may be anticipated.*

And all your other capabilities in gaining your chance will be of no avail if your purpose meets resistance; unless you are equipped beforehand with friendly courage, the *kind of real bravery that is likable.*

Genius

It is highly important to your success that you be able to make the impression that you are a person of *genius.* Genius, analyzed, is no more than the exceptional application of natural ability to doing work. Application demands complete attention. Attention leads to discrimination. Discrimination concentrates, of course, upon the recognition of differences. And differentiation depends principally upon sense training in alertness. Unless a sense is very keen, it cannot make distinctions sharply. *So we get back to the primary necessity of developing all your senses and of keeping them wide awake to perceive and act upon chances for success.*

Memory

Your discriminative power of perception will be well-nigh valueless to you, however, if you are unable to recall whenever needed, all the points of difference possible to utilize in your salesmanship. Therefore you should *train your memory*. We will not enlarge just now upon this factor of the process of making success certain; because in previous chapters and also in the companion book, "The Selling Process," the right methods of developing a good memory are indicated.

Constructive Imagination

The value of *constructive imagination,* not only in planning your entrance to the physical presence and into the mind of the prospect, but all through your salesmanship, cannot be over emphasized. If you are to gain your chance with another man, *you must be able to see imaginary future situations, through his eyes.* In advance of your interview it is necessary that you imagine yourself in his place when a caller like yourself is received.

Some so-called "realists" condemn imagination. They say it is apt to make men visionary and unable to recognize and meet successfully the every-day problems of life. But the *big* men of finance, industry, and politics have become pre-eminent because of the fertility and productiveness of their imaginations. What the "hard-headed" man condemns is not imagination, but *inability to use it constructively.* He deprecates imagination not carried into *action.* Constructive imagination, however, has always been man's greatest aid in making progress.

Four Ways to Re-construct Ideas

In order to develop your constructive imagination most effectively you must follow certain laws with regard to the re-adjustment of parts, qualities, or attributes of things you know. You can re-construct an idea; (1) by merely *enlarging* an old mental image; or (2) by *diminishing* the size of the previous image; or (3) by *separating* a composite image into its parts; or (4) by imaging *each part as a whole.*

Let us illustrate how these laws of constructive imagination might be applied effectively in planning the approach to a prospective employer.

Using Constructive Imagination

He perhaps has an idea that the possibilities of the job you want are limited. You should plan to *enlarge* the picture of your possible service and to show that you could do more things than he is likely to expect of you.

So you can *diminish* his idea of the salary you want, by planning to show him that in proportion to the enlarged service you purpose to render, the pay you ask is not really big.

In order to make him appreciate better just what your contemplated job means, you can *separate* it into the different functions you will perform. The mere fact that the job has a great many parts will be effective in impressing him with the idea that it is worth more pay.

Then you can take each part or function of your job and show it as a *whole* opportunity. For instance, if you are a correspondent, you might demonstrate just how letters of different length could be spaced on the stationery to develop a uniformly artistic impression that would help to get more business by mail.

All your imaginative powers can be made to work *together* to accomplish the one certain result you desire. "Constructive imagination is always characterized by a definite purpose, which never is lost sight of until the image is complete."

Friendly Courage

Thousands of men have failed, after getting right up to the door of opportunity, because they had to turn away in order to screw up their *courage.* No one can hope to succeed if he lacks *the quality of bravery necessary to gain chances.*

True bravery is not cockiness or swaggering. It is simply a *kindly self-confidence* that makes no impression of a threat to others, and gives no suggestion that the man who has it feels there is the slightest reason for being afraid of anybody else.

No One To Fear

Really, if you have planned just how to approach each prospect with a true service purpose, there is no one in the world you need to fear. Lack of courage is usually due to lack of preparation for what might be anticipated. Sometimes a man is fearful of another because of his own consciousness that he has come to that other man principally for the purpose of *taking something away from him*. This consciousness causes a guilty feeling, which undermines courage. If through imaginative planning you know in advance about what to expect, and if you feel your intentions toward your prospect are absolutely square, you will not be afraid to seek your chance anywhere. Your courage will not ooze.

"Right is Might"

True courage is based on a *permanent consciousness of right feeling and thinking, coupled with the sense of power* that is expressed in the maxim, "Right is might." Such courage can be developed by the discriminative-restrictive process with absolute certainty, as is explained in the companion book, "The Selling Process."

Big Mental Outlook

Our study of plans of approach would be incomplete without emphasizing the prime necessity for a *big mental outlook*. To assure your success in gaining the chances you want it is necessary that you vision imaginary situations of the future and fit into them the facts you know now or may be able to learn.

However, you cannot develop maximum skill in gaining your chances if you are unable to learn anything except through personal experience. Personal experience is valuable, no doubt. But you must develop the ability to *think out the significance of other men's experiences*, and must be capable of *applying what you learn to your own imaginary use*.

The big view-point, the ability to learn from observation as well as from experience, will develop in you broad and varied conceptions of other men. It will make you tolerant of characteristics that differ widely from your own. You will respect the view-point of the other fellow, and will recognize that he may be perfectly fair in his attitude and opinions, however widely he may differ from your ideas. Your big mental outlook should make you feel friendly toward him as your prospect, and you can make the approach of *courage that is friendly*.

The Sentry And the Password

Perhaps you will meet opposition to your entrance when you come to gain your chance. It is likely that some sentry in the outer office of your prospect, or the sentry of his own mind when you reach his presence, may halt you at the portal of opportunity with the challenge, "Who goes there?"

Your answer should be spoken confidently, "A friend."

The test will then be made by the sentry, "Advance, friend, and give the countersign."

The secret pass-word to Opportunity is, "Service."

Prove you know the countersign, speak it with courage, and you will find yourself no longer an object of suspicion, no longer regarded as a possible enemy.

You have nothing to fear if you plan to approach your prospect as a true friend who has come with a carefully thought out, intelligent offer of service that he lacks.

CHAPTER VII
Knowledge of Other Men

Unlocking The Other Man's Heart And Mind

We have seen how you can make certain of *gaining* your introductory chance. Now we are to consider the first step in the *most effective use* of this opportunity to begin building your own success.

Let us say that you have chosen a particular man as the sort of employer with whom you want to work. Your prospecting has convinced you that in his business you have found the right market for your present services and a promising field for the future big success you are ambitious to achieve. Therefore you wish to sell him a true idea of your best capabilities. We will assume that you have passed the threshold of his private office, but your object in calling upon him has not yet entered *his thoughts and feelings*.

Before you state the ideas and service intention you have brought, make certain of the best possible reception from him. You need to take every practicable precaution against being rebuffed. You want to assure yourself of a welcome. Having gained this chance to start the sale of your capabilities, it is of vital importance not to take the next step in the selling process *blindly*, lest you stumble. Hence you should *size up* the other man before you announce your purpose in calling. What you may learn from reading his character correctly will help you to gain admittance into his mind for your ideas. It should assure a welcome from his heart for your sincere desire to serve him.

Skeleton Key Unavailing

Golden opportunities to succeed in a particular business cannot be unlocked with a skeleton key of knowledge about human nature. Knowledge of *all* men supplies merely the shaft and general shape of the key blank, which must then be notched and filed to fit the characteristics of the individual whose mind and heart you wish to open for the admission of your ideas and feelings. Unless you can get into that *one* mind and that *one* heart with your service purpose, you will be shut out from the opportunity you want. It is important that you know the traits of men in general, of course. Such knowledge, however, should be supplemented by a *specific* and true conception of the particular man through whom you hope to reach your chance to succeed.

Do not confuse in your present thoughts the process of *prospecting* the characteristics of a man *before* meeting him, with the later process of *sizing him up at the time of the interview*. It is highly important to accumulate in advance as much knowledge as possible of your prospect's individual traits. But what you learned about your chosen future employer before you gained the chance to present your ideas to him in his office should be used *merely as a guide* in sizing him up on the spot.

Stop, Look, Listen

Take nothing for granted now. Through your personal, specific observation either confirm or disprove every item of information that has come to you from other people previous to meeting this man face to face. Your informants may or may not have had correct conceptions of his characteristics. It would be unwise, even unsafe, for you to rely implicitly on *their* judgment of him. You need to be *certain you know him as he really is*; so that you can present your purpose with the confidence a skilled salesman feels when he is sure he understands the principal traits of the prospect he is addressing. In reaching this man you have gained your first chance. You cannot afford to risk losing it by haste. *Do not advance farther in the selling process until you have made certain of the ground you are to tread*. It is very bad salesmanship to begin introducing ideas and feelings to a mind and heart that are unknown to you except from hearsay.

"But," you say, "I'm not a mind reader. And I can't look into another man's heart."

True. Yet you should be able to read the *signs* of his thoughts; which he manifests in his words, tones, and acts. And you need not see into *his* heart to know what it contains; since fundamentally *all* men are much alike at heart. Just look clearly into your own heart at its best. You will find there the basic emotions and feelings that civilized men have in common everywhere.

Character Analysis by Types Not Reliable

Character analysis by "types" is unreliable. I believe as little in phrenology as in palm-reading. I have directed thousands of men in business. Personal experience has proved to me that the *permanent* structure of a particular human body is not an invariably true index to the characteristics of the inner, or ego man who owns that body.

He has had no control over the color of his hair or eyes. He cannot reshape the bones of his face, nor alter the bumps on his head. To believe that such permanent structural details of the "natural" *outer* man determine or denote the peculiar aptitudes of the *inner* man is to credit the exploded doctrine of fore-ordination.

Therefore, when you have gained the chance to present your capabilities for sale to a chosen prospect with whom you believe you will have the best opportunities to succeed, and when you are swiftly shaping your presentation plans to fit his personality, don't size up merely the factors of his make-up with which he was born. You will be apt to mistake his true character if you have come to his office with the delusion that the blonde type of man is fundamentally different *in nature* from the brunette type. Get out of your head any misconception that a man is foredoomed to practically certain failure in a particular career because he has a big nose, sloping brow, and receding chin; and that another man with a snub nose, bulging forehead, and protruding jaw is destined almost surely to succeed if he selects a certain vocation. No "mind man" with a normal, healthy body is limited in his possibilities of success by being born with red, or black, or tow hair; or because the bones of his head happen to be shaped in a particular way. The ego is the master, not the slave, of the body.

True Signs of Character

The true signs of character are to be read only in the words, tones, and movements of a man—and in his muscle structure *as he has developed it* or has left it *undeveloped.* We already have seen in a previous chapter how a mind center and its co-ordinated set of muscles develop each other. So the positive characteristics of the inner man are revealed clearly by the muscle structure built up by his habits of thinking and feeling and action. On the other hand, his deficiency in certain mental and emotional development is indicated negatively by his lack of the muscle structure that naturally would be co-ordinate with such development.

The relation of muscular development to mental development, as explained in an earlier chapter, suggests the one *sure* way to judge a man's habits of thinking. *Observe discriminatingly his various muscle structures, and his muscle activities in detail.* The development of certain sets of *muscles* proves a co-ordinate development of the *mind centers* most directly connected with these muscle structures. Similarly the *mental action* of a man is indicated by his *physical manifestations* with his muscles in movements.

Hence if you learn to read the *mental significance of particular muscle structures and of particular muscle actions,* you will be able to size up both the *habits* of thought (individual characteristics) of a man, and what he happens to be thinking *at the time* you come to present your services or ideas for sale.

Recapitulation

Before going on with our study of the subject of this chapter, let us summarize the preceding pages to make sure that we know thoroughly the somewhat difficult but very important ground we have gone over thus far.

You chose a certain man as your prospective employer because you believe that if you succeed in associating yourself with him you will have the best opportunities to achieve your ambition. You are now standing in his presence. You need to size up his true character quickly in order that you may be sure of presenting your capabilities in the particular way that is likely to be most effective with him. You wish to impress this one man with right ideas of your qualities and their value. You want him to perceive that he lacks and requires just such services as you purpose to offer for sale. You realize it is unsafe for you to jump at conclusions about his characteristics. You pause briefly to size him up before presenting your proposition, rather than to proceed blindly in ignorance of his habits of thought, and with no clue to what he happens to be thinking at the time you call. You must know all it is possible to find out on the spot regarding him.

What Has He Done with His Birthright?

You cannot be certain of his characteristics if you judge him solely by what Nature forced on him. But you can be absolutely sure if you size him up by observing *what he has done with his birthright,* and if you are then able to *interpret* correctly what you *perceive.* Your prospect has had nothing to do with the shape and size of his head. His fair or dark complexion is inherited. He is utterly unable to control the color of his hair or eyes. His *muscle structure,* however, is a *development* that he has accomplished himself. If he has a firm jaw, the jaw *muscles,* not the jaw *bone,* signify the characteristics of a firm mentality. *Judge the physical man he has made by his habits of living under the government of his mind.* Disregard such physical details of his appearance as he cannot help. The *made* man is the true image of the ego. It is this *ego* of your prospective employer you need to know, for your chance to succeed in your purpose with him depends on the *inner* man you must convince and persuade. Therefore restrict your size-up to the discriminative observation of the *muscle signs of his mind habits and mind actions.*

Recall Burbank Method

Recall now, or re-read the second chapter of this book. There you studied the principles of restrictive-discriminative growth—the Burbank method of developing selected qualities of manhood. That chapter related to your cultivation of particular characteristics within *yourself*. The same principles will guide you with equal certainty in acquiring knowledge of *other men*.

Every *mental* characteristic of your prospect about which you need to know has *physical indications that can be perceived, and translated into certain knowledge of details of his character*. You have studied the co-relation of *your* mind and body in mutual development. You may be sure that similar processes of development have produced like effects in the case of the man you have come to see. You know exactly how to grow particular qualities within yourself, by using your muscles to develop corresponding mind centers and vice versa. You can read another man's mind by observing *his* muscle structure and muscle action, and by then interpreting the mental significance of what you perceive.

Men are Alike At Heart, But Differ in Mind

To repeat and emphasize again what already has been said about knowing the *heart* of another man—you need but look into your own breast to find there the finest basic characteristics of the human heart in general. As Kipling wrote, "The Colonel's lady and Judy O'Grady are sisters under their skins." All men are fundamentally alike at the bottoms of their hearts, however much they may differ in the individual traits they have grafted upon their common root of human nature.

So when you are sizing up your prospect, you should comprehend that *the most effective way to get to his heart is through such an appeal as would reach the heart of every man*. Know your own heart surely, then, in order to be certain of knowing his. All human hearts respond similarly to manifestations of courage, nobility, love, faith, honor, and the like. We laugh and cry at the same humor and pathos. Our *feelings* are closely akin. We differ from one another only in our *minds*. Our individual, acquired habits of thought affect but the *degrees* of our several heart responses to the gamut of fundamental emotional appeals.

Exhaustive Prolonged Analysis Unnecessary

Knowledge of another man, then, involves first, comprehension that he is *like* every other man in his *emotions*, and *unlike* all other men in the way he *thinks*. To a trained observer his habits of thought are clearly indicated by his muscle structure and muscle action. Exhaustive prolonged analysis is unnecessary. You can learn to read quickly the mental significance of the comparatively small number of details of muscle structure and action that constitute a fairly complete index to his character. Then you will be able to judge with certainty practically all the traits of which you need to be sure in order to make the most effective presentation of your services for sale to this particular man.

Value of Size-up

The value of such a dependable size-up can scarcely be over-estimated. It is not easy to gain the *initial* chance to present your capabilities to the one man with whom you have chosen to be associated. But it would be tremendously harder to win a *second* opportunity to sell your services after *failing* the first time. By sizing him up aright while you are presenting your qualifications for his consideration, you will be able to *avoid making unfavorable impressions*. You can also adapt your salesmanship to *creating the best possible impression* of your capabilities and their fitness to his **especial needs**.

The Gruff Reception

Sometimes a man seeking to gain the big chance that he believes would open the door to success fails to secure his opportunity because he is disconcerted by a gruff reception that he misconstrues as personal to him. He wrongly interprets *natural* self-defense as a sign of habitual crabbedness.

A big man often thinks he is "hunted" by people who want to make him the prey of their own purposes. The employer you have chosen as the means of reaching the goal of your ambition may feel suspicious of your object in approaching him. He is likely to assume an attitude of extreme reserve, or even of icy indifference. Possibly his manner will be curt and sharp. Size up such a reception as just his way of protecting himself against impositions. His treatment of you is merely a superficial manifestation of the instinct for self-preservation. It indicates nothing more than that he is wary of any one who calls on him with an unknown purpose.

His object in being cold or brusque is to get rid of people who might annoy him or waste his time. He would not assume his repelling pose if he knew *you* had come with a purpose of *true service*, after full preparation of yourself and your selling plans to interest him. Though he does not realize it yet, you will neither pester him nor fritter away his precious minutes.

Melting Ice And Smoothing Roughness

Therefore if your size-up convinces you that the cold, brusque manner is only *assumed*, you need not deal with it as if it were *characteristic*. It indicates no more than the habit of wariness. You should proceed confidently with your selling process, undeterred by the bearing of your prospect. Do not attempt to mollify his assumed harshness. It will take but a few moments for you to *sell him the idea that you have brought him something he really needs*. When he first glimpses your service purpose, his icy pose will begin to melt and his rough tones will be smoothed.

A great public-utility corporation with thousands of branch offices throughout the United States had as its purchasing agent for many years an old gorgon. He was "a holy terror" to new salesmen, but became a staunch customer when once his confidence was deservedly gained. And every employee in the office of this tartar loved him for his true kindness of heart.

Don't Flinch Or Retreat

You may have occasion to call on such an eccentric big man. If you are rebuffed fiercely, don't let it "get your goat." He can have no possible reason for disliking you personally, especially before he comprehends your purpose in coming to him. So disregard his ferocious pose. Though he may treat you as an unwelcome intruder, proceed calmly to the statement of your business. You know that your intention to render him a true service justifies you in taking his time. Therefore his assumed fierce manner should be powerless to disconcert you.

Do not retreat from a chosen prospective employer; *do not even flinch* from him, however ill-tempered and repellant he may appear. You cannot possibly lose so much by standing your ground as you would forfeit by running away from this chance to demonstrate your salesmanship. Countless thousands of men have failed because at the first sign of antagonism they surrendered even more than they might have lost if they had been utterly beaten after the hardest kind of a fight for victory. *They gave up without a struggle, not only all their chances for success, but their self-respect as well.*

Suppose the man you have selected as your future employer does snap at you viciously when you call on him; his ferocity signifies no more than that you must approach and handle him carefully. Your prospecting and your size-up should have convinced you that he is not in fact the crab he tries to appear. Real, thorough cranks are so rare they can be considered as non-existent. It is safe to conclude that any man who acts as if he were sore all the way through all the time is just *acting*. Ignore the irrascibility of the "Everett Trues" you meet. *Superficial, assumed* indications will not help you to comprehend the *inner* man you want to influence. *Restrict your size-up to the signs of that inner man.* While the old gorgon you face is brow-beating you, he may be planning in the back of his head an act of gentle kindness to some one. If he is *habitually* kind, there will be physical indications of that characteristic; in his *tones* and *acts* if not in his *words*. Look for these signs beneath his harsh manner, which is merely a disguise he has put on. "Everett

True" behaves like a domineering tyrant, but he really is characterized by an acute sensitiveness to what is right and just.

Judge By Unconscious Appearance And Actions

When sizing up a man, depend principally upon details of his *appearance* and *actions*. Translate whatever you see or hear into definite discriminative judgments regarding him. His muscle structure and movements indicate certain traits. Of course you should also observe and size up the significance of the words and tones he uses. But a man employs his speech with the conscious intention of making impressions. Therefore it is not safe to rely on a size-up based on what he says. Your prospect may be using his words and tones to hide, rather than to reveal, his inner self.

However, if you know how to separate and classify *details of muscle structure and action*, you can depend safely on specific conclusions based on these indications. The muscle structure of a man is the result of his habits of living, or of his predominant characteristics. He builds it up unconsciously and is unable to disguise it. It can be interpreted as certain proof that he has particular traits. Most of his movements, too, are made without his realizing exactly what they denote of his character and present thoughts. He just "acts natural." Therefore if you read indications of the inner man by analytically observing his *physique* and *actions*, you will gain reliable information about him. He will not know that he is revealing his traits and what he is thinking.

Your Opinions About People

From your earliest childhood to this moment you have been forming first-hand opinions of other people by observing and interpreting their words, tones, and movements. Sizing up men is not a new process to you. But in order to be a certainly successful salesman of yourself you should *observe more intelligently and discriminatively* hereafter. Instead of making up your mind about people without knowing just how or why you arrive at your judgments, classify your intuitions scientifically. Know the reasons for your opinions. You can be sure about the conclusions you reach as a result of your *specific, exact observation of details*. The study and analysis of words, tones, and acts, coupled with a little painstaking practice, will make you an expert judge of other men.

Study Character Unobserved

Do not seem to make an effort to observe the person you are sizing up, for that would impress him disagreeably. Without indicating that you are watching him, mentally note and interpret his muscle structure, his manner of speaking, his gestures, the rate of his physical activity, the way his actions respond to his ideas, the type and tensity of his movements. *Each item you analyze and translate should indicate to you clearly some fact about the inner man.*

Of course you will not be able to read your prospect thoroughly in the first few moments after you meet him. It is possible to make only a partial size-up then. No one would reveal *all* his characteristics in such a brief time. *But each indication you perceive and interpret correctly will aid you to attribute to him certain other, related traits.* For instance, if the actions of a man indicate the characteristic of evasion, you may judge safely that he lacks courage, the highest sense of honor, some of the elements of perfect squareness and trustworthiness. If he has a habit of under-estimating or "knocking," and manifests this characteristic in something he says or does, you may feel certain he is not an idealist. He is likely to be pretty "practical" in his views, and cannot be won by appeals to rosy visions.

Elements of Character are Consistent

Analysis of a man's true character usually shows that its elements are thoroughly consistent. A human being is not a bundle of contradictions, but an aggregation of likenesses. Every man differs from every *other* man; yet, generally speaking, one element of his character is not apt to differ radically from another detail of *himself.* There are exceptions, but in most cases the seeming contradictions in an individual are only apparent opposites. Supposed inconsistencies cause surprise because the true fundamental traits of the person observed are not discerned. The *outer* man often seems to contradict himself. But nearly always the *inner* man is consistent in his various characteristics. This is the reason why your size-up should be *restricted to discriminative observation of indications of the ego.*

Application of Theory

Perhaps you have been thinking, "The *theory* seems to be all right, but exactly how is it *applied?*" So we shall turn our attention next to specific details of sizing up the characteristics of the inner man. We shall see just how his thoughts and feelings may be discerned at a particular time.

We assumed previously that you have called upon the man to whom you want to sell your services. You believe the way to your success lies through association with him. *Your faculties of observation should be trained to size up at a glance whatever traits are suggested by his bearing, his clothes, his manner, his actions, his surroundings.* Whether he is standing or sitting, it is possible for you to perceive and interpret his pose and poise. You can learn much from his walk if he steps forward to greet you. His handshake may tell volumes about his true character. The different ways that men clasp palms are especially significant of their individual traits. You should have a scientific knowledge of handshakes.

Traits Suggested By Nods

Should your prospect merely nod on your entrance, note discriminatively the movement he makes. There are many kinds of nods. The quick, sharp tipping of the head indicates unhesitating, clean-cut decisions. Such judgments on the spur of the moment are not always right, but they are apt to be pretty conclusive. Irregular, jerky nods are signs of irritability, of rash or very impulsive decisions, and often of unreasoning prejudice. The nod made directly forward signifies frankness, dignity, and straight thinking. The tilting of the head a little to one side suggests a habit of indirectness and a tendency to "stall."

Learn to Analyze Smiles

How much of a man's character is illumined by his smile! Ability to analyze smiles *correctly* will enable you to size up the dissembled traits of character behind the *false* smile. Such analytical ability will also show you how to turn to your best advantage the smile of *true* friendliness.

It is possible to judge from the physical aspect, from the facial expressions, from the movements, and from the voice of a man whether he is nervous or phlegmatic, active or passive, healthy or lacking in vigor and strength. A skillful size-up will determine that he is either eccentric or well balanced mentally, that he is thrifty or extravagant, that he is disposed to take comprehensive views or is inclined to give undue attention to trifles and details. He will indicate to a keen observer real intellect or mere intelligence. His emotions also may be read. He reveals himself as generous or selfish; as an optimist or as a skeptic. He shows that he is responsive to heart appeals or is hard hearted, moral or immoral, artistic or lacking in appreciation of art, cultured or boorish.

Discriminative Restrictive Process

To know the significance of your prospect's different *words, tones, and movements — the only means he has for the expression of his ideas and feelings,* just apply to *his* case whatever you have learned in studying *yourself.* Adapt your previous discriminative knowledge to the prospect you are sizing up. Restrict your conclusions about him to the significance of details you observe in his appearance, actions, and speech.

After considerable practice in sizing up you will become familiar with the indications of many different traits. *But in most cases it will be sufficient if you can observe swiftly and interpret in a flash only a few of the commonest character signs.* We will touch briefly upon some of these.

Facial Muscles

Tense jaw muscles, whether large or small, denote the characteristic of persistence. But loose, flabby cheek muscles do not necessarily prove the habit of over-eating, or of sensuality. They may mean that the man who has them does not habitually allow his feelings to show in his face. When the muscles of facial expression are flabby they prove only that they are slightly used. Therefore when you encounter a man with loose cheeks read his characteristics from other muscle-structure signs, and from his actions. Do not misjudge the heavy face as a sign of grossness.

Courage And Bluff

If a man holds his head up easily, and moves it in this upright position without stiffness or effort, you may be sure his back neck and shoulder muscles are strongly developed. Such strong development suggests that he is courageous, for these muscles are directly co-ordinated with the mind center of bravery. Therefore the head and shoulders easily held back and up; not a high chest, signify courage. The bulging chest often indicates no more than pouter-pigeon bluff temporarily put on.

Indications Of Intellect And Power

A man's high chest, however, is a sign that his predominant characteristics are intellectual; because his chest has been developed by the student's habit of upper-lung breathing. The nerves running from the upper part of the lungs are directly connected with the brain centers of *intellect*. On the contrary the nerves that lead from the lower portions of the lungs center first in the plexus through which are manifested the *vital emotions* and the emotions of *sex*. Hence the man who breathes deeply by habit indicates a great deal of vitality and has marked "he-man" traits. He is not of the intellectual type so markedly as he is a man of *power*. The man who breathes only from the upper part of his lungs is not a man of power, but may have a fine intellect.

Significance Of Postures

The postures of the body are significant of characteristics. If your prospect stands with his feet wide apart and his arms folded conspicuously across his high-held chest, he probably has a habit of bluffing. His widely spread feet indicate that he has to prop himself in that physical posture; so it is unnatural to him. Similarly he has had to prop himself in his mental posture. *Push your ideas hard and he will lose his mental balance;* just as he would lose his physical balance if you were to jolt him. He is obliged to prop himself. He is bluffing. You can make him quit. The folded arms and expanded chest of the bluffer mean no more than the high-arched back of a cat. Stroke "Tom" soothingly, and he stops bristling. Stroke the human bluffer tactfully with persuasion, and he will not act pugnacious for long.

The Balanced Body

But if, when making a statement, your prospect stands or walks about easily with his feet close together; if he balances his body without difficulty or artificial postures—it is certain that he has a good deal of determination in his make-up. You cannot influence him to change his mind by making emotional appeals to him. In order to secure the favorable decision of such a man, you will need to use the most conclusive, solid evidence of your capabilities.

Wavering Minds

Suppose your prospect shifts his feet continually and rather jerkily. While you are talking with him, he frequently changes his weight from one foot to the other. He is suggesting that he has little confidence in his own judgment, that he is not sure of his own thoughts. *Take the lead strongly with such a man.* Do his thinking for him. It is up to you to bring his vacillating mind to definite conclusions, following your lead. First make it clear to him that your proposal is really to his interest. Then proceed with a manner of absolute assurance, as if you did not question his doing what you wish. With your skillful salesmanship you can stop his wavering and induce him to act as you indicate.

Quick Thinkers

The *rate* of one's *muscular* activity is directly associated with the rate of one's *mental* activity. The man who *moves* slowly by habit is also a plodder in his *thoughts*. On the contrary, quick actions indicate quick thinking; which, however, may be mistaken. Only the quick motion that is *under perfect control* suggests an *unerring* conclusion reached swiftly. The man who snatches up a pencil with sure fingers, and without fumbling it begins to write at once, demonstrates that he has an electrically fast mind perfectly harnessed to his purpose. When another man reaches swiftly for a pencil but misses his sure grasp at the first attempt; or when the dash of his hand to the paper is followed by a momentary delay for adjustment of the pencil in his fingers or by hesitation before he begins to write, he denotes mere impulsiveness.

Self-Control

Sometimes a quick thinker will purposely develop the habit of making very deliberate motions. This trait is the result of his determined repression of a recognized inclination to act on impulse. He has accomplished perfect self-control in order to guard against the danger of making up his mind too quickly on his first thoughts. But his slowed-down movements will be so *precise* and *certain* as to indicate his characteristic of self-control and that his mind has moved in advance of his acts.

If you have occasion to size up such a man, you should perceive that the movements of his muscles do not correspond with the rate of his mental activity, as a superficial observer might mistakenly conclude. If your prospect sits or stands immobile; or if his actions give no indication of what he is thinking, watch his eyes and his facial muscles of expression. Eyes that fairly dart from one object to another, expressions that flash on and off the face; prove swift mental activity, no matter how quietly the body may be held. For instance, a strong, quick thinker may have his muscles under such perfect control that he will pick up a pencil very deliberately because he has trained himself to repress his impulses. But when he has finished using the pencil, he will drop it cleanly and not let it slip slowly from his fingers. His self-training in precaution applies only to what he does *before* acting on a purpose. The moment he is done writing, he also is done with the pencil. His hand does not linger with it over the paper. Unconsciously his characteristic quickness manifests itself in his inclination to get rid at once of the tool he has finished using.

Tightened Thoughts

Any indication of *muscular tensity* suggests a *tightening of the mind* on thoughts. It is often a sign of mental resistance or of persistency. If, when talking to a man you observe that his muscles seem taut, avoid forcing the idea you want him to accept, for his mind is opposing it strongly just then. Perhaps he has a persistent thought of his own, at variance with yours. Either give him a chance to express his idea in words, so you can dispose of it, or switch him away from it by changing the trend of the conversation. When you perceive that his muscles are normally relaxed, you may safely return to the postponed point. You will encounter lessened mental resistance. Very likely he will then have no impulse to persist in the thought he previously had fixed in his mind.

What a Man's Walk Shows

Note how your prospect walks forward to meet you, or how he moves about his office. If his stride is long and free and easy, it proves that the back muscles of his thighs are strong. Those muscles function in direct co-ordination with the mental action of *willing*. Therefore when a man walks easily with a long, free stride he indicates that he has a strong will. He may be sized up confidently as a fighter for his rights, as a man with a great deal of resolution once he makes up his mind.

Determine Mental Speed

It is very important when sizing up a man to determine the *degree of his mental speed*. If you have brought your best capabilities for sale to a prospective employer, you need to know whether or not he is getting clearly all the ideas you present. It is necessary for you to make sure on the one hand that you are not presenting ideas too fast for his mind to comprehend each point fully. On the other hand, you wish to avoid harping on details after he understands them. It will aid you very much in your salesmanship if you know *just how quickly* the mind of your prospect acts. There is no better way to find out than by noting the speed of his *muscle* response to test ideas. Since the rate of *muscle* activity is directly indicative of the rate of *mental* activity, you can often learn from observing the *movements* of your prospect *how quickly his mind takes in* points you state or suggest.

You might test him by asking that he write a name or set down some figures you give him. If without hesitation he reaches for a pencil, you may be sure his mind responds quickly to your ideas. But should there be a moment or two of delay before he picks up the pencil, his *slower physical response* to your request is to be read as an *indication that his mind does not grasp ideas at once.*

Keep Mental Pace

After making your size-up of the degree of his mental speed, you can govern your presentation by what you have learned. If you are dealing with a mind that acts slowly, give your prospect plenty of time to get each idea you want to impress upon him. But proceed briskly from point to point with the man whose mind grasps ideas instantly. You would make a poor impression on him were you to go at a lagging pace.

It is not necessary, however, to make special or artificial tests to learn how quickly your ideas are being grasped. Observe the facial expressions of your prospect, which will indicate how soon your thought is appreciated after it is presented. Should you say something with a touch of humor, the time it takes him to smile or twinkle his eyes will measure the speed of his mind in catching ideas.

Head and Eye Movements

The movements of the head and of the eyes, according to which are predominant in the case of an individual, tell much of his character. The villain on the stage habitually looks out of the corners of his eyes. So does the mischievous ingenue. But the hero turns his whole head when he looks about. And the look of innocence in the eyes of the heroine is straightforward; her head is pointed directly in line with her gaze. *Apply the principle in your salesmanship.* When you observe a man who turns his head freely and easily for a square look at a person who comes into his presence, size him up as one who is not afraid to face either facts or people. If you note that another prospect glances obliquely at persons or objects, or that he habitually turns his eyes to one side or the other while keeping his head still, judge him to lack the characteristic of frankness. He is likely to be evasive and shifty in his dealings. Perhaps the sign you have perceived indicates no more than that your prospect is "stalling." It is evidence, nevertheless, that his mind is not meeting your ideas squarely. You will need to compel his attention to come back to your point, time and again perhaps.

Strength Of Mind

The full-arm movement denotes strength, and bigness of conceptions. A mere wrist gesture suggests littleness, flippancy, weak traits. Similarly if a man walks from his hips, he suggests the characteristic of strong personal opinion. If he walks principally from the knees, or over-uses his ankles and minces along, he indicates that his mind is not certain and that he holds his opinions weakly.

A straight gesture denotes pure *mentality*. A single-curved movement indicates some *emotion*, rather than only a thought. Action in a double curve suggests *power* behind the expression.

Honor and Straightforwardness

A gesture outward from the chest and on the *same level* denotes the qualities of honor and straightforwardness. If your prospect makes such a motion in response to some idea you present, he is thinking on the same man-level as yourself—he is treating you as his equal.

A characteristic movement of the arm *above* the shoulders signifies vivid imagination, or impracticability. It may be read as an indication of lightness of character or of a tendency to go off on a tangent. Conversely, gestures outward from the *lower* part of the body denote power, or an inclination to depreciate values.

Selfishness

If a man gestures *toward* himself, he indicates limited conceptions, or selfishness, with a tendency to materialize everything. Movements in any direction *away from* the trunk of the body and on its level denote assertiveness, sincerity, creative ability, or willingness to cooperate in thought.

Affirmation And Denial

Vertical movements suggest the *life* of ideas, and symbolize *affirmation.* *Horizontal* gestures accompany the *denial* of ideas and the *death* of interest. The *diagonal upward* curve indicates *idealism.* A similar curve *downward* is a sign that an idea presented to the imagination is *concretely realized.*

Frankness and Dodging

The person who gestures *directly in front* of himself proves he is *willing to meet you face to face* regarding the idea presented. But when a man gestures *slightly* to one side or the other, he is not dodging. His movement denotes only that he is *thinking seriously.* However, if you present ideas to a man who gestures *far* to the right or left, you may feel certain that he is not giving his thoughts in harmony with yours, but probably is trying to get your ideas out of his mind.

Study Tones

While we have emphasized that "muscular indications" are of principal importance in making a certain size-up, the tones and words of the prospect should not be altogether neglected. Often a man will unintentionally reveal in his tones the very things he means his words to conceal. You would not depend on the words of a person if they were contradicted by his acts and tones.

Mental, emotive, and power characteristics are signified by various tone pitches. *The degree of a man's determination* and his *persistence in thought* are denoted by the *number of tone units* he habitually employs when speaking. The *genuineness* of a statement is suggested or disproved by the tone *intervals* in the statement. "Yes" spoken in one unit without inflection means unqualified assent. "Y-es" in two tones may mean doubtful assent, or false agreement, or even a contradiction. The *middle-of-the-mouth* tone proves a *well balanced* mind, in contrast with the *unreliable* mind that is denoted by the *lip* tone, and the *secretive* mind which is suggested by the tone that comes from *far back* in the mouth.

In a five minute conversation an alert observer who has studied a few of the elemental principles of tone analysis can size up a great many of the most pronounced characteristics of a prospect.

Don't Offend By Scrutiny

It is better to make no size-up at all than to *strain* in observing the other man and make him aware of your close scrutiny. Such an inartistic size-up impresses a prospect disagreeably. He feels that you are prying into his personal characteristics. Therefore *teach yourself to observe without seeming to look closely at the object of your size-up.* Learn to observe unobserved; especially to perceive details without looking *sharply.* Your eyes and ears can take in specific points about your prospect without making their keen activity apparent.

Two Parts of Sizing-up Process

When you have learned how to see and hear many details clearly at the same time, *unsuspected by your prospect,* you will be a master of the first essential of skillful character reading. The second necessary element of proficiency in sizing up men is the *relation or association of each detail observed, with the particular characteristic it denotes.* To begin with, *perceive points* about your prospect. Then ask yourself about each, *"What does this mean?"*

Practice Makes Perfect

Of course you will not become an expert judge of other men at once. But get the habit of seeing and hearing *specific indications of characteristics* wherever you go. You will soon find that your mind has been opened to new, clear ideas of people.

It is possible for anyone to become a mind reader. It is necessary only to *note* and *think out* the meaning of character signs and thoughts. Trained specific observation will read and interpret these signs. When you become skillful in sizing up other men, this art will help you very much in gaining the best possible receptions everywhere you go. Also, if you are able to read your prospect's thoughts and character, you can avoid antagonizing his ideas.

Remove Unnecessary Difficulties

Gain knowledge of other men in order to make it easy to sell them true ideas of your best capabilities. It is not *hard* to succeed if you take the *unnecessary* difficulties out of the process of gaining your chances.

CHAPTER VIII
The Knock At The Door Of Opportunity and The Invitation To Come In

Selling is Not a Mechanical Process

The process of selling ideas comprises several steps, part or all of which the salesman may need to take in order to close a particular sale successfully. In our study we are considering step after step in regular order, but the actual selling process cannot be reduced to such exactitude and routine. Before we begin our analysis of this "presentation" step, it should be clearly understood that success in selling ideas is not achieved by going through a *machine-like* process. We follow a regular sequence in these chapters, but it is unlikely that you will ever complete a sale of your services by taking the various steps of the selling process in the precise order of our study.

Be a Fully Equipped Salesman

You may need to use them all in order to succeed in a specific instance. Again, without taking many of the steps here analyzed, you might be able to gain the success opportunity you most desire. *The object of this book is to fit you for any and every condition you are likely to meet* in your efforts to gain opportunities for your ambition. It is improbable that in order to get your desired chance and to make the most of it you will have to *use* all you learn of the secret of certain success. You cannot afford, however, to run an *avoidable risk* of being at a loss regarding what to do at any stage of the process of selling to a selected prospect true ideas of your best capability. You need to know the most effective ways to deal with situations that may never happen, but which, on the contrary, *might* be encountered. You cannot start *confidently* on your quest for success unless you are *fully* equipped.

Reducing the Odds Against You

If you believed it would be necessary for you to do everything contained in this book in order to gain the opportunities you desire, you likely would feel very skeptical about succeeding. You might think, "A single little slip and I'd lose out. It's a thousand to one against me." The fact is that the odds on the side of failure are very heavy in the case of an *ordinary* man. If you can *reduce* them only a little *in your own case,* you will get a start towards success because of the slight lessening of your handicap.

Value of Knowing a Single Step

I recall a man who mastered but three principles of *prospecting needs.* With this limited knowledge of salesmanship he was able to induce a great financier to open the door of opportunity and take him into a field of rich chances to earn a fortune. Another friend of mine got his start solely from knowledge of a manufacturer's principal hobby. What he knew about the "single tax" enabled him to plan a sure approach to the mind of the factory owner. A young lawyer in Chicago seized upon a chance for fame and wealth in his first meeting with a poor, seemingly unsuccessful inventor. In each of these instances a single step of the selling process, taken correctly, carried the salesman through the door of opportunity and brought him within reach of the beginnings of success.

Get Ready for Imaginable Happenings

You may not need to knock at that door, nor wait for an invitation to come in. In *your* case, perhaps, the door stands open, with a "Welcome" mat just outside. Yet if you *do need* to knock with your ideas for admittance to another man's mind, and if it ever becomes *necessary* for you to win a welcome, this chapter will prove valuable reading. You will be helped to gain your desired chance, and the danger of your failure will be minimized, if you *know how* to knock and exactly *what to do* to assure your welcome.

Even the master salesman can never be absolutely certain of the reception he will have from any prospect. Therefore he "goes loaded" for all imaginable contingencies. You, the salesman of yourself, should be likewise prepared with knowledge of how each and every step in the selling process may be taken most effectively. Whatever emergency arises, you must be ready to take the fullest advantage of a favorable turn, and equally ready to reduce as much as possible any disadvantage you encounter.

Knocking and Getting In

Of course it will avail you nothing if you succeed only in *reaching* the particular man through whom you have planned to gain success. And after you meet him it will do you no material good to *size him up* correctly; if you are then unable to hold his *attention* to your presentation of ideas. Your preliminary skillful salesmanship would all be wasted. Evidently, in order that you may continue the process of gaining your chance, it is necessary that you should know how to knock on the door of his mind in such an *agreeable but compelling* way that he will be *forced* to let his attention come out *pleasantly* to you and your purpose. Hence right knocking at the door of opportunity immediately follows the size-up as an essential part of the process of making success certain.

It is necessary next for you to know how to prevent a turn-down on the front porch of your prospect's mind, and how to insure *the admission of your ideas to his thoughts*. You can compel your prospect to open the door of his attention, but in order to get *inside* his mind and secure his *interest* in your purpose, you must win his *willing invitation* for your ideas to enter his thoughts and make themselves at home there.

Certain Success Methods

We have seen how you can make certain of gaining your chance to reach the door of opportunity. You can size up surely your prospect's dominant characteristics and what he is thinking. Likewise you can guarantee to yourself, first the attention, and second the interest of the man you have come to see. It is necessary only that you use the methods of the master salesman to *compel* the opening of the door and to *induce* the extension of welcome to your ideas.

Our Old Acquaintance Again

Here again we meet our old acquaintance, the discriminative-restrictive method. You must *discriminate* between the process of knocking at the door of opportunity and the process of securing the invitation to come in. Then, in *practicing* these related but different steps of the selling process, it is necessary that when you knock you *restrict* yourself to the use of the methods that are most effective in gaining *attention*. Similarly you should restrict yourself to using the very *different* methods of securing *interest*, when you work to get an invitation for your ideas to come inside the other man's mind and make themselves at home there.

Process of Compelling Attention

Psychologists define "Attention" as "that act of the mind which holds to a given object perceived by one or more senses, to the *exclusion* of all other objects that might be perceived at that time by the same or other senses." A knock at a door attracts attention because it temporarily diverts the previous attentiveness of the mind to other things, and concentrates it on a new object of attention. The sense of hearing is *struck*. Whether or not the mind is *willing* to hear, it *cannot help perceiving* the sudden new sound. Its attention is *forced*. The instant the knock is heard, the mind is compelled to drop or suspend what it has been thinking about; though this *exclusive* new attention to the knock may last but a fraction of a second.

Our *senses* function under the control of the sub-conscious mind. It is futile for us to *will* that we *won't* hear, or see, or taste, etc. We *have* to take in sense impressions, whether we want to do so or not. Therefore, if you employ restrictively the *sense-hitting* method, you can force the man upon whom you call to give his *attention* to you or to the presentation of your ideas.

Inducing Interest

It is necessary to discriminate, however, between the use of the avenues to reach the mind center of *attention*, and the use of very *different* ways into the mind center of *interest*. If you start wrong, there is very little chance that you will arrive at the right destination. The center of interest is wholly under the control of the *conscious* mind. Your prospect can refuse to be interested, if he chooses, despite your determination to interest him. *His interest must be induced.* Any attempt to *compel* it is apt to have a fatal result. Nearly always such an effort to force interest develops antagonism, instead.

But there are methods of *inducing* interest that are just as sure to succeed as are the sense-hitting methods by which attention may be compelled. This *double step* in the process of selling the true idea of your best capabilities in the right market can be taken with absolute *certainty* of success if you know and practice the principles in accordance with which the master salesman sells his ideas of goods to prospects. We are to study these principles now, as applied to the sale of your qualifications for success in the field you have selected.

Exclusive Agreeable Attention

When you enter the office of your prospect—your chosen future employer, for example—he will be giving his attention to *something*. No one, while he is awake, can be wholly *non*-attentive. Your function, at this stage of the selling process, is to compel him to stop paying attention to something or somebody *else*, and to give *you and your ideas* his exclusive attention.

Avoid Making Unfavorable Impressions

Of course good salesmanship makes it advisable also to avoid creating a *disagreeable* impression while forcing yourself and your ideas upon the attention of your prospect. The *conscious* mind governs a man's likes and dislikes. So if you knock compellingly at the door of *that* mind to gain attention, you may arouse very *unfavorable* attention. For illustration, a boisterous greeting of your prospect, or a very noisy entrance into his office, would doubtless compel his attention by the direct hammering on his senses.

But the attraction of his attention to you would affect the operations of both his conscious and sub-conscious minds, and his conscious mind would be disagreeably impressed. His compelled attention, therefore, might result in your being thrown out.

Gaining Both Attention And Interest

However, you can knock at the *sense* doors of the *sub-conscious* mind with such unobjectionable sense-hitting methods that while agreeable *attention* will be *compelled* thereby, you can also be sure that a favorable impression on the conscious mind of the prospect will be *induced*. For illustration, if your prospect is evidently busy at his desk when you are admitted to his office, you might compel his attention by entering very quietly and by standing in silence without interrupting him until he has had an opportunity to finish what he is doing. His sound sense would be struck, paradoxically, by your exceptional quietness. His sense of equilibrium would also be affected by your perfect poise while waiting. Your whole attitude would impress him so favorably that his especial interest in you would be induced. His greeting would be pleasant.

Suppose your prospect looks up from his work when you enter his presence, and you approach close to his desk; if you are immaculate in dress and body, you will appeal agreeably to his olfactory sense. The law of the association of ideas will then begin to work in your favor. Your prospect will get subconsciously a conscious impression of your clean character.

You might wear a fresh flower in your buttonhole and so strike several of his senses pleasantly. But unless the flower is inconspicuous and in good taste it would make an unfavorable impression.

Good Impressions

Let us assume now that when you enter the office of your prospect, he is disgruntled about something. You can take some of the heat out of his ill temper by your appearance of cool self-confidence and good nature.

There are many more such *favorable sense impressions* which you could make by simply standing in manly erectness while waiting to receive the exclusive attention of your prospect. You might employ all the sense-hitting features of bearing and manner referred to above. The effect of the sum of these would be the *forced agreeable attention* of your prospect. He simply could not help noticing the various items that would strike his different senses; nor could he help being agreeably impressed; though he might not give you any indication of the effect you had compelled.

Continual Attention Necessary

It is highly important that you should be able first to *gain* the favorable attention of your prospect, and second to *hold* it until his interest is aroused. It may also be necessary for you to *regain* his attention if it is temporarily lost and diverted to some other object. The master salesman realizes it is essential to have the attention of his prospect *continually centered* upon the ideas presented, *throughout the selling process*. Only a poor salesman of ideas would go right on talking, even though it might be clearly evident that he did not have the exclusive attention of the man addressed.

Regaining Attention

When you proffer your capabilities for purchase by a prospective employer, do not make the mistake of continuing to present your best selling points if you have any doubt that his attention is exclusively yours. *Stop your selling process if his attention wanders or is diverted.* Use the sense-hitting method to compel it to *come back* to you and your ideas. If some one should enter his office while you are talking to him, or if his telephone should ring, stop short in your presentation. (Your sudden silence, in itself, will be attention compelling.) Do not go on with your sales presentation until the interruption is over. Then use some sense-hitting method of making sure that his attention is again concentrated on you and your ideas.

Sense Hitting

An acquaintance of mine who had especially fitted himself for business correspondence, typed striking paragraphs taken from form letters he had devised and pasted the slips of paper on stiff filing cards. He carried with him to his interview with the president of a large corporation about thirty-five or forty of these cards. His prospecting had indicated that in the course of the half hour he had planned to take up with a presentation of his capabilities this executive would be interrupted often by telephone calls and the entrance of subordinates. The salesman's size-up also revealed that his prospect's attention was likely to wander to the things on his desk. From time to time when the correspondent was presenting his ideas the president reached out his hand and picked up a paper. Evidently he was inclined to give but flighty attention to his caller.

Striking More Than One Sense

The salesman, however, had "come loaded" for exactly this situation. He had worked out his selling plan in detail. As he developed idea after idea, he used a device for regaining attention by hitting at the prospect's senses of *sight* and *hearing*. Just as soon as the president's hand wandered to a paper, the salesman ruffled the cards he held, quickly selected one, and clicked it down on the desk top before his prospect. He had to do this perhaps a dozen times before he felt confident he had clinched the interest of the executive. If the salesman had used words merely, what, he said in presenting his ideas to the prospect might have gone in one ear and out the other. But his action of ruffling the cards struck the president's senses of sight and hearing compellingly; as did the clicking of the card on the desk top when it was presented for reading. Repeatedly the return of the prospect's wandering attention was forced subconsciously; yet no disagreeable impression was made on his conscious mind. In the course of half an hour the correspondent succeeded in selling his services at a very satisfactory salary.

"Come Loaded"

If you similarly "come loaded" for sense-hitting, you will be able to get your prospect's attention originally, and to regain it whenever it is temporarily lost. In advance of your call on the man to whom you want to sell your services, think out things you can do that will strike one or more of his senses forcibly, without making disagreeable impressions. You can take with you to the interview specimens of your work, or testimonials; and hold them in your hand where they will attract notice. Or you might plan to use attention-compelling gestures.

Tone Variations

Changes of tone will make the other man "perk up his ears" if his attention wanders; so plan to introduce variety into your manner of speaking. Don't just open the spigot of your mind and let your ideas run out in a monotone. Variety of voice is pleasing, as well as attention-compelling.

I know a salesman who is in the habit of using a spotlessly clean big handkerchief to help him keep the prospect's mind concentrated on the proposition being presented. Whenever the other man's attention is diverted, this salesman whisks his handkerchief from his pocket and touches his lips with it. The flash of white hits the sight-sense of the prospect and brings back his wandering attention to the salesman.

Sense Hitting Should Help The Sale

But such devices are superficial. *The best sense-hitting means of compelling attention, directly relates some sense effect to the salesman's purpose.*

The correspondent who ruffled his cards and clicked them down on the prospect's desk would not have been so successful if on each card he had not pasted a specimen of his work as an efficient letter writer. If he had brought a pack of blank cards, for example, the repeated use of his device for getting attention might have irritated the other man. To analyze the illustration further; if the correspondent had brought the specimens of his work on letter paper, not pasted on stiff cards, they would have been much less effective. He could not have ruffled them, and would have been unable to make the clicking sound he used to hit the other man's ears.

Suggesting Capability

Suppose you apply for a situation as a bookkeeper or an accountant. One of the best sense-hitting devices you could use to compel attention to your ability would be a collection of complicated tabulations in your handwriting, made neatly without a correction or an erasure. Such an exhibit of painstaking workmanship, if complemented by a neat, attractive personal appearance, would *force* the employer to *notice* you and the proofs of your qualifications. You certainly would make a most favorable impression. Your prospect would imagine his books and records as you would keep them. When presenting the evidences of your capability as an accountant, you could suggest other qualities than those mentioned—such as the proper pride of a good workman, serious earnestness, dignity, keen intelligence, etc. Such *suggestions made with the aid of sense-hitting devices* would help you to complete the sale of your services.

Make Your Qualities Stand Out

Perhaps you wish particularly to impress your qualities of alertness, energy, love of work, and physical stamina. Then sit or stand easily erect when you call on your prospect. If you should slump or loll in your chair, you would suggest that you lacked the very characteristics on which you are depending to get the job.

Make your best qualities stand out noticeably in your bearing. Should you apply for a position of great trust, requiring the exercise of the finest discretion, be sure to look the other man frankly in the face and let him see into your eyes. Also modulate your tones to the pitch of discretion and confidence. Your manner, your expressions, your voice will all draw attention to your fitness for the chance you want.

Original Methods

Such illustrations as have been given above should be understood as merely suggestive of ways to use the sense-hitting method of compelling attention. *Do not copy* the suggestions offered. *Think out for your individual use a collection of sense-hitting devices of your own.* Then you will be able to select various ways to gain and to re-gain attention when you are in the presence of a prospect. No matter what may be your ability and ambition, *there are features of your character and your service capacity that you can utilize to make direct sense appeals.* Find out for yourself what they are, and plan how to use them most effectively. If you cannot gain attention to your qualifications, or if you are unable to recall wandering attention, you may lose the chance you have succeeded in getting. *Insure yourself* against the possibility of such a disaster; so that your previous good salesmanship in securing an interview will not all go for naught.

Out-of-the-Ordinary Things

If you do something *out of the ordinary*, the force of your sense-hitting will be much greater than if you employ only common devices for gaining attention. It is better to *do* something that compels attention to your recommendations than to *say* "I want to call your attention to these letters."

Danger of Distracting Attention

However, there is always the danger that in gaining attention by *unusual* means you may attract too much attention to the *device* you use, and so distract notice from the *proposition* you are presenting for sale. Therefore be sure that whatever extraordinary thing you do to compel attention *contributes directly to your main purpose* and does not lead your prospect off on a *side track* of thought.

A business house once got out an advertising novelty and had samples distributed by the salesmen as gifts to their principal customers. The novelty was an ingenious mechanical device. It attracted so much attention to itself that when a salesman put it on the desk of a prospect before beginning his sales talk, the attention of the other man was drawn from what the salesman was saying and was given to the novelty. The prospect would pick up and examine the advertising device while the salesman was presenting ideas regarding his standard line of goods. As a result, many of the best points of the sales talks were unnoticed. The advertising novelty was a detriment. The sales volume fell off while it was being distributed. The slump was traced directly to the mistake of having the *salesmen* pass out the attention-compelling device *which was not related to the staples of the house line.*

The Remedy

The distribution was made by mail thereafter, in advance of the salesman's call. It was effective then as an introduction for the traveler; because by the time he came to see the prospect, the novelty of the advertising device had worn off. It was no longer an attention-distracter.

Three Ways To Compel Attention

Remember that the attention of your prospect is always given to *something*. If another object of attention is more compelling than *your* means of forcing his notice, your attempt will fail. Therefore be sure that your attention-getting device has at least one of three points of superiority.

(1) It can be *stronger* than the other appeal to the same sense. If your prospect's attention to what you are saying wanders because a phonograph starts to play in the next room, you can recall it to your presentation by slapping your hands together to emphasize a point, or you can change your tone suddenly. His sense of hearing will be struck compellingly by your device.

(2) Your appeal for attention can be made to *more* senses than are being reached by the distraction. The phonograph music hits only the ears of your prospect. Besides slapping your hands together or changing your tone, you can supplement such appeals to his tone sense by an appeal to his sense of sight. You can make a gesture, or display a letter for him to read just at that moment.

(3) Your appeal can hit the senses of your prospect more *insistently* than the other. If the phonograph music proves very attractive to him, you will need to *keep hammering* at him with forceful changes of voice, with gestures, by touching him, or by doing something else to make his attention to the music "let go."

Summary

To summarize the most effective method of gaining attention—*hit each sense to which you appeal as strongly as you can, without making a disagreeable impression, strike as many senses as possible, and keep on using your sense-hitting device as long as necessary to get or to recover exclusive favorable attention.*

Many a man has gained success because he first gained attention. He stood out from the crowd, or was able to make his qualities noticeable. When one is fully qualified for success, he may need only to attract attention to his capabilities; then he is likely to be given the chance he wants.

"I'm Not Interested"

Often, however, the salesman is discomfited after he gains attention. The prospect halts the selling process by declaring, "I'm not interested." Suppose you are able to compel your prospective employer to notice you favorably, but he balks there and shows no inclination to buy your services. He has listened attentively to all you have said. He has concentrated his mind upon you, and has not wandered in thought to other subjects. Yet you perceive that he is inclined to put you off or to turn you down. Evidently, in order to prevent such a contretemps, you need to resort now to a *different selling step*, which you have not taken previously.

It is necessary that you have at your command a way to induce interest. This interest-inducing means must be as *sure* in its effects as the sense-hitting method of compelling attention. Otherwise you could not be certain of success with the selling process. If the effectiveness of every step cannot be assured in advance, you will not rely confidently on salesmanship to achieve your ambition.

Discriminate Between Attention And Interest

Probably you have never worked out in your mind exactly *the reasons why you are interested* in particular things and in certain people. Let us make an analysis. Your *attention* might be attracted so strongly to a vicious criminal that for the time being you could think of no one else. Yet his fate might be a matter of such indifference to you that you would have absolutely no *interest* in the man. But suppose you should see in his face, or in an expression of his eyes, something that haunted your memory appealingly. It would induce you to read the newspaper accounts of his trial. You would feel a little sorry for him, on learning that he had been sentenced to a long term in prison. Very likely you would say to yourself, "I suppose he is a mighty tough character, but I believe there is something in him that isn't altogether bad." Your intuition would tell you he possessed undefined traits that you like. In *your own liking* for these characteristics that you vaguely discerned in him when you saw him, *is the key to the interest he induced.*

What and Whom We Like

What do we like? Whom do we like?

Things that are *like* our own ideas. People who are *like* the ideas we have about likable people. Interest is all a matter of recognizing points of likeness.

In order to draw your prospect beyond the attention stage of the selling process, and to induce his interest in your "goods," you must impress on him suggestions of the similarity of your ideas to ideas already in his own mind. *He will like your ideas in proportion to their resemblance to his own way of thinking* on the same subjects. So you should express yourself as nearly as possible in his terms, and attract his interest by making him feel that your mind and his are much alike.

Non-Interest

One day I was sitting in the private office of a very wealthy philanthropist. A salesman presented a letter of introduction to the millionaire, who in turn introduced me to his caller. The newcomer thereupon proceeded to present most attractively a business proposal. He offered my friend an excellent opportunity to make a good deal of money by joining an underwriting syndicate. The millionaire at once declared he was not interested. "I have all the money I want," he said, and bowed the salesman out. The ideas that had been presented to him were altogether *different* from his own financial motives.

Interest

That same afternoon another promoter called upon my friend with a project for investment in a house-building corporation. This second salesman evidently had prospected the philanthropist and had planned just how to interest him. He did not stress the profits to be made from investment in the stock of his corporation, but referred to them in a minor key. He emphasized the need of the city for more homes, and cited instances of distress due to the housing shortage.

My friend was thoroughly interested. He took home the salesman's prospectus for further study. Since he was a good business man, he satisfied himself that the investment would be profitable. But he subscribed for fifty thousand dollars worth of securities principally because they represented a project *like his own ideas* of the way money should be put to work for human happiness.

Know Prospect's Likes and Dislikes

When you call on the man you have selected as your future employer, go equipped with all the prospecting knowledge regarding him that you have been able to get. Be sure you know his strongest likes and dislikes. Size him up on the spot, for the purpose of supplementing what you have previously learned about him. Hit his attention with sense-appeals related to his peculiarities. Then, in order to make sure of his interest, present some idea that is of the kind *he* especially likes. He will open his mind and welcome your idea at once.

The Man of Quick Decisions

Suppose he has a reputation for brusqueness and quick decisions, and is impatient about any waste of time. You probably would help your cause by looking him straight in the eye and saying bluntly something like this:

"I want to work for you because you are my kind of a man. Ask me any questions you want, now. You won't have to call me on the carpet for information about my work after you hire me. Pay me two hundred dollars a month, and I won't be back in this office to get a raise until you send for me."

I know a young man who secured a good job from an "old crab" in just that way, within three minutes after they first met.

Two men sought the position of office manager of an automobile company. The owners of the business were thorough mechanics who had designed their own car, but who were comparatively unfamiliar with office operations. They were not at home outside their factory.

Mistake of Speaking Different Language

The first candidate for the vacant position brought the finest recommendations of his qualifications for office management. The other applicant had had much less experience, and was not nearly so well qualified. But the first man was a poor salesman of his capabilities. He failed to recognize, when he explained his ideas to the partners, that he was talking to a pair of mechanics. They did not understand the language he used. His presentation of his qualifications as an office manager would have impressed an employer accustomed to sitting at a desk. But the partners were intuitively prejudiced against the capable candidate who was so very *unlike themselves* in all respects.

Speaking the Same Language

The other applicant was shrewd. He used salesmanship in presenting his lesser qualifications for the position. He talked in terms borrowed from the language of shop practice. He compared the plans he suggested for the office supplies stock room, with the "tool crib" in the factory. He explained his idea of office organization by using as a model a chart of the plant departments. He compared office expenses with factory overhead.

The owners of the business understood very little about the subjects he discussed, but he used words and expressions that were familiar to them. So his ideas, as he presented them, impressed the partners as *like their own way of looking at things*. The better salesman, who knew how to interest his prospects, got the five-figure job; though he was a less capable office executive than the disappointed applicant.

Fitting Ideas To Prospect's Mind

Do not try to sell another man particular ideas because *you* like them. You are not the buyer. Sell him ideas that *he* likes. Fit the ideas you bring him to the characteristics of his mind.

If you judge him to be a quick thinker, do not hesitate in indecision a moment longer than is necessary for you to make up your mind confidently. On the other hand, should he be a deliberate thinker, be careful not to make an impression that you are rash or impulsive in your decisions.

Clothes and Interest

If he is inclined to be finical about his dress, or over-particular regarding orderliness, he will be interested if your garb is punctiliously correct and if you suggest to him the habits of precision. I read a little while ago the story of a young man who lost the chance to become the confidential assistant of a noted financier. The young man missed his opportunity because he made the mistake of wearing a soft collar when he called for the final interview with the financier.

Avoid False Pretense of Interest

Do not, of course, put on false pretenses, to make your prospect like you and your ideas. Remember that you must *live up* to a first good impression. So appear nothing, say nothing, do nothing that is untrue to your best self. But without any dishonesty you can indicate that your way of thinking has points of similarity to the slant of the other man's mind. If he is a Republican, while you are a Democrat, and the subject of politics comes up, do not pretend to be an elephant worshiper. Admit your party allegiance casually, and remark that you are not hide-bound in your political faith, but open-minded. Maybe he will employ you with the hope of converting you to Republicanism.

Few Direct Opposites

There are few ideas regarding which honest men are diametrically opposed on principle. You can suggest to your prospective employer the idea that you are in accord with his way of thinking; though you may differ widely in many respects. You need not emphasize the *degree* of your likeness in mind. Certainly it would be very poor policy to stress your differences of opinion.

Like Breeds Like

Any likeness of your suggestions to the ideas of the other man will impress him agreeably. He will be pleased to find the points of resemblance, and they will help to gloss over a possible prejudice in his mind against you. The association of your similar ideas on a subject will suggest to him imaginative pictures of your association with him in his business. "Like breeds like." He will place you mentally in a situation where the likable qualities he has found in you might be employed to his satisfaction.

Inside the Door

Then you will be safely *inside the door* of his interest. Without realizing it, your prospect would like to bring about the condition he has imagined. He is beginning to want you in his employ; though as yet he has no deep-seated desire for your services. Objections to you may spring up in his mind, but you certainly have been successful throughout the processes of getting his response to your knock, and of securing for your ideas his invitation to come into his thoughts for a better acquaintance with your purpose.

Unwelcome Guests

After admitting your ideas to his mind, he may wish he had not welcomed them. He may find objectionable things in you or in your proposal. Sometimes a man responds to a knock on his door, and becomes sufficiently interested in the caller to invite him to enter the house; but regrets afterward that he extended the welcome. This change of heart and mind is usually due to something done by the visitor after his admittance. However, we are not considering just now any step of the selling process beyond winning a welcome. In later chapters we will study how to make the most effective use of hospitality and the things to avoid that might impress the host as abuses of the privileges of a guest.

Furniture of The Mind

Ideas have been called "the furniture of the mind." We have already seen that they are the developments of *repeated sense impressions*. A particular mind center is partly or wholly furnished with ideas in proportion to the man's use of his sense avenues to bring in ideas from outside himself. The doors of the mind swing inward most readily when the new mental furniture brought along a sense avenue matches the ideas already in the mind center. Doubtless the young man who lost the interest of a great financier by wearing a soft collar would have been able to hold it if he had dressed according to his prospect's ideas.

One Likable Thing Helps

If there is one thing about you that another man dislikes, it disproportionately tinges his entire attitude of mind toward you. On the other hand, if you have one especially likable feature, it tends to lessen the disagreeable impression of things about you that the other man does not like.

So, when you come to a prospect as a salesman of your best self and have gained his attention, avoid making disagreeable suggestions to his mind, and have at your command a number of sense appeals you are sure he will like. You certainly will secure his interest if you follow this selling process.

To win his interest you need not induce your prospect to like you *all through* or in *every respect*. If he likes but one thing about you at first, he will be interested enough to give you the chance to develop more interest. *The interest that produces the fruit of acceptance is often a growth from only one seed sown by the salesman of ideas.*

Avoid Over-Emphasis

At this stage of the selling process it is not wise to plunge ahead fast. Do not go to the *extreme* on any subject that you find is interesting to your prospect. His interest may be mild, and he might be prejudiced if you seem to display excessive concern about something that he considers of minor importance. I recall the experience of a man who was complimented on keeping an appointment to the minute. He *over-emphasized* the virtue of punctuality and irritated his prospect, who was not always on time himself. The job went to another applicant.

Moderate Attitude

Be moderate in your attitude when you work to secure the beginning of interest, lest you raise an obstacle in your path. Until you are sure you have won a considerable degree of interest, you cannot lead strongly in any direction without running the risk of losing some of the advantages you have gained. Therefore at the interest stage proceed warily. "Watch your step."

Hobbies

Be especially careful not to gush over a hobby of your prospect, in which his interest may not be so great as you suppose. *Hobbies are dangerous.* Don't harp on one. It requires consummate art to show enthusiasm about another man's hobby without arousing his suspicions regarding your sincerity.

Art of Knocking and Winning a Welcome

Throughout the various steps of the selling process, salesmanship is an *art*. The art of knocking at the door of opportunity and of winning the invitation to come in lies in *making favorable out-of-the-ordinary impressions in unusual ways.* The salesman himself, his methods of presenting his services for sale, and his qualifications—all should stand out distinctly, and make impressions of his individuality. He should not seem like a common applicant for a position, but should suggest to the prospective employer that he is a man of uncommon characteristics and especial capability.

The Process And Effects

That is the way to make a good impression. Such an impression of an extraordinary personality first affords pleasure, then excites a degree of admiration, and next arouses a certain amount of curiosity that is nearly akin to interest. If you please your prospect in your initial impression on him, he will like you and begin to feel *personal concern* about your application.

Analyze, Discriminate, Restrict

In order to qualify yourself for taking this step of the selling process effectively hereafter, analyze the impressions you make now. Discriminatively select the good and bad details. Then restrict your future practice in perfecting the art of inducing interest, to the development and use of your pleasing qualities only.

The Interesting Opening

Most men begin an interview with a prospective employer indefinitely or in merely general terms. Naturally they confront a wall of non-interest. You have come, remember, on a mission of service. Please at once by presenting the idea that you know a particular service which is lacking and which you can supply. Break the ice of strangeness between you and your prospect by an appeal first to his human side through a smile of *genuine friendliness* and by looking straight into his eyes so that he can see into your heart.

Then in a business-like way get right down to business without hesitation. Show enthusiasm, which is contagious if not overdone. Base your enthusiasm on real optimism. Indicate temperamental youthfulness in vigor and courage. Say something original—something strong, maybe a little startling; but it must be self-evidently true. By all means avoid anything that suggests parrot talk or indefinite thought. Do not expect the other man to listen with interest to a statement proceeding from premise to conclusion.

Headlines

Use headlines prominently and often to summarize the body of your proposal. Headlines attract your attention and induce your interest in particular newspaper items. Employ headline statements for the same purpose in selling the idea of your capabilities; just as surely you will get attention and interest.

A noted sales manager who had been earning a large salary made up his mind that satisfying success for him was to be gained only through a business in which he would be partly an owner instead of just an employee. He called together a group of financiers and introduced his purpose by saying to them, "Gentlemen, I have an idea in which I have so much confidence that I will resign my $75,000 a year job to develop it. I want to explain it to you and to have your co-operation in financing a project I have worked out." His headline statement secured instant interest, of course.

There is something about yourself or your capabilities that you can put into headlines. In forcible, vivid language you can strike some senses of your prospects. Think of headline statements about your services. Write them out in advance. You may be certain they will produce the same psychological effect as headlines in the newspapers.

Sense Doors Always Open

Use the sense avenues to introduce agreeable suggestions into your prospect's mind centers of attention and interest. Then you will be employing the *unusual* methods of a master salesman, who devises ways of using every possible sense appeal.

The sense doors are always open. They are held open by the subconscious mind. If you understand your way through them there will be no doubt about the effectiveness of your knock at the door of opportunity, or about getting an invitation for your ideas to enter the mind of the other man.

CHAPTER IX
Getting Yourself Wanted

Show a Need For Your Services

A great many salesmen mistakenly believe that if they can interest a prospect thoroughly in their goods, he is almost sure to buy. When this stage is reached, they think they only need to keep his interest growing to close the sale. If, instead, it drags on interminably, they are utterly at a loss regarding what *more* they should do to secure the order.

Do not fall into a similar error when selling true ideas of your best capabilities. Not only is it necessary that you induce your prospective employer's *interest* in your personal qualifications, but you need to make him realize there is a *present lack* in his business which you can fill to his satisfaction. *You must get yourself wanted.*

You might make an excellent first impression on the man you have chosen as your future chief. He might listen attentively to your presentation of ideas, and question you so interestedly that you would expect him to say at any moment, "All right. The job is yours." Then, instead of engaging your services, he might remark, "I'll keep your name on file." Or he might say, "I know a man who probably could use you. I'll give you a note to him." You would win a cordial farewell handshake from your prospect, but not an acceptance of your proposal to work with him. You would leave without the job. *Your failure would be due to your inability to get yourself sufficiently wanted.*

See Yourself Through Your Prospect's Eyes

Now imagine yourself in the place of this employer. See your application through his eyes. Unless you can look at yourself from the prospect's viewpoint, you may not comprehend your deficiency in salesmanship.

The employer upon whom you called said to himself while you were trying to sell your services, "Here is a very attractive man. He presents an interesting proposition. But I have no real need for such an employee; therefore it would be poor business for me to engage him, much as I should like to do so. I am sorry that at present I have no place for him in my organization. He's a man I'd like to keep track of, so I'll file his name and address for possible future reference. Meanwhile I'll give him a note to my friend Smith. I hate to turn him down cold; he's such a fine man."

Evidently the employer did not feel a *lack* in his own business. You failed to make him realize any *need* for your services.

Proving A Need

Contrast with this illustration the case of an efficiency engineer who secured his chance to overhaul a factory by demonstrating to a manufacturer that he needed a new order-checking system. The engineer "beat" the old system and brought to the manufacturer's office a lot of goods he had secured that could not be checked. His salesmanship compelled attention, induced thorough interest, and proved there was a hole that should be filled. When the lack was shown convincingly, the manufacturer wanted it satisfied. The sale of the engineer's services was quickly closed.

Getting Yourself Wanted Is Only One Step Ahead

Do not jump to the conclusion that you are sure of the job you desire, just as soon as you get yourself wanted. You are not yet at the end of the selling process. The prospect has only been conducted successfully another step forward toward your goal. *The moment after he realizes the lack in his business, he is apt to question most critically your qualifications for filling it.*

Analysis Naturally Follows Desire

As soon as a man begins to feel a real tug of desire for anything, he examines it with new, increased interest to make sure there isn't something the matter with it. The suit of clothes that only induces his interest in a shop window is passed by after a look. However, if he says to himself, "That's the kind of suit I want," he goes in and examines the workmanship and the cloth, in search of faults. The salesman may need to overcome certain objections of his prospect before the order can be secured.

But we have not reached the objections stage of the uncompleted sale. That is the subject of the next chapter. Let us retrace our steps to study the essence of the art of getting yourself wanted.

Two-part Process of Getting Yourself Wanted

There are two parts to the process. First, you must show the prospect what he lacks; that in his business there is *an unoccupied opportunity for such services as you believe you are capable of rendering to his benefit and satisfaction.* Second, you need to *picture yourself filling the place and giving the service;* to show him imaginatively *your qualifications at work in his business.*

Sincerity Of Service Purpose

Of course it is primarily necessary that you believe in your own capability, and in the value to the other man of the qualities you have brought to him for sale. Unless you have this feeling yourself, you will not be likely to draw out his reciprocating desire for your services. You are not dealing now with his mind. *Desire proceeds from the heart. It is emotional, not mental.* The least suspicion of your insincerity would check your prospect's feeling that he wants you as an employee. You must feel that you have come with a purpose of genuine service, and you must draw out his similar feeling.

Desire Comes Out of the Heart

When you knocked at the door of your prospect's mind, and when you sought to induce his welcome for your ideas, your object was to get him to take your thoughts *into* his head. The line of action is *reversed* at the desire stage of the selling process. Until now *you* have been the moving party. You have been getting yourself and your ideas into his consciousness. But while attention and interest are *receptive* processes, the emotion of genuine desire starts with an *outward moving impulse from the prospect*. It isn't enough that he open his heart and let you enter, as he has admitted your ideas to his mind. *If he really wants you, his feeling of desire will come out after you.*

Service Value is Appreciated

You have revealed to your prospect a lack in his business, and have pictured yourself filling it to his satisfaction. You have done him a double service. It is human nature to *appreciate* such a genuine service, and to *want more* like it. The first service is accepted with appreciation, but when the square man wants more *he makes a move to get it, and expects to pay for it.* As soon as you have shown the lack and your ability to fill it, and have pictured yourself "on the job," it will be natural for your prospect to want you there in fact.

The colored porter who washed the windows and scrubbed floors in the general offices of a manufacturing corporation was ambitious to rise in the social scale and to earn a larger salary. One evening he went to the private office of the president, and presented for sale an idea of his capability for a different job.

Official Welcomer Wanted

"Boss," he began, "You-all ain't got nobody dere to de front doah to make folks feel welcome-like when dey comes in heah. Down in Virginny my ol' gran-pap useter weah a dress suit ever' day an' jist Stan' in de front hall of his ol' massa's house, a-waitin' to bow an' smile to comp'ny whad'd come in. If you'll jist rent me one o' dem dar suits, Boss, I could stan' out in the front office an' make folks feel we wuz glad to see 'um, lak' mah gran'pap did. When ennybody comes heah now, dey ain't nobody pays much 'tention to 'um. You'd orter git somebody on dat job, Boss; an' I reckon I'm jist 'bout cut out foh it, suh."

The colored man compelled attention by presenting himself at the door of the sanctum. He induced interest in his proposal. Then, in addition, *he pointed out a lack and that he could fill it*. Immediately the president *visioned* the old darkey as an official welcomer, and *wanted* him. *He reached right out for the service offered*. The sale was closed at once, and the colored man shone in his new glories within a week.

Conflict of Heart and Mind

Often a man desires with his heart things that his mind does not approve. Therefore when you work to get yourself wanted, *appeal to the heart of your prospect, rather than to his mind*. Then if *his* mind raises objections to his desire for your services, *your* mind at a later stage of the selling process will overcome or get around his mental opposition. When the time for that step arrives, *his heart* will already have been won as *your ally*, and will help you dispose of the objections *his mind* has raised.

Get Yourself Liked

As a preliminary to getting yourself wanted, get yourself *liked*. Make such an impression, do and say such things, as will draw out of the heart of your prospect *a friendly feeling* for you. You know of people who have been boosted to notable successes because influential men took personal interest in their advancement.

I recall an office boy who was always ready to perform little extra services. He held his employer's overcoat one day, and the boss rather absent-mindedly handed him a tip. The boy shook his head and declined the dime.

"I didn't do that for a tip. You always treat me fine, and I just like to show you I appreciate it."

The boy's *heart had spoken*, and the employer's *heart responded at once with an especial liking* for the lad. The seed of personal interest having been planted in the heart of the president, his liking grew. The boy was advanced to better and better positions. He made good on his merits, but he was helped very much because his employer *wanted* him to succeed.

The Common Heart of Man

Reference has previously been made to the fundamental likeness of all men at heart and to their differences in mind. Send out with your voice an appeal to only the *minds* of your audience—read a table of statistics, for example—and it will affect all your hearers *differently, depending on the mental characteristics of each individual.* But tell a story of great courage, of self-sacrifice, of love—*the same fundamental effect* will be produced on all the *hearts* in the audience; though, of course, the various individuals will respond with *different degrees of emotional intensity.*

As has been said before, in order to look into the heart of another man you need but see clearly into your own. There you will find all the emotions of human nature, no matter how you may differ from other men in mentality. Hence if you would prompt the heart of another man to want your services, just *do the things he would need to do to win your liking for him.* Imagine the cases reversed, and be guided in your selling process by what you see.

Popular Men

To look at this step from another angle—*if you would be likable, you must find other men likable.* If you like people only within a limited range, you will similarly narrow your own likableness. If, however, you genuinely like all men—like them for their faults and frailties as well as for their merits—you will appeal to the intuitive heart of any other man. You will draw out his liking for you because *the magnetic power of your own heart will not be restricted* to pulling your way the friendly feelings of only a few people. Instead, you will be a "popular" man, a man who is *generally* well liked.

You meet certain men whom you like at sight. You desire further acquaintance, or friendship with them. But these men have not prepared themselves to suit *you* in particular. Most *other* people who meet them have the *same feeling* toward them that you experience. The men you like at sight, and who make friends wherever they go have developed in themselves *feelings of friendliness for all men.* As like breeds like, liking draws liking.

Artificial Methods Never Deceive The Heart

If you try to develop particular traits, only because you believe they will attract other men to you, you will not make your nature likable. Such *artificial methods* of making yourself attractive *never deceive heart intuitions.* You will not become popular by proceeding *selfishly.* But if you develop within yourself a heartfelt interest in your fellow men, if you are full of genuine desire to serve them with your friendship, *you will attract the liking of nearly all the people you meet.* They will want to know you better and to be your friends.

No Insulation Against Human Magnetism

There is "no sich critter" as a natural grouch. A man who has that reputation is *repressing his natural emotions*—that is all. He does not express his true feelings. He attempts to deny that he has them. *But they are inside him, and you can pull them toward you* if you bring your likableness to bear upon his heart. He will feel the tug, and will be drawn to you by your magnetic power. *There is no insulation that can prevent the pull of human magnetism.* So treat the crab with a feeling of real liking for the human nature inside, and don't be discouraged by his shell. Be more than ordinarily likable when you have to deal with a surly prospect. Exert all the magnetism you have. He will feel drawn to you. You will get yourself wanted.

J. Pierpont Morgan, Senior, was noted for being unapproachable. But it is said that he took a great liking to a certain newsboy who never acted afraid of him and who treated him as an ordinary mortal. This gamin always had a cheery word for everybody. That he made no exception in Mr. Morgan's case won the heart of the austere financier, who helped the boy to get an education and to start in business.

Do Not Over-sell Likability

The emphasis placed on the importance of likableness as the *principal* factor in getting yourself wanted may have made you forget the *primary* necessity of showing your prospect *a real lack in his business, and that you are capable of filling it.* It is possible to attract an employer's liking for you, whether he has a place for you or not. But his liking will do you no good unless you can also make him see he has a need for you.

Success is not to be won by getting in where you are not wanted, however likable you may be. You must sell the idea of your service *value* as well as the ideas that your services would be *liked*. You *cannot over-develop* the quality of likableness, but you *can over-sell* it, to the detriment of your own best interest.

A Winning Personality Sometimes Fails

One of the most conspicuous failures I know is a man who has "a winning personality." Times without number his genuine agreeableness has won him fine chances to succeed, but in the positions he has held he has never studied the needs of his employers for other qualities than likability. Consequently he has fallen down on all his big chances. Today he is just a popular door man for a big department store. His intelligence and his physical ability are so evident that he is an object of pity and wonder as he smiles and bows to customers of the store. Undoubtedly if he had studied the different opportunities he has had, and had fitted himself into all the requirements of a particular situation, his winning personality would have helped him higher and higher toward the mountain peaks of success instead of leaving him on an ant hill.

Three Impressions Necessary

Of course the mind of your prospective employer acts in co-ordination with his heart when you attract him so much that he really wants the service you proffer. He imagines you rendering that service. He thinks what "might be" if you were associated with his business. He paints mental pictures that please him, and he wishes his vision to come true. But when he begins to imagine you rendering service, the picture of your agreeable personality will not be pleasant to him if he sees that he doesn't really need you. *In order to get yourself wanted it is necessary that you show him the lack, and that you can fill it, and that you would be likable when filling it.* If you make these three impressions on the mind and heart of your prospect, your success in your purpose will be assured. You will not fail to get yourself wanted.

Desire is Turning Point Of the Sale

In salesmanship "desire is the determinant of the sale." By this is meant that *when the salesman sufficiently stimulates a real desire in his prospect, he has climbed the highest grade of difficulty.* If he is skillful, the selling process from then on should be comparatively easy sledding. You realize that if you can get yourself wanted by an employer, the matter of landing a job in his business should not be hard. We therefore are considering now *the turning point in the process of selling the true idea of your best capabilities in the right field.* After you get yourself wanted, the odds are no longer against you, but grow increasingly in your favor. If, having succeeded in getting yourself wanted, you then fail in your ultimate purpose, you should blame no one but yourself.

The Use of Tactful Suggestion

A very skillful use of *tact and diplomacy* is necessary to success in pointing out to a prospect something that he lacks, and your capability for filling that lack. A man is apt to resent your "picking flaws" in his business. He is likely to regard you as an egotist if you *assert* that he needs you. You will not get yourself wanted if you make the impression that you are a critical fault-finder with "the big-head." Rather, you should pattern after the example of the professional salesman of goods. In the processes of persuasion and creating desire he employs the arts of *suggestion in preference to making direct statements*. He is a tactful diplomat. Learn from his methods, as explained in "The Selling Process."

You have come to a chosen employer, with a real service purpose; but be careful not to *offend* in your presentation. Do not bring him your idea for improving his business as if it were a great discovery you have made. He won't like it if you open his eyes to his lacks in that fashion. You might better suggest that while you have perceived what he needs, you have no doubt he either has seen it already or would have perceived it if his time and attention had not been engrossed by other things. You will be liked if you so present a picture of the lack and of yourself satisfying it.

Rubbing the Prospect the Wrong Way

You are apt to get yourself cordially disliked if you rub your prospect's pride in his business the wrong way.

An accountant sought an opportunity to become the auditor for a manufacturing corporation. He had gained considerable "inside knowledge" of the company's lax business methods. But when talking to the president he exaggerated the relative importance of these defects. In his eagerness to impress the executive with the need for an auditor, he over-drew the danger from leaks in the company's accounting system. The president was exasperated. His pride was stung. What had been said reflected on his capability as an executive. So he turned savagely on the accountant.

"If we're so rotten as all that," he snarled, "how could we make money and pay dividends? No doubt you are right in your criticisms of our methods. But if I had a man like you around here, continually finding fault and picking everybody and everything to pieces, the whole business would be demoralized. The ideas you have brought to me are worth a thousand dollars, and I'll give you my check for that, but no crepe hanger can work for me."

Avoid Teaching

When you present your capabilities for sale, don't suggest that you think your prospect's business will go to the "demnition bow-wows" if your services are not engaged. *Understate the lack and your fitness to fill it.* You may be sure the employer will appreciate fully the value of the new ideas you bring, and the worth of your services.

Pope's Rule

None of us really like "teachers." Nowadays the most successful educational methods follow the rule laid down by Alexander Pope, "Men must be taught as if you taught them not; and things unknown proposed as things forgot." Do not suggest that you are a "know it all." Much less make the impression that the other man does not know. Communicate to him the idea that you believe he has overlooked the lack to which you call his attention. With modest confidence present your capabilities. You need not assert in words that you will fill the bill. Your prospect can see that. In everything you suggest and say, show that you genuinely like him and his business. Manifest sincere admiration. *Make him feel that you have come to his office because you especially want to work there. That will make him want you in his service.* Use suggestion to increase his desire for you.

Reduce Resistance By Suggestion

Direct presentation of ideas indicates an intention to inform, to teach, to direct the mind of the other man. Every human individual, whether a child or a centenarian, *re-acts in opposition* to such an effort at instruction. There is something in all of us alike which makes us wish to think and decide for ourselves. Hence the value of the art of suggestion in getting yourself wanted.

Ideas you *suggest* enter the mind of the other man so unobtrusively that *he does not realize you originated them.* He has no feeling that you intend to influence his mind. Consequently he makes no resistance to the suggested ideas. *It never pays to reason when selling an idea; because reasoning invariably brings out a reaction of opposition.* You will not create a desire for your services by presenting them *logically,* or by making an *argument* regarding your capabilities. One of the greatest students of the human mind assures us that "most persons never perform an act of pure reasoning; but all their acts are the results of imitation, habit, suggestion, or some related form of thinking."

Three Reasons For Using Suggestion

Suggestion is remarkably effective in persuading and in arousing desire because:

First, *every "suggested" idea is accepted as absolutely true unless it is contradicted by other ideas already in the mind of the prospect.* This is because the prospect thinks a *suggested* idea is his. He adopts it and makes it his own. That is, his mind takes the suggestion and interprets it in terms of his own thoughts. Of course he believes what he himself thinks. *Say* to a prospective employer that you would particularly like to work in association with him, and he may believe you are "shooting hot air." He will have no such feeling if you tell him details about his business that have especially interested you. *Show* him that you have been studying and observing his methods. Give him to understand that you have also investigated other businesses. Thus without *saying* it, you *suggest* to his mind that you have come to his office because you really would prefer to be employed there. He will believe the suggested idea; though he might have scoffed at the statement.

Suggestion Avoids Contradiction

Second, *suggestion is effective in persuasion and in arousing desire because suggested ideas which include no comparisons or criticisms very seldom arouse contradictory attitudes of mind.* The suggested idea enters the mind of the other man quietly, unaccompanied by a blare of the trumpet "I Tell You." Opposing ideas are not aware of its presence until it has supplanted them. *Suggest* to a chosen employer that he *means* to be up-to-date, and he agrees. If you *say* his methods are behind the times, he will be apt to defend them instead of following your lead along the line of suggested improvements.

Suggested Ideas Tend to Action

Third, *every suggested idea of action tends to result in the action itself; whereas a direct attempt to secure action is almost sure to result in opposition.* Human nature works that way. Your prospect, being unconscious that a particular idea of action is suggested to him, does not have his will stimulated to prevent that action. If you come to your prospective employer and *ask* for the job you want, he will be on the *defensive*. But if you *suggest* to him that he wants you—that he lacks and needs such services as you present—*he will be impelled to the affirmative action of offering you the job.*

Selling Henry Ford

When I was originally engaged by Henry Ford, it was in the capacity of a public accountant, for an audit of the business of the Ford Motor Company, and later for the installation of an accounting system that would tell accurately every month "where they were at." Back in 1904-1905 the Ford Motor Company was not showing any more profits than many other motor car manufacturers organized on similar lines. After I completed my work as an accountant, Mr. Ford talked with me about taking a permanent position with the Company in the capacity of "Commercial Manager." That title covered responsibility for the distribution of products, advertising, collections, selection of branch managers and their corps of assistants, operation of branch houses, appointment and direction of agents, employment and control of the entire sales force, etc., etc. The position was much broader than that of Sales Manager, as it included also the accounting and organizing of nearly every department of the business.

For several years prior to that time I had sold my services as a public accountant and organizer to many large concerns throughout the country, including twenty-eight different automobile companies. I believed in my ability, not only to organize a selling and distributing force for successfully marketing a standard product, but also to extend that force over a world field and to control it in all the details of its operations, from opening the mail to the declaration and payment of dividends, more efficiently than the average sales or commercial manager. So I had no hesitancy in undertaking the Ford job, which, even at that early date, I visualized as culminating in a big one.

When I finally engaged my services with the Ford Motor Company on a permanent basis, the business was represented by only a few hundred scattered, unorganized, uncontrolled, and non-directed dealers. My work during the following twelve years was concentrated on developing and enlarging yearly this small hit-or-miss distributing aggregation into a compact force of thousands of well-trained, highly efficient sales and service representatives of the Ford Motor Company. They were all Ford "boosters," and by their loyalty and intensive co-operation they "put across the Ford" in the big way that today makes the little car so conspicuous everywhere throughout the world.

Statement Avoided Suggestion Used

Note that while my experience with the Ford Motor Company as a public accountant convinced me that what the business needed then was a commercial manager and sales organizer, and I believed myself fitted for the position, I did not make that statement to Mr. Ford; because it would have been poor salesmanship. He might have thought me entirely qualified to deal with figures, but not so capable of handling sales agents and dealers.

So I never *said* to him that I was the man he needed. But I *suggested* it by presenting my ideas of how the job should be done. He accepted my ideas as good, and was influenced by the natural suggestion that resulted from them. He told me that he wanted me to become Commercial and Sales Manager. It was the opportunity for success that I most desired. I got myself *wanted* without having to overcome any *resistance* in the mind of the man with whom I had chosen to work.

Negative Suggestions

You recognize how true to human nature are incidents of this sort. You know how powerful is the force of *affirmative* suggestion. But have you appreciated how surely desire is killed by *negative* suggestions? If you make *displeasing* impressions, you will get yourself *not* wanted. Therefore you must *be careful to avoid certain things your prospect would not like, just as you should be careful in doing things that are likable.*

Speak the Prospect's Language

If your prospecting and sizing up of an employer indicate that he is very painstaking, suggest to him how particular you have been to prepare yourself in knowledge of his needs. If he is a man who weighs ideas carefully, suggest to him your qualities of judgment and decision. Perhaps he is characterized by a marked constructive imagination. Suggest that you, too, have imaginative power. Bring out conspicuously the particular elements of your qualifications that are most likely to *suggest ideas akin to his own.* Speak those phrases of the language of suggestion which he best understands, and that are most likely to impress him with *the idea that you and he think alike.*

Deceptive Suggestions

A caution is necessary here. In any suggestion that you make, *convey neither more nor less than the actual truth* regarding your capabilities. *Avoid any possibility of deception.*

I recall the case of a young man who quite won the heart of a dignified bank president whose tastes were very quiet. The young man studiously avoided the slightest appearance of flashiness in his dress and manner. He spoke in modulated tones. His movements were subdued. He had exactly the quiet pose that suited his prospective employer. The banker stressed his appreciation of the characteristics manifested by the applicant, and the young man "overdid it" by suggesting that he was *always* decorous in his manner.

The bank president had occasion to entertain a visiting financier who wanted to go to the ball game. A few seats away the young man whose application was being considered rooted boisterously for the home team, unconscious of the contradiction he presented to the suggestions he had made in the banker's private office. The new impression was made more disagreeable because the boisterous behavior suggested to the banker that the young man had not conveyed a true idea of himself previously. When he came next morning for the answer to his application, he received a cold "No."

The young man really was not boisterous except on the rare occasions when he let off steam, as at a ball game. If he had conveyed the *truthful* impression that he was *nearly always* quiet, and had taken pains to admit that *occasionally* he "let loose," but only in proper surroundings, he would not have killed his chances by the negative suggestion of untruthfulness.

Motive of Suggestion

After all it is your *motive* that determines the right or wrong use of suggestion in getting yourself wanted. If you keep carefully in mind a purpose to *suggest less instead of more than the truth* about your capabilities, you need not fear that you will offend by over-drawing the picture of your real self.

If *your* motive is wrong, it will lower the quality of *your* manhood. If you suggest a wrong motive to the *other* man, the effect is to lower *his* manhood qualities in considering you. *It is particularly important not to stimulate a motive that may afterward operate to your detriment.*

Over-Suggestion of Ability

I know a young man who was so eager to show his willingness to work that he suggested absolute tirelessness. His employer, though he appreciated what this young man did, kept overloading him. Finally the employee broke down and made a serious mistake. He was unjustly dismissed from service because *he had encouraged his employer to depend on him altogether too much, and disappointment resulted.*

Do not pretend a higher degree of ability than you possess. Attempt no more than you can do well. You will succeed in getting yourself wanted if you *manifest promise of growth* in capability. If you are a sapling, do not pose as a full grown tree of knowledge.

Selling Out To Competitor

Sometimes it happens that a man can present his capabilities for sale and appear especially desirable to another man because he possesses certain knowledge the employer would like to have. Maybe you have sought to gain your chance by carrying to a competitor of your former employer the latter's secrets. If you come with the suggestion that you will sell out, you are offering a service that does not command full respect, and you are appealing only to the *lower motives* of your prospect. You do not thereby get *yourself* wanted. He wants *what you know*. What you have learned fairly by working for one man, you have a right to sell fairly to another man, of course. But do not suggest that this special knowledge is the *principal element* of your desirability. Suggest, rather, that it is *only incidental to your all-around fitness* for the job you want.

Self-Respect

Use what you know without pandering to the lower motives of your new employer. Impel him to like you for what you *are,* and not merely for what you *bring*. Open his eyes to your *better* nature, not to the *worst* side of you. *He will see in you the better qualities of himself and appreciate them.* Have your own motives right; then there will be no danger that you will appeal to the wrong motives of the other man.

Of course you must have the highest respect for your own motives. This necessitates high character. *You must be honest in the very structure of your being.* You need, too, *absolute faith in yourself and in your proposition,* and faith in the *desirability* of your service to the other man. Finally, you must be *consecrated* to the motive of rendering him *service*.

Postpone Criticism Until Desire Is Stimulated

It is poor salesmanship to let your prospect begin to analyze your faults *until you have made yourself thoroughly pleasing* to him. Before you complete the selling process you should admit your own faults, rather than let him discover them. *But skillfully postpone this step until you get yourself wanted.* Then your prospect will be inclined to *co-operate* in disposing of objections to you; whereas *if criticisms arise too soon in the selling process they may prevent him from liking you thoroughly, and may check your purpose before you get yourself wanted.*

Right Time to "Face The Music"

A merchant received an application for employment in his private office from a young man who created so pleasing an impression that the employer decided to make him his secretary. He outlined his ideas to the applicant, who entered into them most enthusiastically; thereby increasing the liking of his prospective employer for him. Then the young man sat up straight in his chair, looked the merchant squarely in the eye, and said, "No one in this city knows it, but when I was eighteen years old I stole ten dollars and was sentenced to the reform school. That was seven years ago. I never have done anything dishonest since, and I never will again. But you have a right to know my whole record before you employ me in a position of such trust." If the candidate had confessed his blemished record *before* making himself thoroughly desirable, it is practically certain that he would not have won the place. He got it because *he handled the objection after instead of before creating the desire* for his services.

Concentrate On Suggesting Qualifications

We shall consider in the next chapter how to meet and handle objections, how to deal with your faults. But as we postpone our study of that step in the selling process; so should you postpone consideration of your faults and shortcomings, until you get yourself wanted. Do not dodge direct questions, but courteously request that you be permitted to answer them a little later. *At this stage* of selling the true idea of your best capabilities *concentrate upon the moderate, truthful suggestion of your qualifications.*

Gaining Prospect's Confidence

The first result to be desired in selling is the *confidence of the buyer.* Use all your manly qualities to win this confidence *deservedly.* Then when you honestly admit your faults and shortcomings, you will be aided to win out in the end by the confidence you have already inspired in the other man.

Very often the applicant for a position fails to get it because he merely presents the *abstract* idea that his services are for sale. *He does not picture himself in actual service.* The presentation of abstract ideas is an appeal only to the *interest* or mind side of the other man. The presentation to his imagination must go *beyond* his interest, if his *heart desire* for the services is to be secured. Therefore it is highly important to your success in getting yourself wanted that you plan how you actually would serve on the job, and when you are talking with your prospective employer, *speak as if you were at work.*

Picture Yourself At Work

If you imagine yourself fitted into a particular job, and *show yourself there to the mind's eye* of your prospect, he will have to go through the mental process of *getting you out* of the imaginary job. That will be much harder for him than it would have been to *keep you out* in the first place. If you merely present the services you *could* render, and don't picture yourself as *actually rendering* them, you haven't won even the imaginary job. *But if you do paint yourself into a chosen place, and can make your prospect see you in that position, the suggestion will impel him to copy imagination with actuality. He will consider you as if you were on the job.* Evidently when you have won this advantage, he will be inclined to want to keep you at work, unless you do something or manifest some quality that makes you undesirable.

No Doubt About Success

Getting yourself wanted is a process that can be brought to a successful conclusion with absolute certainty. It is not difficult to understand human nature if you are willing to see clearly into yourself. It is only necessary, then, that you subordinate your personality to the personality of the other man. *Learn what he wants, and avoid showing him that you want something from him. Show him instead that you can supply what he lacks.* Complete and round out the process by suggesting the particular qualities in yourself that your prospecting and size-up have indicated to be the qualities *he especially likes.* He will want you then. He can't help it.

CHAPTER X
Obstacles In Your Way

Mountain Climbing

There is no great mountain in the world that has a natural, smooth road with an easy grade all the way to the top. Mountain climbing requires some hard work. It involves getting around, or going over, or removing many obstacles that block the path upward.

You will encounter similar difficulties, obstacles, and resistance on your way to success. *If you cannot pass them, your ambition will be defeated.* You will quit the climb, discouraged; or will be driven back, a failure. In order to *assure* your success you must now ascertain dependable ways to conquer obstacles. This advance knowledge will make them seem less formidable. Since you will have definite plans for dealing with the difficulties that may obstruct your path, you will not feel hopelessly blocked when you face them.

Knowing How

No great mountain has ever been scaled by a novice ignorant of the science, and unskilled in the art of climbing to supreme heights. But an expert mountaineer learns from mastering one peak something about how to climb others. He develops ability to conquer any and all obstacles he may meet. He proves repeatedly that what would be impossible to a novice is a *certainty* to him. He starts the most difficult ascent with absolute confidence that he will gain the top.

Obstacles and Resistance

You likewise can feel sure of your ability to reach the highest peaks of success. In preceding chapters you have been shown how to take advantage of the *easiest* way up by following the guide marks of salesmanship at every step. Now we are to study the obstacles you will encounter, in particular the objections the prospect may raise to frustrate your purpose. At this stage of the selling process you will be like a mountaineer fighting in the Alps. It will probably be necessary that you overcome or evade considerable human resistance while you are climbing toward your goal.

Let us assume that you have already gained a chance to sell your capabilities to the particular man through whom you expect to succeed. He has heeded your knock and welcomed you into his interest. You have made such a presentation of your desirability and service value that he wants you to be associated with him. But now it will be natural for him to begin a critical analysis, seeking whatever faults he can discover or imagine in you or your proposition. *Your success or failure in your ultimate purpose is likely to depend on how you handle the criticisms he raises.* Therefore it is of vital importance that you learn in advance *sure ways to gain your goal despite normal opposition.*

Objections Are Natural

Recognize first that it is *natural* for your prospect to raise objections, whether he is favorably impressed or not. His resistance to your purpose may be only a *precaution.* Perhaps it does not indicate *opposition* at all. He may want you to convince him you are all right; so that he will feel entire confidence in his own judgment when he finally does as you wish. Or he may object for no other purpose than to test you thoroughly. If this is the case, his sympathies will all be with you while you are dealing with the obstacles he puts in your way.

Evidently objections of this sort should not be handled the same as the objections of opposition. It is necessary that you distinguish between the two kinds and that *when dealing with each specific objection you determine in your own mind what is its source.* There should be nothing in your method of handling the obstacle that might *antagonize* your prospect. You should take fullest advantage of his every inclination to *cooperate* with you in his thoughts and feelings. He may be "pulling for" you strongly when he seems to be "bucking" the hardest.

Objection is Favorable Sign

An objection really is a favorable sign. If you call upon a prospective employer who, after hearing your presentation, begins to find fault with it and with you, or tries to evade your proposal, you may be sure that you have carried him along a considerable distance toward the accomplishment of your purpose. *He objects or evades because he is on the defensive.* "You have him going." He is wary, and so takes measures for self-protection. *The moment your prospect begins to raise objections in your way, he indicates that he is not entirely comfortable in his own mind about escaping from your salesmanship.* He has felt the tug of desire; but he does not feel sure yet that you deserve his confidence, or else he has a pretty positive idea that in this matter of your possible employment his interests and yours are different. He is looking out for himself.

Welcome Opportunity To Strengthen Yourself

However, you have come with a *true service* purpose. You believe he *needs* you; that you can *satisfy a lack* in his business. You feel your interests and his are alike, not different. You know that you have no intention "to put anything over on him." You want your prospect to be absolutely satisfied with what you propose. Therefore you should welcome every chance to convince his mind and win his confidence. *An objection affords you an opportunity to overcome it, and so both to strengthen your proposition and to weaken his resistance.*

Don't Set Up Straw Men to Knock Down

You should not, however, bring up objections that the *prospect* has not raised in his own mind. That would be putting up a straw man and knocking him down, which is profitless and unconvincing. Of course you must clear the path when there is no other way to proceed, but do not block it yourself. Sometimes it will not be advisable to clear the path. If you can get around a difficulty you see, without attracting your prospect's attention to it, you will be wise to go some indirect way to your goal.

Suppose, for example, that you know the salary you want is higher than your prospect has been accustomed to pay. It will be good salesmanship for you not to refer to the amount you have in mind, until after you have carried him along with you to consider the profits he will make from engaging your services. Since you plan to show him that these profits will pay your salary, you will be wise to avoid the matter of your compensation until you have approached nearer to the successful conclusion of your selling process.

Avoid Troubles by Forethought

Almost every difficulty and opposition you are likely to encounter can be anticipated. Don't wait until you come face to face with an obstruction in the way of success. Let forethought carry you imaginatively into just such a situation. *Think yourself out of a possible difficulty before you actually get into it.* Then you can win the respect of your prospect by proving on the spot that you are not a man who can be dodged or blocked, or cornered. *Every time you pass an obstacle, you will be a long step nearer to success* in selling your services.

Suppose an employer says to you, "You are too young. You have had no experience in this line of work." You cannot *deny* your youth and you should not *defend* it as if it were a fault. Nor can you claim experience you have not had. But it is unnecessary for you to indicate any feeling that inexperience is a demerit. An ordinary applicant might be discomfited by such resistance to his purpose. If you are a skillful salesman, you will be prepared to deal with this very obstacle and will turn it to good account. You can say at once:

Value of Adaptability

"Because I am young, I am adaptable to your methods, instead of being set in ways that might differ from yours. True, I am not experienced. Therefore, I haven't any wrong ideas to unlearn. Think of me as raw material that won't have to be re-made, and that can be easily shaped as you want to form it. I realize it will take some work on your part, *but the product will be satisfactory to you when it is done.* It seems to me that the only question involved is whether or not I would make it worth your while to do the work on me. The fact that I have come to you of my own choice proves I really want to be employed here. I assure you now that I will make my services worth any pains you take to teach me your methods, and I will be just as eager to remain as I am to start."

Use Objection As a Sales Help

Analyze this method of dealing with any particular obstacle. *Plan to get rid of the obstruction completely, leaving the way ahead smoothed.* When the objection of the prospect is so skillfully disposed of, his *desire* for your services is stimulated. He *wants you more, because he likes you better* now that you have cleared away the obstacle. Thus you have utilized the objection as a *help* in selling yourself successfully. Just so a mountain climber uses the rocks he encounters as holding places to help him climb higher.

Your prospect may say that he has no need for such services as you offer. He may state reasons why you are not needed in his Business. *But if you have prepared yourself thoroughly, each disclaimer of his lack, every suggestion of an objection, will give you an opportunity to prove in some specific way your service value to him.*

The president of a manufacturing company had an ironclad rule that all positions in his business were to be filled by promotion. He never hired a new employee except to start at the bottom. A competent young office man applied for a situation. He was turned down flatly. The company's policy was quoted as the reason. He met this obstacle in a new way.

Making an Exception

"One of the principal reasons I came to you, Mr. Blank, is that I hope to benefit from your rule myself. I want to get into a company where I will know that the way to advancement is sure without going outside for my chance. But by my experience in other employment I have developed certain capabilities that would warrant you in making an exception to your rule, in my case.

"You do not audit your own books. Yet you have been self-auditing your methods of office operation. Another thought I want to suggest. You know that in the royal families of Europe the stock runs down because they don't get in fresh blood. I would not advocate a change in your general policy. But you have already made an exception to your rule in having your books checked by a public accountant whom you engage by the year for that purpose.

"I propose to bring in the outside viewpoint for the study of your office system, with the expectation of suggesting possible improvements. I want to introduce fresh blood, and yet to become part of your organization family. It is sound business for you to engage me because I am from the outside. You need an auditor of your operations as much as an auditor of your accounts."

This view of the matter had never been presented before to the employer. It won him over to the proposal. The new man broke in where every preceding applicant had failed.

Apparent Objections

Thus far we have considered *actual* obstructions, *real* blocks in the salesman's way. Now let us turn our attention briefly to obstacles that are only *apparent*, to resistance that is but a *feint*.

Your prospect may try to put you off. Or perhaps he will attempt to evade uttering a downright refusal, and instead will make some sort of an excuse for not doing what you wish. If you dignify these *artificial* or merely *apparent* obstacles by treating them as *real obstructions*, you will hinder your own progress toward success.

Danger of Losing Ground Gained

You have secured your chance to present your services for purchase. You have made real progress toward the successful accomplishment of your ultimate purpose. *Nearly always if you let yourself be put off for any reason, without making a definite advance toward your final goal, you will lose some of the ground already gained.* When your prospect attempts to evade the issue by making an excuse or by postponing further consideration of the subject, *he tacitly admits that your position is strong*. But if you have to start the selling process all over again at another time, if you let him put you off when your position is strong, *you will be weaker when you attempt to resume your sale.*

Do One of Two Things

Should you be put off, do one of two things. *Either disregard the evasion entirely and go straight ahead with your selling process*; or, if you consent to the postponement or evasion, *take advantage of your strategical position of strength to make a definite advance toward the accomplishment of your purpose*. For examples of the two methods let us consider supposititious cases.

Driving Ahead

Your prospective employer might say, "I'll think over your application. Come in next week and I'll let you know my decision." You can handle this evasion effectively by going directly ahead and proposing, "I am perfectly willing that you should think over my usefulness to you, but during the week you are considering me for future employment, let me actually work on the job. If you decide that you don't want to keep me, tell me so at the end of the week and there will be no charge for my time." *You will be driving straight toward your goal, not even pausing when he attempts to put you off.*

Strengthening Position

This effort at evasion or postponement might be handled in a different way. You could say to the prospective employer, "Very well. I will return in a week for your decision. Meanwhile I will submit some additional references as to my character and energy. I ask also that you permit me to save a week instead of wasting it. I should like your permission to spend this next week in your office, studying the job. Then if you decide to employ me, as I believe you will, I will be already broken in." Such a proposal is hard to refuse. While you would consent to the postponement or evasion of decision, *you would be strengthening your own position*.

Make Progress

In one way or the other you can make progress. Either you can brush the evasion aside and carry your prospect through to the closing stage of the sale of your services, or you can close an intermediate sale on the spot, as in the second illustration.

Forcing Real Objection

Do not, therefore, treat evasions and postponements as real obstacles. Even in case you cannot induce your prospect to go ahead with you, or close an intermediate sale, *you can avoid being blocked* by his attempt to put you off. When he sees that he cannot get rid of you by his subterfuge, he will be forced to make a *real* objection. He will not give you another weak excuse after you have disposed of his first attempt to evade. When he tries to block you by making a real objection, after the failure of his excuse or postponement, he will fall right into your plan of the sale. *You will be all ready for the objection he states.* You will know exactly how to handle it and turn it to good account so that his opposition will be weakened and you will add to your strength.

Let us suppose your prospect comes out with the flat statement, after you prevent him from putting you off, "No, I have made up my mind not to add any new employees for the present." He thinks that settles the question. In reality it affords you a sales opening. You retort, "Your attitude is perfectly right. You do not want to add to expense. I should feel the same way myself, were I in your position. However, I am not going to be an *expense*. I shall be a *money-maker*. I know you have no objections to increasing your profits." His opposition would have given you your lead.

Unsound Objection

A man applied for a position in a bank. Business in general was dull; so the president tried to put him off. The position sought offered any one filling it opportunities to develop increased business for the bank along certain lines. Thus the objection of dull times was plainly *unsound*. The applicant felt, however, that it would be a mistake to urge very strongly his ideas about increasing the business. He believed the president would not accept them if fully stated. So the young man met the attempted evasion by drawing the banker on to a step that committed him only to the *beginning* of the program outlined.

"I appreciate that business is not rushing at present," he said. "Therefore you will have time to study how I propose to develop some new business. If you were very busy, you would not be able to investigate my plan thoroughly. You may not care to put it into effect just now, but while you have comparative leisure let me give you an illustration of ways in which my idea can be worked out.

"It is unnecessary to discuss salary or a definite engagement at present, if you prefer to wait awhile. But with your permission I should like to come in here for a month and demonstrate a few of my ideas in actual practice. At the end of that time I will show you a chart of the results."

Evasion Turned to Selling Aid

The evasion was turned into a selling aid. The banker, naturally desirous of making additional profits, could not very well turn down such a proposal. He would have felt a little ashamed to accept services without paying for them. Therefore he gave the applicant a chance and agreed to pay him a moderate salary from the beginning. The new man went to work immediately, and very soon demonstrated such value that his compensation was increased to an entirely satisfactory amount.

Don't Fight Back

Already in this chapter you have been warned against handling an objection in such a way that the natural antagonism of the man who makes it will be increased by your method of dealing with his opposition. When he resists you, or puts obstructions in your way, you of course must take the measures that are necessary to enable you to proceed with your purpose, notwithstanding the obstacles he raises. *But if he acts antagonistic, be careful not to appear to fight back.* Avoid making the impression that you regard him as an *opponent*. Your difficulty in closing the sale will be lessened if you keep him from feeling at any time that he needs to adopt measures of *self-protection* against you.

Diplomacy And Tact

When your progress is obstructed, it is necessary that you use a very high degree of diplomacy and tact. This will carry you much farther toward your purpose than any manifestation of naked force. Of course you must meet many objections squarely. You will encounter obstructions that cannot be avoided, opposition that will not step aside. There will be occasions when it will be necessary for you to employ force. But you can always conceal "the iron hand in the velvet glove" if you exert your force in *tones* and with *gestures* or *movements*, rather than by making *word* statements. *The art of suggestion can be employed as effectively at the objection stage as at any other step of the selling process.*

Let us assume that you are a greenhorn. But you believe yourself capable of filling a certain position. You apply for it. Your prospective employer questions your capability because you lack experience. He refuses your application, and declares he is unwilling to run the risk of having you make mistakes that might be expensive to him.

Using Suggestion Instead of Statement

You know that you are very careful, and that you would not take any important action on your own responsibility if you were in doubt whether or not you were right. You feel that his objection is unsound; that he is exaggerating caution. But it would certainly be a mistake for you to say, "Nonsense!" That would make him bristle.

Of course you want to show him that you do not take his objections seriously. You can make the right impression by smiling at his statement. You can reinforce the effect of your smile by making a horizontal gesture with your hand. If you shake your head slightly, force will be added to your denial of incapacity or rashness. It may not be necessary for you to *say* anything. Possibly your suggestion will be stronger if you simply ignore the point he has raised against you. Usually, however, in such a case it is best to employ a few quiet words in disposing of the objection; *though chief reliance should be placed on the suggested meaning behind the statement.*

Your Stake In Your Opportunities

I recall the case of a man who handled an objection of that sort by first smiling while shaking his head and making a gesture of negation, and then said, "I could not lose much for *you*, but if I were reckless or irresponsible I certainly would lose for *myself* this opportunity that you see I want very much. I have a great deal more at stake than you. You may be sure I shall not risk losing my chance to succeed, by causing you any losses." The tone used was the heart pitch of sincerity, with the final assurance in the deeper tones of power. The tone and the manner of the applicant for the position indicated such strength that the prospect felt the weakness of his objection and did not persist in it.

Direct and Qualified Admissions

When you make a *direct admission* of the point the prospect raises against you, *have a strong answer ready and give it to him at once.* Otherwise you will not rid his mind entirely of the objection. In most cases it is preferable to make only an *indirect* or *qualified* admission of the point raised. Then the objection, not having been strengthened by your full confirmation, can be overcome without the use of much force or power.

Straight-out Agreement With the Objection

If your prospective employer says to you, "We are not making any money. I do not intend to put on a new man," diplomacy requires you to admit unequivocally the truth of his assertion that his business is not profitable. He may be exaggerating a temporary condition, but he would take offense if you should question his blunt statement. Therefore agree with him, and having prepared the opening with your tact, *introduce to his mind agreeable ideas of satisfying his want for profits.* You might say, "I realize business is poor. That is one of the reasons I come to you just now. If you were making plenty of money, you would not appreciate the value of my ideas for increasing your profits. The results of the work I propose to do might not be sufficiently conspicuous among other large earnings to attract your especial notice. This period of depression gives me the very opportunity I need to prove to you that I would be a money-maker, and not an expense to you. Surely you would like to have me demonstrate that. All I ask is a chance to convince you. Judge me by the results."

Analyze this unequivocal admission of the validity of the objection. Such cases can often be handled most effectively by granting the point raised, directly and without any reservations, and then answering the objection in such a way that it is completely removed as an obstruction. This is good salesmanship.

Indirect Admission

Suppose, however, you feel the objection of poor business is unsound. Let us assume that this prospective employer you are interviewing has a dull season every year. Therefore the condition of which he complains is simply normal, and his objection is put forward as an excuse for rejecting your application. *In such a case you do not want to make the obstruction more formidable by fully admitting its validity. Yet tact forbids you to deny its soundness.* It will be better salesmanship to recognize indirectly the point raised than it would be to give your full agreement with the objection, as in the above example of an unequivocal admission. You might use such an answer as this:

"That is True, But"

"I notice, Mr. Blank, that you are making some extensive repairs on your factory. Though this involves additional expense in your dullest season, you are having the work done now because this is your slackest time. True, your profit showing at present will not be so good as it would be if you did not make the repairs. But the earnings of your business will be improved during your busiest season and you will avoid the extra expense of interrupting your production when it is at the maximum. This, of course, is the time to have your repair work done. It would not be good business to put it off.

"My proposal that you engage me now is directly along the line of your own policies. What I would do in your office might be called repair work. Your dull season is the time to have it done. I can introduce my efficiency ideas now without disorganizing your operations. Then, when you are busiest, the new system will be in perfect working order, for your service."

Adapt Solutions To Your Own Problems

When you study illustrations of the application of basic principles, do not give them merely superficial consideration. *Examples are of slight value unless they suggest to you how you should use your imagination to make illustrations of your own in actual practice of the principles.* Whatever your need for help in selling your services, and whatever difficulties you may have to overcome or get around, you will find in the pages of these books *cues* to the methods of certain success. Evidently, however, the scope of the series of chapters must be somewhat limited. None of the answers to the major problems of salesmanship are omitted from the contents, *but you must apply and fit the given solutions to your individual necessities.*

Two Bases of Objections

Turn your thought now to the different bases of objections. It is of the utmost importance that you know whether the obstruction is raised by the *mind* or by the *heart* of your prospect. *Mental* resistance can be met and overcome by *ideas*, by points introduced by *your* mind into the *mind* of the *other* man. His *heart* may not be involved. But if there is "feeling" in his opposition, it is necessary that you displace it with a different *feeling* toward you and your proposal. The heart of your prospect must be turned from antagonism to friendliness, if it is involved in an objection. Therefore when a point is made against you, *decide from the evidence whether the obstacle raised has an emotional or a mental basis.* Treat it accordingly. Use your own *mind* principally in dealing with the purely *mental* objection of the prospect. But depend on drawing out *his heart with yours if his emotions are involved* in his opposition.

Mental Basis

Suppose you have a plan about engaging in a certain business. You have worked it out carefully and are confident that it is "a winner." But you need financial backing. So you go to a man who has money, and apply to him for a loan. He listens to your plan. When you finish explaining, he refuses your request. He uses the mental tone of cold business when he states his reason. "You offer me no security. I am not in the habit of lending money without it." His words and manner indicate that he has listened to your plan without the slightest feeling of sympathy for your purpose. His *emotions* have not been stirred. He is turning you down simply because his *mind* is opposed to the form of investment you propose for his money. It would be futile for you to make an *emotional* appeal to this man, in the hope of getting rid of his *mental* objection. He would be disagreeably impressed were you to attempt to stir his heart. You cannot offer him the security he has in mind, but you need not be balked for that reason. It is possible for you to make an appeal to his mind only, and to suggest to him ideas of security that he has not considered.

"Mr. J.P. Morgan," you might remind him, "when asked the basis upon which he loaned money, replied, 'Character, principally.' I offer you the security that Mr. Morgan considered most important. You know my reputation is good. You perceive that my plan is sound, and that I have thought it out thoroughly. You do not expect me to lose money. I have proposed to protect you as fully as possible by agreeing in advance that I will take no step until after your approval has been given. Therefore, in addition to my character, I am offering you the security of your own mature, sound judgment on all operations.

A New Idea Of Security

"Don't you believe that my squareness, guided by your advice, would secure you? I have applied for a loan of only ten thousand dollars. You will absolutely control the expenditure of the money. You know, therefore, that at the worst I could not have a large loss. I have offered you life insurance to protect you against the possibility of my death within the next five years. It is altogether improbable that I should have a loss of as much as a thousand dollars in the new business. Certainly you have sufficient confidence in my ability and integrity to believe that I could and would repay you a thousand dollars with interest before the expiration of five years. I expect, and you expect, that my venture will prove successful. I have planned a sound business enterprise, free from the dangers of speculation. With the cooperation of your judgment, your loan would be a secure investment. I believe you are now convinced of that."

Reaching Heart Through Mind

Notice that the objection is dealt with powerfully; yet there is no appeal that is aimed away from the prospect's *mind*. For this very reason his sympathy with the proposal is likely to be stimulated. *Such salesmanship often has the effect of enlisting the heart of the other man after removing the objection of his mind.*

Objection on Emotional Basis

Let us assume now that the prospect refuses to make the loan to you because he has been imposed upon before by some one he has backed. He may really want to lend you the money, but his heart has been so embittered by his previous experience that he turns a deaf ear to your proposition. His opposition is based chiefly on feeling. His heart, not his mind, is at the bottom of his refusal of your request for a loan. He would not be reached by the appeal that would be effective with the man in the first example. This second prospect should be addressed something like this:

"The experiences you have had hurt you, principally because they have made you lose faith in men. This, not the money involved, was your greatest loss. So long as you have only those experiences to think about, you will be unable to get back your former belief in human nature. You would like to recover it. You would be happy to feel that the men who abused your confidence were exceptions, and not the rule.

Selling a New Feeling

"If you will lend me ten thousand dollars, and I make good my promises to you, your new experience with me will go a long way toward restoring your lost faith in men. It is natural that you should feel embittered, but the taste in your mouth is unpleasant. Back me up. I will help you get rid of your bitterness, and will replace it with a glow of satisfaction. You cannot doubt that I will make good. You should not let your old prejudice stand in the way of the gratified feeling you will have when I prove to you that all men are not unworthy of trust. After I justify your confidence you will be happier for the rest of your life."

In the illustration the objection is dealt with *emotionally; because its basis is feeling.* No *mental* appeal is made. The salesmanship in this example is the direct converse of that in the previous illustration.

The Best Rule

Usually, however, it is best to counteract objections by making appeals to *both the heart and the mind* of the objector. In most cases it is safe to assume that his mental opposition involves his feelings to some degree, and it rarely happens that an objection is so purely emotional that the mind of the prospect does not take part in it at all. So the rule of masterly salesmanship is to use neither the appeal to mentality nor the appeal to feeling *exclusively,* but rather to *stress one or the other, while using both.* If the objection appears to be based *principally* on opposition of *mind,* it is more important to reach into the prospect's *mind* with the answer than it is to draw out his *heart;* and vice versa.

Emotional and Mental Tones

If the thought behind the objection arises principally from *feeling,* it will nearly always be expressed in an *emotive tone.* By this pitch of the prospect's voice you can determine whether he is speaking chiefly from his heart or from his mind. Conversely, of course, the *mental* objection will be pitched in the high "head" tone. One of the most difficult features of dealing with opposition from the other man is uncertainty as to *how much he means* of what he says and does. It would be a mistake to take his resistance too seriously or too lightly. Therefore it will aid your salesmanship a great deal if you are able to discriminate between the mental and the emotional tones in which opposition is expressed. You can reply accordingly.

The Power Pitch

It is almost as important that you recognize *the pitch of power* when it reenforces the words of objection, and that on the other hand you note when the power tone is *lacking*. In the first case you will need to reply with considerable force, whether you appeal to the mind or the heart of the prospect. But when his objection is stated in a powerless tone, even though it may be accompanied by curtness or bluster, you need not waste much force on your answering appeal to his mentality or his emotions.

Keep Ears Alert

The mental tone, as we recall from previous study, is pitched higher than either the tone of feeling or the tone of power. The medium, heart tone is vibrant. It rings with sincerity. The power tone is deep, and most sonorous of the three. *Keep your ears alert for these indications* your prospect will give you unconsciously when he opposes your purpose. The discriminative reading of the tones of objections will greatly reduce the danger of "getting your wires crossed" when you reply.

Suggest Strength Without Antagonism

If you have to deal with opposition expressed in the tone of power or with gestures of force, you will be safe in concluding that considerable *feeling* is behind the objection. Therefore it will be necessary for you to put *both feeling and power* into your answer. You should be careful, however, when you meet such resistance, not to make the impression that you are engaged in a contest of power with your prospect. *Throughout the selling process avoid any suggestion that you are fighting back.* Use the tone of force, not to indicate that your strength of purpose is greater than the strength of the resistance, but just to *emphasize the basic soundness* of your proposition. Thus you can suggest that you are sure of your ground, while you do not dispute the force and sincerity of the other man in making his objection.

Suppose, for example, you apply for a situation in a wealthy firm, and one of the partners turns you down most emphatically by saying that they can't afford to engage any new men at present. You realize the firm may be losing money temporarily, but you believe that your services in the capacity you have outlined will be valuable to the partners. You can come back firmly and not retreat an inch from your position. You need not *antagonize* by manifesting your determination to have the merits of your proposal given due consideration. You know your prospect feels pretty strongly on the matter of increasing his payroll while business is unprofitable, but you should make him recognize that you believe so thoroughly in your earning capacity that you feel you would justify him in disregarding the temporary depression, while he considers your service worth.

Units of Tone

As we have noted previously, it is important to know, at the time an objection is put in your way, *whether or not it is really meant.* When deciding in your mind on the right answer to this problem, you will be helped very much if you size up not only the tone pitch of the objection, but also the *units* of tone employed by the prospect in his expression of opposition. If he refuses your application, but uses just *one* tone, you may be sure his negative is not strong. If you do not strengthen it to stubbornness by antagonizing him, but use tact to get rid of his resistance, you will not find it difficult to melt away the obstruction.

However, should the "No" be spoken in two or more tones, with increased stress at the end, your prospect certainly means his rejection to be final. His mind is fully made up for the time being. It would be poor salesmanship to butt your head against his fixed idea, just as it would be foolish to tackle a strong opponent when he stands most formidably braced to resist attack. But the two or three toned negative does not mean that the idea behind it is fixed in the prospect's mind *forever*. Any one is prone to change his mind, *unless he is kept so busy supporting a position taken that he has no chance to alter his opinion.*

Preventing Stubborness

Therefore leave alone at first the rock you encounter. Get behind the boulder by taking a roundabout path. Then quietly dig the support from under the negative idea. If you make no fuss while you are undermining the obstacle, it will be likely to topple over and roll from your path without your prospect's noticing that it has disappeared. If his interest is diverted from it, there is no reason why he should turn his mind back to a stubborn insistence on his objection. Should he be conscious that the rock of his earlier opposition has rolled away, he will probably think it lost its balance. He will not realize that you subtly undermined it and got rid of it by your skillful salesmanship.

A salesman of an encyclopedia met a prospect who refused to give favorable attention to him and his proposition.

"No sir-e-e!" declared this objector, shaking his head emphatically. "No more book agents can work me. The last slick one that tried to swindle me is in ja-a-il now, and I put him the-ere!"

He gloated in two or three tones.

Turning Back A Turn-down

"Good for you!" praised the undaunted salesman, who had come prepared for adamantine obstacles in his path. "If more book buyers would see that such rascals get what's coming to them, the rest of us salesmen, who represent square publishers squarely, would not have to prove so often that we are not crooks like some fellows who have happened to precede us in a territory. Please tell me the name of the man who swindled you. He might hit my publishers for a job after he gets out of jail, and I want to warn the boss against him. Sometimes those slick rascals pull the wool over our eyes, too. We are always on the lookout to avoid getting tangled up with them."

The salesman pulled out his note book and pencil. When the name was given, he wrote it down painstakingly. He asked the prospect to spell it for him; so that he would be sure to get it right. Then he thanked the man who had said he would have nothing more to do with book agents. Having "got around" the objector, the salesman proceeded with his selling talk on the encyclopedia, as if he had not been turned down flatly to begin with. In less than half an hour he had secured the signature of the prospect to a contract for the finest edition.

Be Ready for Opposition

If this salesman had not been thoroughly prepared to meet the strongest kind of mental and emotional opposition, he could not have come back so quickly with the appropriate answer that undermined the obstacle. You should be likewise ready for the "tough customers" one hears about. *Practice in anticipation various ways of handling every imaginable objection.* Then, when you face an actual difficulty, you will either have on the tip of your tongue a solution of the problem, or your forethought will assist you to devise on the spur of the moment the way to work out the right answer. Again we observe the importance of full preparation, in assuring successful salesmanship.

Two Essentials Of Resourcefulness

No quality is more important to the salesman than *resourcefulness*. Its first requisite is *knowledge*, particularly advance knowledge of the points that are likely to come up in the course of the selling process. The second is a *mind trained to act quickly and effectively in using* its knowledge. If you have these two essentials of resourcefulness, no objection will ever catch you napping. It will do you no good to look up the right answer *after you leave the prospect*. Nothing can be more exasperatingly worthless than an idea of something you "might have said" but could not think of until *too late*. Have all your facts on tap. And be practiced in making use of them in every imaginable way. Rare indeed will be cases that you are not prepared to handle successfully.

Practicing "Come-backs"

I know a salesman who trained himself in resourcefulness by typing on about fifty cards all the objections to his goods or proposition that he could imagine. For ten or fifteen minutes every evening he played solitaire with these cards. He would shuffle them, held face down, and then deal off, face up, objection after objection. He never could tell which was coming next. In a few weeks he had trained himself to give an answer instantly to each objection, and to utilize it as a help instead of a hindrance in his selling. Thereafter opposition and criticism from prospects had no terrors for this salesman. He was able to get rid of objections so swiftly, surely, and completely that they never had time to grow formidable in the mind of the other man.

Adaptive Originality

Only a little less important than resourcefulness in meeting objections, is *adaptive originality in answering them*. The "pat, new" reply is always very effective. But do not unduly stress the value of the factor of *originality* alone. It must be coupled with *adaptation to the particular viewpoint of the other man*. You must speak his language, if you would be sure of making him understand you perfectly.

Use Prospect's Language

For example, suppose you apply to a watch manufacturer for a position in his office. He seems inclined to question your dependability. You will make a hit with him if you quote a detail from one of his own ads and say, "I have a seventeen jewel movement," and then particularize that number of good points about yourself. Such a reference preceding a specification of your qualities would be adaptive originality. *It would be an expression exactly fitted to the way this prospect thinks.* So it would be more effective than an ordinary answer to the objection. Adaptive originality in disposing of objections is a manifestation of tact and diplomacy—the fine art of letting the other man down with a shock absorber instead of jolting him to your way of thinking.

Keep Train of Thought on Main Track

When your prospect starts objecting, it is up to you to prevent him from wandering far afield. At the objections stage, as at every other step in the selling process, *you should dominate the other man*. Tactfully keep him concentrated on the subject and on your application. If he starts to grumble that some man he has engaged previously was "no good," you can smile and reply, "You would not give *me credit* for *anybody else's* fine work, and of course you do not *blame me* for what *that* fellow did."

You know what points are relevant to the subject you have come to discuss, and what are not. *Discriminate, and make the prospect follow you.* Restrict your treatment of his objections to points, means, and methods that will keep his ideas from switching onto side-tracks of thought. *When he wanders away from the subject, do not ramble with him.* Promptly and diplomatically run his mind back on the main line of your purpose. *You are operating a through train to success. You must not be diverted into picking either daisies or thistles by the right of way while your salesmanship engine stands idle.*

Patience and Calmness

Tact and diplomacy include the qualities of *patience* and *calmness.* You cannot deal successfully with opposition if you are impatient or flustered. Patience understands the other man and avoids giving him offense; because it comprehends his way of thinking and is considerate of his right to his opinions. *Calmness denotes a consciousness of strength. Hence it inspires admiration.* Keep your patience open-eyed. See ahead. Do not chafe restlessly because the present moment is not propitious. A better chance for you is coming. Because of your vision have faith in your power to *make* it come. Whatever may happen, be self-possessed when you meet it. You can give no more impressive proof of your bigness. Your calmness will win the confidence of the other man. It will help in making the impression of courageous truth. Only an honest purpose can meet attack with quiet fearlessness.

Win Admiration by Keeping Upper Hand

The chief danger to the salesman at the objections stage is that he may lose control of the selling process. Be on your guard to prevent the other man from dominating you by his opposition. You have the advantage at the start. He cannot be so well prepared to make objections as you should be to dispose of them effectively. *Keep the upper hand.* If you have not antagonized his feelings, your prospect will admire you when he sees that he cannot dominate you and realizes that you will not let him have his own way. You will build up in him a favorable opinion of your manhood, intelligence, and power. *He cannot help appreciating your art in handling him.*

Make Desire Grow

Dispose of each objection in such a way that you will get yourself wanted more and more as you remove or get around the obstacles encountered. *The prospect's desire for your services should grow in proportion as you overcome his opposition.* It is possible to use objections, or rather their answers, to strengthen your salesmanship so greatly that it will be easy to gain your object—- the job or the promotion you seek.

Hard Climb Leads to Supreme Heights

Therefore do not quail from the obstacles you meet. Recognize in each an opportunity to succeed in demonstrating your capability; a chance to increase the respect, confidence, and liking of your prospective employer. *Remember, if there were no difficult, steep mountains to scale, the supreme heights of success could not be gained.* So, with shining face, climb on and up undaunted!

CHAPTER XI
The Goal of Success

"Nearly Succeeded" Means "Failed"

After an applicant for a position seems to have the coveted opportunity almost in his grasp, he is sometimes unable to *clinch* the sale of his services. He does not get the job. His failure is none the less *complete* because he *nearly* succeeded. *No race was ever won by a man who could not finish.* However successful you may have been in the earlier stages of the selling process, if your services are finally declined by the prospective employer you have interviewed, your sales effort has ended in failure.

When one has made a fine presentation of his capability, and therefore feels confident of selling his services, it shocks and disheartens him to have his application rejected. "It takes the starch out of a man." He is apt to feel limp in courage when he turns his back on the lost chance to make good, and faces the necessity of starting the selling process all over again with another prospect. It is harder to lose a race in the shadow of the goal than to be disqualified before the start. The prospect who seems on the point of saying, "Yes," but finally shakes his head is the heart-breaker to the salesman.

Making the Touch Down

Of course, as you have been reminded, even the best salesman cannot get *all* the orders he tries to secure. *But he seldom fails to "close" a real prospect whom he has conducted successfully through the preliminary steps of a sale.* Each advance he makes increases his confidence that he will get the order. The master salesman does not falter and fall down just before the finish. He is at the top of his strength as he nears the goal. All his training and practice have had but one ultimate object—a successfully *completed* sale. He knows that *nothing else counts*. He does not lose the ball on the one-yard line. He pushes it over for a touchdown. He cannot be held back when he gets that close to the goal posts. You must be like him if you would make the "almost sure" victory a *certainty*.

Don't Fear To Take Success

Perhaps the commonest cause of the failures that occur at the closing stage is the salesman's *fear of bringing the selling process to a head*. He is in doubt whether the prospect will say "Yes" or "No." His lack of courageous confidence makes him falter when he should bravely put his fortune to the test of decision. He does not "strike while the iron is hot," but hesitates until the prospect's desire cools. Many an applicant for a position has talked an employer into the idea of engaging his services, and then has gone right on talking until he changed the other man's mind. He is the worst of all failures. Though he has won the prize, he lets it slip through his fingers because he lacks the nerve to tighten his hold.

Keep Control At the Close

Doubt and timidity at the closing stage, after the earlier steps have been taken successfully, are paradoxes. Surely each *preliminary* advance the salesman makes should add to his confidence that he can *complete* the sale. His proved ability to handle objections and to overcome resistance should have developed all the courage he needs to *finish* the selling process. Closing requires less bravery and staunch faith than one must have when making his approach. Now he knows his man, and that this prospect's mind and heart can be favorably influenced by salesmanship. Is it not a contradiction of good sense to weaken at the finish instead of pressing the advantages already gained and crowning the previous work with ultimate success? Yet there are salesmen who seem so afraid of hearing a possible "No" that they dare not prompt an almost certain "Yes."

When you have presented to your prospective employer a thoroughly good case for yourself, *do not slow down or stop the selling process.* Especially avoid letting *him* take the reins. Thus far *you* have controlled the sale. *Keep final developments in your own hands.* Go ahead. Smile. Be and appear entirely at ease. Look the other man in the eye. Ask him, "When shall I start work?" *Suggest* that you believe he is favorable to your application. *Even speak his decision for him,* as though it were a matter-of-course. If the previous trend of the interview justifies you in assuming that he has almost made up his mind to employ you, pronounce his probable thought as if he had announced it as his final conclusion. *He will not be likely to reverse the decision you have spoken for him.* His mental inclination will be to *follow your lead,* and to accept as his own judgment what you have assumed to be settled in his mind.

Reversing a Negative Decision

A stubborn merchant made a dozen objections to hiring a new clerk. The young man cleared them all away, one after another, as soon as each was raised. But the employer leaned back obstinately in his chair and declared, "Just the same, I don't need any more clerks." This was but a repetition of an objection already disposed of. The applicant concluded, therefore, that he had his man cornered. The salesman smiled broadly at the indication of his success. He stood up and took off his overcoat.

"Well," he said, "you certainly need one less than you did, now that I'm ready to begin work. I understand why you have been putting me off. You wanted to test my stick-to-it-ive-ness. I'm sure I have convinced you on that point. You needn't worry about my staying on the job. Shall I report to the superintendent, or will you start me yourself?"

The merchant drew a deep breath; then emptied his lungs with a burst of astonishment mixed with relief. He could not help laughing.

"I meant to turn you down, but you say I've made up my mind to hire you. I didn't know it myself, but you're right. I believe you are the sort of clerk I always want."

Expect the Prospect to Say "Yes"

Remember, when you face your prospect at the closing stage, the *motive* that brought you to him. You came with the intention of rendering him *services from which he will profit*. You want your capability to be a "good buy" for him. Your consciousness that your motive is *right* should give you strengthened *faith* in yourself and in the successful outcome of your salesmanship. It should fill you with the courage necessary to close the sale.

Neither hesitate nor flinch. Confidently prompt the decision in your favor. Believe that you *have* won and you will not be intimidated by fears of failure. Your prospect is unlikely to say "No" *if you really expect to hear "Yes."* Even if he speaks the negative, still *believe in your own faith*. I know a man who, a minute after his application was flatly rejected, won the position he wanted. Unrebuffed, he came back with, "Eventually, why not now?" His evident conviction that he was *needed* gained the victory when his chance seemed lost.

Don't Be Afraid to Pop The Question

We all laugh at the young swain who courts a girl devotedly for months and uses every art he knows to sell her the idea that he would make her happy as his wife; but who turns pale, then red, and chokes whenever he has a chance to pop the question. Often the girl must go half way with prompting. When, thus encouraged, he finally stammers out his appeal for her decision, she accepts him so quickly that he feels foolish. Women are reputed to be better "closers" of such sales than men.

You smile at the comparison of courting with salesmanship. Yet the selling process is as effective in making good impressions of the sort of husband one might be as in impressing an employer with the idea that one's services in business would prove desirable.

Selling a Future Husband

The young man bent on marriage needs to prospect for the right girl, to secure an audience, to compel her attention, to regain it when diverted to other admirers, and to develop her curiosity about him into interest. He must size up her likes and dislikes; then adapt his salesmanship to her tastes, tactfully subordinating his own preferences to hers. If she is athletic, he will play tennis or go on tramps with her, however tired he feels after his work. If she is sentimental, he will take her canoeing and read poetry to her, though he may prefer detective yarns. Throughout his courtship he will do his utmost to stimulate in her a desire to have him as a life partner. Whatever objections she makes to him, he will get rid of or overcome.

Suppose he has taken all these preliminary selling steps successfully, and at last the time comes for pinning the girl down to a definite answer to the all-important question, is there any likelihood that it will be a refusal? Of course not! If his earlier salesmanship has been masterly, the reasons why she will be inclined to accept him in the end are of much greater weight and number than any causes for rejection that she may have thought of previously.

Never Weaken At the Finish

He should not fear to close the sale. He has been "going strong" until now; why should he weaken at the finish? The master salesman does not quaver then, or doubt his success. He asks his prospect's decision bravely and with confidence, or he assumes it as a matter of course and kisses the girl. His heart beats faster than usual, but he is not afraid of hearing "No."

You should feel the same way after leading your prospective employer successfully through the preliminary stages of the process of selling your services to him. Do not falter now. *Promptly emphasize the idea that the weight, amount, and quality of your merits are fully worth the compensation previously discussed.* If you are *sure* of that, if you have valued your services from *his* standpoint, and not just from *your own*, you will feel no doubts about the acceptance of your application. You will put your prospective employer through the process of decision as courageously and confidently as you first entered his presence.

Getting the Decision Pronounced

Sometimes a prospect will be convinced, but will not express what is in his thoughts. Therefore *it is not enough to bring about a favorable conclusion of mind*. Until this has been *pronounced or signified*, it may easily be changed. Hence the *effective process of decision includes both the mental action of judgment and its perceptible indication.* Often a prospect who is *thinking* "Yes" will not *say* it until he is prompted by the salesman.

A Lawyer Sums Up the Case

When a lawyer is trying a case, he endeavors to bring out the evidence in favor of his client and to make the jury see every point clearly. He shows also the fallacies and falsities of opposing testimony. But after all the evidence has been given, the case is not turned over *immediately* to the jury for decision. If that were done the lawyer would miss his best chance to influence the jurors to make up their minds in his favor. They are not so familiar as he with the facts and their significance. They would be apt to attach more importance to some details of testimony, and less to others, than the circumstances warrant. So, to assist the jurors in arriving at their verdict on the evidence, the lawyer *sums up the case.* He lays before their minds his views, and tries with all his power and art to convince them that his word pictures are true reproductions of the facts in their relation and proportion to all the circumstances surrounding the issue.

Preponderance Of Evidence

The *object* of the lawyer when he addresses the jury is to make the convincing impression that *the testimony in favor of his client far outweighs the evidence on the other side.* He adjures the twelve men before him to "weigh the evidence carefully." He declares the judge will instruct them that in a lawsuit the verdict should be given to the party who has a "preponderance" or greater weight of proof on his side. *At this closing stage of the case the lawyer acts as a weighmaster.* He wants to make the jurors feel that he has handled the scales *fairly*, that he has taken into consideration the evidence *against* him as well as the facts *in his favor*; and that the preponderance of weight *is as he has shown it*—so that they will accept *his* view and gave him the verdict. If he feels a sincere conviction that he is right in asking for a decision on his side, he makes his closing address with the ring of confidence. He looks the jurors in the eye and asks for the verdict in his favor as a matter of *right*. He does not beg, but claims what the weight of the evidence *entitles* him to receive.

Treat Your Prospects As Jurors

The jury that will decide on your application when you apply for a position will usually consist of but one man, or will be composed of a committee or board of directors. Treat him or them *as a jury*. Remember that your capabilities and your deficiencies are *on trial*. Close your case with the same process the skillful lawyer uses when he sums up the evidence and weighs it before the minds of the jurors. Do what he does *as a weighmaster*. Avoid making any impression that you are not weighing your *demerits* fairly, though you *minimize their importance*; also miss no chance to impress the *full weight* of your *qualifications*. The essence of good salesmanship at this stage of the process is *skillful, but honest weighing*. That means using *both sides* of the scale, to convince the prospect that *the balance tips in your favor*. He will not believe in the correctness of the "Yes" weight unless you show the lesser weight of "No" *in contrast*. Then he cannot help *seeing* which is the heavier. *Decision on the respective weights is only a process of perception.*

The Process Of Perception

Let us suppose the employer has asserted the objections that you are not sufficiently experienced to earn the salary you want, and that you don't know enough yet to fill the job. It would be poor salesmanship to try to convince him that you have had a good deal of experience. If you exaggerate the importance of the things you have learned, he almost surely will judge you to be an unfair weighman of yourself. So you should tacitly admit your inexperience and treat the value of experience lightly by reminding him that his business is unlike any other. Then bear down hard on your eagerness to learn his ways and to work for him. Thus you can make him perceive the two sides of the scale *as you view them*.

Tipping the Balances Your Way

It is possible for you so to tip the balances in your favor, though previously the mind's eye of your prospective employer may have been seeing the greater weight on the unfavorable side. *It is legitimate salesmanship to influence the decision of the other man in this way.* Your weighing is entirely honest; though you sharply reverse the balances. Certainly you have the right to estimate the full worth of your services, to depreciate the significance of points against you, and to picture your desirability to the prospect as you see it, however that view may differ from his previous conception. *If your picture of the respective weights is attractive and convincing, the other man will adopt it as his own and discard his former opinions about you.* Not only will he accept the idea of your capabilities that you make him perceive; he also will see that your deficiencies are much less important than he had before considered them.

Serving Hash For Dessert

Beware of a mistake commonly made by applicants for positions who do not understand the art of successfully closing the sale of one's services. When they try to clinch the final decision, *they just repeat strongly all their best points. They make no mention of their shortcomings.* For dessert, in other words, they serve a hash of the best dishes of previous courses. Is it any wonder that such a close takes away any appetite the prospect may have had?

What would you think of a lawyer who had closed his case by simply reading to the jury all the testimony that had been given on his side, but who had made no reference to the opposing evidence? If you were a juror, would you vote for a verdict in favor of the side so summed up? Of course you would have heard the testimony of both parties to the case, but *you would not feel that the lawyer who ignored the evidence against his client had helped you to arrive at the conclusion that he had the preponderance of proof on his side.* On the contrary, you probably would be inclined to attach to the opposing evidence *greater weight than the facts justified,* and would discount whatever the lawyer claimed for his client. You, yourself, would act as weighmaster; and would give the other party to the suit the benefit of any doubt in your mind as to the contrasting weights of the testimony pro and con. *The lawyer's failure to weigh all the evidence before your eyes would make the impression on you that his view of the case was unfair to his opponent.* If you felt at all doubtful, you would be likely to vote against him in order to make sure that the other side received a square deal.

Weigh Both Pros and Cons Before Jury

The jury that is to decide favorably or unfavorably on your application for a position will feel similarly inclined to reach a negative conclusion if in closing you omit the process of weighing the pros and cons, and emphasize only your strong points. It is good salesmanship to stress these at the finishing stage, but they should be pictured *in contrast with lighter objections* to your employment. In order to *convince* the prospect that the reasons for employing you outweigh the reasons for turning you down, you must show his mind *both sides of the scale.* If you fail to do this, his own imagination will do the weighing and is certain to bear down with prejudice on every point against you. It will also depreciate your view of the points in your favor. The other man will make sure that *he* is getting a square deal on the weights, since he will believe *you,* too, are looking out only for Number One.

To Make Certain Do The Weighing Yourself

The *certain* way to make your prospect perceive that the reasons for accepting your proposal are of greater weight than any causes for turning down your application is to *do the weighing yourself.* First be sure the heavier weight *is* on your side. When you fully believe that, use all the arts of salesmanship to *make the other man see the balances as you view them.* Then he can come to but one conclusion, that the "preponderance" is on your side. *Just as soon as you make the respective weights clear to his perception, he will be convinced.* He cannot deny what his own mind's eye has been made to see.

Get Prospect Committed

Therefore bringing about a favorable *mental conclusion* is not at all difficult. The judgment that your services would be desirable is no harder to gain than a decision that the weight of one side of a scale is greater than the other. Any one who looks at the balances sees at once which way they tip. The rub is not in getting the decision *made* but in getting it *pronounced.* The sale is not completed until the prospect has *committed* himself.

Now is the Acceptance Time

He feels that his mental processes are his own secret, which you cannot read; so he will not guard against the conclusion of his *mind* that you would be a desirable employee. But for some reason he may be unwilling to *express* his thoughts to you just then, however thoroughly he is convinced. He naturally prefers not to say "Yes" at once; so that he may change his mind if he wishes. *You will endanger your chances of success if you let him put off action on his decision.* To-morrow he is likely to see the weights in a different light and to imagine less on your side and more against you. *Now* is the time to close the sale, when he cannot help seeing things *your way.*

Two Stages Of Closing

You know that sometimes a juror will be convinced in his own mind, yet cannot bring himself actually to vote according to his mental conclusion. Perhaps he is a "wobbler" by nature. So a girl may decide in her thoughts that a certain suitor would make a good husband, yet she may hesitate to accept him just because that step is *final.* These illustrations impress the importance of *discriminating between the two stages of closing a sale.* The success of the salesman is made certain only by his knowledge and skillful use, first of the art of *vivid weighing,* and second of the art of *prompting the prospect to action on his perception of the difference in the balances.* At the closing stage we have encountered again our old acquaintance, "the discriminative-restrictive process."

Closing a Procrastinator

A friend of mine who has an advertising agency wanted to secure the business of a prominent manufacturer who was inclined to vacillation. The prospect was always timid about acting and had the reputation of a chronic procrastinator. My friend went ahead with the selling process in ordinary course until he had proved the desirability of his service and had shown that there was no really weighty reason why the contract should not be given to him. He knew he was entitled to the decision then, but he did not wait for the timid man to pronounce it. The advertising agent knew the characteristics of the prospect and had planned just how he would handle the finishing stage of the selling process so as to get the order promptly.

The Clincher Held in Reserve

He held in reserve a closing method that a less skillful salesman probably would have used earlier in the sale instead of reserving it especially for the end. As soon as he had completed the weighing process my friend took from his pocket a sheet of copy he had prepared for a first advertisement along the line he had proposed. This had been worked out carefully in advance, just as if the order had already been given for the advertising service. My friend laid the sheet of copy before the prospect, who was taken completely by surprise.

"I knew you would want this service as soon as I explained it to you," said the salesman. "Therefore I prepared this ad for the first publication under the plan I have submitted, and which I am sure you approve. There is no question that you will get much better results from this copy than you have been receiving from the advertising you are doing now. Naturally you want to begin benefiting from my service as soon as possible. I'm all ready to deliver the goods. Just pencil your O.K. on the corner of this copy. I'll do the rest."

From Pencil To Pen

With a smile of confidence the salesman held out a soft lead pencil. *The moment the other man involuntarily obeyed the suggestion by accepting the tendered pencil, he was started on the purely muscular process of pronouncing his approval of the proposition likewise tendered for his acceptance.* The informality of the off-hand request that he "pencil his O.K." kept him from being scared off. He did not feel that he had yet committed himself fully. Probably, with characteristic timidity, he would have shied from signing a formal contract at that moment. But he hesitated only slightly before he scribbled his initials on the corner of the proposed ad. Then he handed the pencil back to the salesman. The advertising agent picked up the approved copy, and at once laid before the prospect a formal contract. Simultaneously he tendered his fountain pen. *He had started the advertiser to writing his name, and did not let the process stop.*

"Now just O.K. this, too," he directed, "and the whole matter will be settled to your complete satisfaction." Then, to prevent the procrastinator from backing up, the salesman reached for the telephone on the advertiser's desk. "With your permission, I'll call up the——magazine and reserve choice space for this ad. It won't cost any more and by getting in early we'll make the ad most effective."

Decide For, Then Commit The Prospect

My friend manifested complete confidence that the sale was *closed*. By continuing the process of affirming the decision, he prevented the prospect from backing up after making his pencilled O.K. Being thus committed informally, the usually vacillating advertiser could not well avoid using the pen put into his hand to sign the formal contract laid before him. Without speaking to him, the salesman pointed to the dotted line while he called the telephone number he wanted. *The prospect wrote his name before he had time to stop the impulse that the advertising agent had started.* The salesman had both *induced* the mental *decision* in his favor, and *impelled* its *pronouncement*. Really he first *made up the prospect's mind for him,* and then *committed him to the decision so made* without the other man's volition.

Both Processes In Right Sequence

Only by performing both processes in right sequence at the closing stage can a sale be finished under the control of the salesman. If the *favorable conclusion* as to the respective weights of negative and affirmative is not first worked out before the mind's eye of the prospect, anything done to *commit* him to a decision will likely kill the salesman's chances for success. The prospect whose mind is not yet made up favorably, who does not clearly perceive that the preponderance is on the "Yes" side of the scale, will almost surely say "No" if his decision is *prematurely* impelled.

Discriminate And Restrict

Hence it is important that the salesman discriminate between the two closing stages, and that he restrict his selling methods at each stage to the selling processes that are effective then. He must not get "the cart before the horse," as the ignorant or unskillful closer is apt to do. The poor closer does not understand the "discriminative-restrictive" process. He lacks comprehension of the distinction that should be drawn between the methods he *previously* has used and what is now required to *finish* the sale. Let us be sure we know how to discriminate; so that our work at the closing stage may be restricted to the processes that are required to assure success in taking the particular step necessary.

New Process Necessary To Close

Throughout the series of selling steps that precede the closing stage, the continuing purpose of the salesman is to make the prospect *see* the proposal in the true light, as the salesman himself views it. When the selling process draws to a conclusion, the purpose of the salesman changes. Now he wants the prospect to *decide* and then *act upon* what has been shown to his mind's eye. If the salesman is to control the close, he must do something *new* to prompt decision and to actuate its pronouncement.

The unskillful closer, instead of changing his previous sales tactics, nearly always devotes his final efforts to making the prospect *see more clearly* the pictures already laid before his mind. He tries to impress the prospect with a *re-hash of perception*, by emphasizing more strongly than before the favorable points brought out clearly at earlier stages. Of course it is important that at the close of the sale the prospect have all these points in view, but it is not good salesmanship to emphasize only the appeal to his *perceptive* faculties. The guest who has had a good dinner does not need to be told just afterward what he has eaten, or reminded of the courses by having them brought in again.

Logic and Reason Won't Win

As it is a mistake to serve at the close of a sale only a re-hash of favorable points; so is it bad salesmanship to rely on a dessert of "logic and reason" for the finishing touch. *Logic and reason provoke antagonism. They are ineffective in bringing about either a favorable conclusion of mind or action on such a decision.*

If you have presented your capabilities fully to a prospective employer, do not wind up by marshalling reasons why he should engage you. Avoid the use of the "major premise, minor premise, argument, and logical conclusion." *You cannot debate yourself into a job*, for the judge is made antagonistic by your method, which puts him on the defensive. It is human nature to resist a decision that logic tries to force. No man arrives at his conclusions of mind by putting himself through a reasoning process. A normal person does not need to reason about things he knows. *He knows without reasoning.* He attempts to use logic only when he is *uncertain* what to think. If logic is used by the salesman to convince the other man, it will be ineffective because it is an unnatural means that the prospect almost never employs to convince himself, and of which he is suspicious.

Why Reasoning is Futile

A major premise is but an assumption unless it is already known. If it is known, why should it be proved? Since the correctness of the conclusion depends entirely upon the validity of the premise, it is evidently absurd to attempt to prove a truth from the basis of an admitted assumption. The reasoning process that starts from a truth already known, and arrives at a truth that must similarly have been known, is utterly useless and a waste of time. Hence, *if you use the reasoning process you will either fail to convince your prospect by starting from a premise that he does not know, or you will irritate and unfavorably impress him by seeming to reflect on his intelligence when you prove to him something he already knows.* That is the wrong way to bring your man to a "Yes" decision.

If the whole process of the sale could be summed up in just one logical statement at closing, it might occasionally be practical for the salesman to apply reasoning with good effect to help him secure the decision. But the four steps, first and second premise, argument, and conclusion, must be applied to every point that is made with reasoning. Since the force of the conclusion is largely lost unless the major premise is an absolute truth recognized by everybody, there is danger of confusion, and no possibility of convincing the prospect by such methods. Besides, a multitude of reasoning processes would be necessary to cover all the points presented by the salesman and all the objections raised by the prospect. Moreover, as we have seen, the whole procedure of "a logical close" falls back upon itself unless everything the salesman hopes to prove was known and admitted to be true before he began to reason it out.

Favorable Decision Defined

Favorable decision is the prospect's mental conclusion that it is better to buy than not to buy; better to accept than to refuse. The process of securing decision is not complex; it is very simple. As has been said, the salesman needs only to weigh before the mind's eye of the prospect the favorable and unfavorable ideas of the proposal. *Any weighing of two mental images always results in a judgment as to which is preferable, or that one course of action would be better than the other.* The mind is never so exactly balanced between contrasting ideas that it does not tip at all either way.

Weighing Ideas of A Steak

The skill of the salesman weighmaster, used legitimately before the mind's eye of the prospect to tip the scales of decision to the favorable side, is illustrated in the story of a butcher who had been asked by a woman customer to weigh a steak for her. He knew that the weighing process *in her mind* included more than the balancing of a certain number of pounds and ounces on the scale. Against the reasons for her evident inclination to take the selected steak, she would weigh its cost, her personal ideas of its value, and other factors of the high cost of living.

Skillful Close of The Sale

The butcher wished to bring her quickly to a favorable decision. He wanted to make up the customer's mind for her in such a conclusive way that she would be prevented from hesitating over the purchase. As a weighman of pounds and ounces he only wanted to show the prospect that he was honest. But in order to tip *the buying scales in her mind* he put into the balances, on the side opposite the cost of the steak, the heavier weight of buying inducements. First he did the actual weighing of the steak; then he added on the "Yes" side of the scales of decision *ideas of the excellence and desirability of the meat.* He followed immediately with a *suggestion of action that would commit the prospect to buying.*

"Two pounds and five ounces, ma'am! Only a dollar and forty-three cents. It's the very choicest part of the loin. You couldn't get a cut any tenderer than that, or with less bone. Would you like to have a little extra suet wrapped up with it?"

Three Effects Produced

The butcher thus combined in his close *three effects.* He brought about *judgment of the prospect's intellect,* plus *increased desire* for the goods, plus the *impulse to carry the desire into action.*

First, by emphasizing, "Two pounds and five ounces!" in a *heavy* tone, and by depreciating the cost, "Only a dollar and forty-three cents," spoken *lightly,* he implied that the *value* of the steak far outweighed the *price.* Thus judgment of the prospect's intellect was effected.

Second, to stimulate increased desire for the steak, the butcher skillfully put on the favorable side of the scales of decision the weight of *a suggestion of excellence.* He said temptingly, "It's the very choicest part of the loin." At this point he also employed *contrast,* to make the prospect's desire stronger still. "You couldn't get a cut any tenderer than this, or with less bone."

Third, this skillful salesman prompted *the immediate committal of his customer to a favorable decision.* He impelled her to this affirmative action by suggesting, "Would you like to have a little extra suet wrapped up with it?" He put a question that was *easy* for the prospect to answer with "Yes." Once she accepted the suet offered free, she tacitly accepted the steak at the price stated. *It is skillful salesmanship to make it easy for the buyer to say "Yes" or to imply the favorable decision indirectly.* The butcher might have been answered with "No" if he had asked, "Will you take this steak?" But he himself nodded when he made the proposal that he wrap up the extra suet. The woman was thus impelled to nod with him. The sale was closed, artistically, in a few seconds.

When you plan how you will close a sale of true ideas of your best capability, *work out in advance a similar weighing process, followed at once by an indirect prompting of acceptance of the decision you suggest.* Shape and re-shape your intended "close" in your mind until it includes the three effects the butcher produced.

Put a "Kick" Into the Close

Put a "kick" into your stimulation of desire at the closing stage. *Paint the points in your favor brightly and glowingly, though in true colors. Conversely paint all objections to your employment unattractively.*

Suppose you are applying for a secretarial position. It would be good "painting" to close something like this:

"I am going to learn to do things *your* way. You would not want a man in the position who was *experienced*; because he would do things some one else's way, not yours. My inexperience really means I am adaptable to your methods. I'd become exactly the sort of secretary *you* want. For instance, how do you prefer to have your mail brought to you—just as it is opened, or with previous correspondence and notations attached?"

Such an alternative question, *answered either way*, leads the prospect through the stage of favorable decision and implies his committal to acceptance of the services offered. It can be followed by the direct proposal, "All, right, I'll bring your mail that way." *Such a close is practically sure to succeed.*

Using the Negative Positively

A man who was not at all prepossessing applied to me one day for a job. He conducted the sale of himself very skillfully, but I meant to put him off. It was our dull season, and his looks didn't make a hit with me anyway. However, he realized there was a good deal on the negative side of the scale, and he weighed his disqualifications honestly; though he depreciated the importance of his unprepossessing appearance. Then, in contrast to the negative side, he showed me very weighty and attractive reasons for employing him. He started by grinning good-humoredly.

"I'm not a prize beauty," he remarked. "But the other day I was reading about Abraham Lincoln, and the book made me feel encouraged about myself. I don't believe I'm any homelier or any more awkward than he was. I don't expect to be a parlor salesman, anyhow, or to rely on my good looks to get orders. I plan to succeed by work. I'm going to be on the job early and late and every minute between. I'll believe in what I'm selling—down to the very bottom of my heart. I'll make anybody see I'm in dead earnest. I look honest, and I am. I'll be square with customers and with you. I guess that out in the field a reputation for always being willing to help, and for telling the truth straight, will count more than anything else. I know I'm inexperienced, but that's a fault I can cure mighty soon." He grinned again. "I'll start right away to get the greenness off, if you'll tell me where to hang up my hat."

His good nature warmed me into smiling with him. I could not help feeling inclined to try this man. I decided to give him his chance at once. He started my impulse to accept his services, and I pronounced the decision in his favor that he prompted. Of course he made good. That was a foregone conclusion. He had mastered the selling process, and was an especially fine closer. He succeeded in getting more than his quota of orders the first year. Selling never seemed to be hard work for him.

Two Ways To Prompt Pronouncement

The pronouncement of the prospect's decision can be prompted, his favorable action can be brought about, in *two ways*. First, as we have seen, *the salesman can suggest, directly or indirectly, the action he wants the other man to take*. Second, *the salesman himself can do something* that the prospect will be impelled to *imitate*.

Impelling Imitation Of Action

For example, when you apply for a position, and have completed the process of weighing the points in your favor in contrast with the less weighty reasons for not employing you, lean forward slightly in an attitude of easy expectancy. *The prospect's mind will be inclined to imitate your physical act*. He will lean toward acceptance of your services. Your act will tend to bring you together. Your magnetism will draw his.

Or you might extend your hand. He will have an impulse to reach out his in turn. It is natural for a man to take a hand that is courteously offered. The moment after you reach toward the prospect say, "Let's shake hands on it." Once his fingers start moving toward yours in imitation of your action, it will be easy for him to commit himself.

Five Essentials Of Good Close

Now let us review the essentials of good salesmanship in closing, which we have been analyzing. We can summarize under five divisions the entire process of completing a sale most effectively and with the practical assurance of success.

First, *the salesman must have definite, certain knowledge that the mind of the prospect has reached the closing stage; that it is time to end* the "testimony" and to *begin* weighing the evidence. If the salesman has kept control of the selling process throughout all the preceding stages, he will know when the selling point is reached, *for he will be there himself,* with the prospect he has "safely conducted" thus far.

Second, at this "right time" it is necessary to *change former sales tactics promptly,* and to *start contrasting* the affirmative and negative ideas that have previously been brought out.

Third, the salesman should weigh these contrasting ideas so *vividly* that the mind's eye of the prospect will *see* the scales and *perceive* the greater weight on the "Yes" side, *as the salesman pictures it.*

Fourth, it is important that the salesman *color* the affirmative ideas very *alluringly,* and increase the contrast by painting *unattractively* everything on the negative side of the scale; so that "No," besides appearing much *lighter* than "Yes," will seem *uninviting.*

Fifth, the selling process should be brought to a climax by the salesman's *suggestion* or *imitation* of some *act* designed to *commit* the prospect to *acceptance* in an *easy* way.

Unbalancing The Process

Nothing so *unbalances* the process of securing a favorable decision and its pronouncement as any indication of fear, doubt, or hesitancy in the attitude of the salesman. Therefore, even though you may be uncertain as to the outcome of your selling efforts, *do not show it.* Long before you came to the decision point, you passed the worst dangers on the road to the end of the sale. Surely your courage should be *strongest* at the closing stage.

Light Dissipates Fear and Doubt

Fear usually arises from something *unknown;* it is due only to *darkness.* Since you *know* now just what closing involves, and *light* has been shed on the problems of getting the prospect's "Yes," your fears and doubts should be dissipated. *You should not hesitate to end the sale you have controlled successfully throughout previous stages.* Our analysis has revealed that closing is no more difficult than winning attention to your proposition in the first place. As a result, your present attitude toward closing is *positive.* Your courage and self-confidence have been built up. You realize just *how* success in finishing a well-conducted sale can be made practically *sure.*

Negatives Must be Avoided

Certain *negative* attitudes at the closing stage should be avoided. Especially do not throw into the scales of decision any little pleas for *personal favor*, with the hope that in so doing you will increase the weight on the "Yes" side. Such tactics almost invariably tend to tip the balance *un*favorably. A plea of this sort is equivalent to an admission that the ideas you have presented *for* buying do not *themselves* outweigh the prospect's images *against* buying. You suggest to him that you are trying to push the balance down on your side by putting your finger on it, by "weighing in your hand," as unfair butchers sometimes do with a chicken they hold on the scales by the legs.

"As a Personal Favor to Me"

The prospect will instantly perceive your action. *His mind, acting on the principle of the gyroscope, will resist by greater opposition any push of the personal plea.* If you ask a decision as a personal favor, your prospect will lose confidence in the true weight of the ideas on your side that you have already registered in his mind. You are much more likely to hurt than to help your chances for success by making a personal plea. Even if it should prove effective, what you get that way would be alms given to a beggar, and not the earned prize of good salesmanship. *Never buy success at the cost of self-respect.* To be a successful *beggar* is nothing to feel proud of.

"Treating" At Close

Do not attempt to "*treat*" your prospect by flattering him at the closing stage. Such "treating" is a tacit admission that your goods of sale, your best qualifications, have not sufficient merit to sell at their intrinsic value. Or you practically confess that you are not good enough salesman to win out with just your goods and your ability to sell yourself for what you claim to be worth. *Flattery is a call for help.* It is like the bad salesmanship of trying to buy an order with cigars or a dinner. Never "treat" at the closing stage, for to do so is to admit *weakness* when you should be your *strongest*.

"No" Seldom Is Final

Of course you should not take a first or second "No" as a *final* answer. Even if the prospect indicates that he is inclined to decide against you, *continue confidently to heap images in favor of buying on the "Yes" side of the scale until you have used all the honest weight you have to put in the balance.* He will not respect you as a salesman if you quit at his first "No." *It is up to you to tip the scales of decision your way.* Remember that you should not bring the other man to the judgment point *until after you have aroused and intensified his desire to a very great degree.* If you have made him want you at all, you will disappoint him if you then fail to put enough weight on the "Yes" side of the scale to win his decision to employ you.

When you receive a "No," understand it to mean, "No, that is not yet enough ideas for buying your services." Keep right on putting weight into the "Yes" side of the balance until it tips your way. *Do not consider any "No" final until you have run out of both contrasting weight and attractive colors; so that you cannot change the scales.*

Stick it Out Here and Now

If it is possible for you to "stick," don't be put off when you come to the closing stage. *All the weighing you do at the present time will be valueless lost effort unless you complete the selling process here and now.* When your prospect tries to put you off, he tacitly admits your weights are right. Otherwise he would say "No" and be done with you. You really have won his mental decision. A continuance of skillful salesmanship will enable you to get him to act favorably without delay or further evasion.

Entertainment In Court Room Out of Place

Some salesmen make the mistake of mixing *entertainment* with the closing process. Earlier in the sale you may be able to secure excellent results by entertaining the prospect with clean jokes and good stories. But the close is the stage at which he arrives at his mental conclusion as to the "preponderance" of the evidence. *Jests and light conversation are out of place when the judge is performing his functions in the courtroom of the mind.* An amusing remark or a witty quip at this juncture would suggest that the scales of decision in the salesman's own mind were somewhat unbalanced. Your attitude when you are weighing "Yes" and "No" before the prospect should be *pleasant,* but *quiet* and *serious, as is becoming to a convincing weighman.*

When you work to secure a favorable decision, you are weighing evidence with the purpose of impelling the prospect to take your judgment or to weigh the evidence just as you do. It is necessary all through the process that he be made to feel you realize you are aiding in the performance of a *judicial* function. He must have complete confidence in your intention and ability to handle the scales honestly and with serious pains to determine what is the right judgment about your proposition. Your levity at the closing stage would lessen the effect of honest, serious, painstaking weighing of the images for buying in contrast with the images against buying. So get the funny stories out of your system before you come to the decision step of the sale, or else keep them bottled up inside you and don't pull the cork until you are safely at the celebration stage.

Tones and Acts When Weighing

Do not forget when closing to add *force* to your words by *tones and gestures that emphasize ideas of the contrast in weights* between the two sides of the scale. By your light tone you can indicate the triviality of objections to your proposition. With the heavier tone of power you can suggest the great weight of the favorable ideas. If you use *broad gestures of your whole hand and full arm,* you can seem to pile a large heap of points on your side of the scale. Conversely you can indicate the smallness of objections by moving *your fingers only,* as if you were picking up a tiny object. Demolish unfavorable points with a strong gesture of negation, as by sweeping your arm horizontally. Give life to the ideas on the favorable side of the scale by accompanying your words with up and down gestures that signify vitality.

Do Not Show That Closing Is Hard Work

Your physical condition or outward appearance will help or harm your chances for success at the closing stage. You should not manifest the least indication that you are under a strain of anxiety as to the outcome, or that you lack the strength to control the completion of the selling process. Why should you not have a feeling of ease when you reach the close? *If your bearing suggests your self-confidence, it will give the other man confidence in your capabilities.* When a salesman has to "sweat blood" to finish a sale, he indicates that it is usually mighty hard work for him to get what he wants. This impression suggests to the other man that there must be something wrong with the proposition or it wouldn't take so much effort of the salesman to put it across. *Any element of doubt at the final stage will almost surely delay or kill the salesman's chances to close successfully.*

Make Sure of A Good Batting Average

Recall once more that the measure of success in selling is not 100% of closed sales; every possible order secured and none lost. *Success is made certain when failures are reduced to the minimum and successes are increased to the maximum of practicability.* There can be no question that if you use the *right processes* in closing, your chances for success will be so greatly increased that your batting average of actual sales should take you far above the failure line. Your career as a salesman involves *continual* selling. You must make sale after sale. However skillfully you employ the right process at the closing stage, you may not accomplish your purpose the first time you try. *But if you keep on selling your services in the right way, you will be as absolutely certain to succeed as the master salesman of "goods" is sure of closing his quota every year he works.*

CHAPTER XII
The Celebration Stage

What Are You Going to Do With Success?

You know now the *certain* way to get your chance to succeed in the vocation of your choice. You are convinced that a *good salesman* can create and control his opportunities in any field, can bring himself to good luck in the right market for his services. You are resolved to master the art of selling, and so to insure your future against any possibility of failure. You feel confident of success; because you are willing to earn it by the diligent study and practice of salesmanship. There is no doubt in your mind that when you become a skillful salesman of your best capabilities, you can get a chance to succeed. *Now what are you going to do with success after you gain it?*

Suppose you had sold yourself into the very opportunity you want, suppose you had won the coveted job or promotion, *how would you celebrate?* It has been said that a man shows his real self either in the moment of his failure or in the moment of his success. Let us assume that you have reached your present objective. You stand at the goal, a winner. Does your victory *intoxicate,* or does it *sober* you with the realization that you have but opened the way to limitless fields of bigger service ahead? Has success gone to your *hands* and made them tingle with eagerness to grasp more chances to succeed, or has it gone to your *head*?

The Stepping-Stone to More Sales

The celebration stage of the selling process should be the first stepping-stone leading to another successful sale. Often it proves to be a stumbling block that marks the beginning of a downfall to failure. Rare is the man who is not spoiled a little by achievement. *Success is the severest test of salesmanship.*

Spoiled by Success

I recall a chief clerk who worked more than a year for promotion to the position of assistant manager. He earned the better job, and was assigned to the desk toward which he had been looking longingly for sixteen months.

Then he "celebrated" by starting to take life easy. He developed a manner of superiority. He acted as if the little foothill he had climbed was a big mountain. He sunned himself on the top, basking in complacency because he had risen above his former clerkship.

One day he was called into the manager's office. He came out chop-fallen and took his personal belongings from the assistant's desk. Another man was promoted to the place he had failed to fill. He went back to his clerk's stool and is roosting there today.

Egotism's Downfall

I know a salesman who closed so many orders the first time he covered his territory that he came back to headquarters with an inflated idea of his importance. He strutted into the president's room and boasted of what he had done. The delighted head of the business gave him a cigar and invited him to tell the story. The salesman betrayed such egotism that his employer was disgusted. The president was plain-spoken. He warned the successful salesman against getting a "swelled head."

The egotist felt insulted. He resigned his position, arrogantly declaring that he would not work for a house where results were so little appreciated. He was cocksure of himself. However, when he offered his services to a competing firm, his application was turned down. The rebuff stunned him. He did not realize that his egotism disgusted the second executive as much as the first. The salesman's spirit was broken. He has never since been more than a fair peddler.

Giant and Pigmy Successes

Think of "successful" men you know. *Compare them as they are now with the men they used to be before they succeeded.* As they rose did they loom bigger and bigger in your respect, or grow smaller and smaller in admirable qualities? There are so-called successful men whose characters seem to be dwarfed by the mountain tops they attain. Other men grow to be giants and overshadow any eminences they climb. The littleness of the last Kaiser and Crown Prince of Germany was only emphasized by their elevation above the common people. On the other hand the bigness of Lincoln and Roosevelt was so tremendous that their personalities towered above even the highest honor in the world.

Breaking Training

When football players are fighting for the championship of the season, they are governed by rigid rules of living. *They keep themselves fit* by strict diet, by the avoidance of all dissipations, by hardening exercise, and by recuperative rest. But after the "big game" is won, they break training. They stuff themselves with rich food until their bodies and minds are sluggish. Then they celebrate their victory by some sort of jollification that lasts half the night. *The next day a second-rate team could beat the champions.*

A man who has kept himself lean, hard-muscled, and healthy all the way to the achievement of his ambition is apt to take on flabby flesh and gout when he succeeds. The celebration of Thanksgiving is an ordeal from which one does not recover for weeks. Turkey and mince pie immoderately eaten are poisons. Our annual Feast Day is more deadly than the Fourth of July.

Rusting in Self-Satisfaction

A great many people "break training" mentally as well as physically at the celebration stage. *Their minds and muscles turn flabby after they succeed. They are so proud of their accomplishments that they rust in self-satisfaction.* Then, usually too late for remedy, they find themselves afflicted by the rheumatic twinges of deep-seated discontent with what they have done.

We are all familiar with the tragedies of the farmer who sells his acres and moves into town "so that he can take life easy," and of the business man who retires from his "daily grind" to enjoy the fortune of success. So long as they remained at work they were vigorous in mind and body. But nearly always men who give up their accustomed activities begin to develop mental and physical ailments soon afterward. They age and break down in a few years. *In order to stay well, one must keep going. It is far less wearying to walk than to stand still. Normal fatigue of mind and body are not so exhaustive of mental and physical energy as torpid idleness.*

Advance or You Will Slip Back

Probably you do not think of quitting work for a long time. You look at your future retirement as a remote possibility. Very likely you feel it is premature to consider "your declining years" now, when you are in the full vigor of ambition. *But if you stop advancing, in order to celebrate your progress thus far, you have quit working your way ahead. If you stay contented with what you have done, even for a little while, you have temporarily retired from the game of success and are in danger of rusting into a partial failure. If you do not continue moving ever upward, you will slip into a decline without realizing that you are going back and down.*

The Zest for Work

The successful salesman thrives on his work, and pines for it when he "lays off." He welcomes the end of his annual vacation with more zest than its beginning. He celebrates each order gained by planning at once how he will get another. He is like Alexander, who sighed only when there were no more worlds to conquer. He is as perennially tireless as Edison, the wizard who is never weary. *To the true salesman there is no enjoyment equal to selling*. He often declares that he "would rather sell than eat."

Pattern after Master Salesmen

You know the importance of being a *good salesman*. You have studied the methods he uses throughout the selling process. Now at the celebration stage pattern after the *masters* of the profession. Do not get into the bad habits of the *mediocre fellows who slacken their efforts after each success*, and who need the spur of necessity to make them do their utmost.

When a good salesman has booked an order, and has taken pains to make a fine last impression on his customer, he does not go to his hotel and play Kelly pool, or otherwise spend the rest of the day just loafing around. Only the poor salesman celebrates in such a way; *thereby showing that his successes are so rare he is not used to them*.

Starting After The Next Chance

The good salesman looks at his watch the moment he is out of his customer's sight. He makes a swift calculation of the time it will take him to reach and sell the next man on his list. If he has no other prospect nearby, he starts looking for one that minute. His keen eyes catch every name on the business signs he passes. *His imaginative mind is planning how he can use the order he just has closed, to influence some other buyer to make a contract*. If there are no additional customers for his line in the town, he sprints to the station to catch the first train up the road. *He does not waste a minute getting to his next selling opportunity*.

Pepper and Poppies

Some pretty good salesmen never win the grand quota prize in a sales contest *because they take so much time out for celebrating the big orders they close*. If they land a fine contract in the morning, they don't try to do much selling that afternoon. The prize-winning salesman, too, is delighted to secure a big order. But he doesn't say to himself, "That will put me 'way ahead on the sales record for today." Instead he grins and thinks, "This is *my day*. I'm going to fatten up my batting average while I'm going good." *Success is pepper to him, not the poppy drug that slackens energy*.

Continual Accumulation

You have worked hard to get the chance you now have. You have paid for it with your best efforts. *It represents an accumulation of your salesmanship.* The good job or the promotion you have gained is like a savings account. Let us compare it with the first hundred dollars a thrifty man puts into the bank for a rainy day. Would he celebrate the accumulation of that moderate amount of money, the first evidence of his ability to save, by quitting the practice of spending less than his earnings? Would he then say to himself, "I am now successful as a saver"? Would he stop putting a few dollars in the bank every Saturday, just because he already had a hundred?

The Building Process is Gradual

No. He would *continue* to save until he had enough "units of thrift," enough hundreds of dollars, to take a *longer* step toward success. He would invest his accumulated savings in a lot, or house. Perhaps he would start a business of his own. After his investment he still would continue to save. So he would *build* his success.

All building is a gradual, continual process. The bricks are laid *one after another*. It takes many to complete the structure. *Likewise a series of minor successes must be built into a major accomplishment.* It does not rise all at once.

If you are tempted to pause where you are in order to celebrate, ask yourself, "*Is this really the celebration stage?*" Probably you will find you have only laid the corner-stone, or made an excavation for the foundation of your success. You would not think of having a housewarming because you had finished the basement walls. Nor would you consider it an occasion for especial jollification the day you erected the scantlings around the first floor joists. Not until the walls are up and the roof is on, not until the house is plastered and papered and painted, not until it is finished would you think of standing on the sidewalk to look it over pride fully and exult, "I did that. It's a good job."

Repeated Building

But if you complete *one* house, you will not only feel the satisfaction of accomplishment, you will also want to build *another* that would be a great improvement on the one just finished. You will be *healthily dissatisfied with what you have already done*. Very likely you will sell the first house at a profit, and straightway start to put up a better building on another lot.

In time you will sell that, too. You will continue the procedure until you become a master builder of houses, and continually achieve more and more success.

We have assumed that you now are successfully in possession of an opportunity. You have sold yourself into the very job you want, or into a better position that you believe will afford you fine chances to advance. *Do not slump or relax in salesmanship. Do not think back, or spend much time contemplating your present success. Look ahead to your next sale* of true ideas of your best capabilities. *The successful salesman is a quick repeater.* He counts his accomplishments in *totals*, not by units. He has successful *"years,"* each made up of about three hundred successful working days. He plans in *campaigns*; so he is not inclined to over-celebrate the winning of a battle.

Make Each Goal a New Starting Point

Samuel McRoberts, vice-president of the great National City Bank of New York, started working for Armour & Company at a small salary in the early nineties. He was a young man who was always *healthily ambitious to keep moving ahead.* He "ate up" the minor work assigned to him, and celebrated the completion of each task by asking at once, "What next?"

In a few years he had risen by successive promotions to the position of treasurer of Armour & Company. But that wasn't a *goal* to McRoberts. It seemed to him only a *good starting point* to bigger successes in the financial world. He became a director of several banks, an officer in important railroad and other corporations. *He continually enlarged his service value* until he was called to New York's greatest bank, and took his place among the masters of American finance.

He did not loll back in his chair then and start taking it easy. *He packed more and more accomplishments into every day.* When the war began, he went to Washington to take executive charge of the job of procuring ordnance for the fighters. He held a post analogous to that of Lloyd-George when he was Minister of Munitions for Great Britain. McRoberts made good as a brigadier general, and after the war resumed his success in business. Whatever he did, wherever he worked, Samuel McRoberts *smiled welcomes to more opportunities for service, and reached out his ready hands to grasp them.*

Celebrate by Tackling the Job Ahead

That is the way to celebrate—by tackling the job ahead. There is no end to the selling process. One sale should lead directly to another. The good salesman celebrates only the opportunity to get the next order in prospect. He may chuckle to himself over the sale just closed, but he does his rejoicing on his way to a new selling chance.

Dynamic Confidence Static Complacency

You haven't "arrived" yet. You are just well started. *Keep moving, and you will never "see your finish."* Your successes thus far should have developed a considerable degree of *self-confidence.* Be careful not to let that *dynamic* quality change into the *static* element of *self-complacency.* Never be satisfied with what you have done. *Always have the zest of appetite for more to do.* Add every day to your success chances.

Do not lose either your self-respect, or the respect of the men with whom you are associated, by *ceasing to grow. Do more than you are paid for, and pretty soon your job will be unable to hold all your earning capacity.* You will be promoted to bigger opportunities. *If you shrink in the place you occupy now, your future chances will shrivel to fit your smaller size.* The way to get a better-paying job, to win a bigger, more profitable field for your salesmanship, is to *crowd your present position with your capabilities.* Burst out of your limited territory and spread over more ground.

. Serving Friends

Render your utmost possible service to other people. Celebrate each opportunity to form a friendship. *Make some one like you for what you are willing to do for him.* Hold your friends, once they are made. As Emerson advised, "Be concerned for other people and their welfare. Put their interests sometimes ahead of your own. You can love your fellow men so much that you will never trample on their rights; and while you yourself keep climbing, raise as many of them as you can along with you. That is the way to make friends."

Celebrate the good fortune of your business associates, rather than your own. When a big contract is closed by your employer, be as tickled over it as he feels. Genuinely rejoice in his success. *Have no envy of the man above you, then when you rise to a higher level the men below you will not be likely to feel jealous.*

Ford and Schwab

Why has Henry Ford won so unique a place in the personal regard of the everyday man? Ford is one of the richest men in the world; yet he is not hated. What is the reason for his general popularity? He is not an idler. He has celebrated each success by taking on another job. And he always has given a hand-up to the other fellow instead of kicking him down so that he might climb higher because of his failure. He has understood and sympathized with the hopes and viewpoint of people who work. As a result countless men and women, most of whom never have seen him, think of Henry Ford as their friend. His finest success is not signified by the millions of money he has accumulated, but by the millions of friendships he enjoys.

Charles M. Schwab, too, is popular. He is a man whom people like. Because he was so successful in winning friends, rather than for his generally recognized business ability, he was made the head of the Government's ship-building program in the war. Other men were eager to work with and for Charles M. Schwab. The co-operation of thousands of friendships, new and old, more than anything else enabled him to succeed in his big, patriotic job. How much more he has to celebrate in his wealth of good will than in his great fortune of dollars! Schwab has been called the most successful salesman in the world, which is another way of saying that he has no equal in ability to make other people both trust and like him.

The Truest Wealth

You may never accumulate millions of dollars. *That in itself is not success. Many wealthy men are failures in life. But with the aid of masterly salesmanship you can so enrich yourself with friendships and the opportunities they bring that making all the money you want will be merely incidental to your real success.* Let every accomplishment be a stimulus to better selling of your service. Celebrate successful sales of your ideas by undertaking to sell more true ideas about your best capabilities in a larger field of usefulness.

The Revolving Door

The good salesman goes from opportunity to opportunity through a revolving door. As it closes on one selling chance, it opens on another. He steps directly from a finished sale into the prospect of getting an order elsewhere. So he never stops selling.

You have sold yourself some knowledge of salesmanship. Do not rest contented with what you have already learned. These chapters should but whet your appetite for more opportunities to master the principles and methods of selling true ideas of your best capabilities. So as you close this book, reach out your hand to open another. You cannot over-study the subject of salesmanship. *Never be satisfied with what you know.* Continue to search for more golden knowledge, and make it yours by practicing everything you learn.

Failure Impossible to The Good Salesman

▸ It is impossible to fail in life if you become a master salesman of the best that is in you. You will be sure to succeed. So here is Good Luck to you! Keep on making it for yourself, and you never will run out. CERTAIN SUCCESS WILL BE YOURS.

It is you that you offer for sale,

>With your traits ranged like goods on a shelf,
>And the first thing to do, without fail,
>Is to make a success of yourself.

>EDGAR A. GUEST.